LETTERS WRITTEN IN A MAHRATTA CAMP DURING THE YEAR 1809

LETTERS
WRITTEN IN
A MAHRATTA CAMP DURING
THE YEAR 1809

DESCRIPTIVE OF THE CHARACTER MANNERS DOMESTIC HABITS AND RELIGIOUS CEREMONIES OF THE MAHRATTAS

THOMAS DUER BROUGHTON

A NEW EDITION WITH AN INTRODUCTION BY

M. E. GRANT DUFF

GYAN

Published by

Gyan Publishing House
5, Ansari Road
Daryaganj, New Delhi-110002
Phone: 011-47034999, 9811692060
E-mail: books@gyanbooks.com

Distribution Network
gyanbooks.com
India, USA, Canada, UK, Australia, France

ISBN : 978-81-212-3703-1 (PB)
First Published, 1892

2nd Impression 2020

Printed at: Gyan Press, Delhi.

Letters Written in A Mahratta Camp During the Year 1809
Author: Thomas Duer Broughton

LETTERS

FROM A

MAHRATTA CAMP

SOLD BY

SIMPKIN, MARSHALL, HAMILTON, KENT AND CO., LTD., London
Sole Trade Agents for the United Kingdom

THACKER, SPINK AND CO.	Calcutta	,,	*India*
E. A. PETHERICK AND CO.	Melbourne	,,	*Australasia*
OTTO HARRASSOWITZ . .	Leipzig	,,	*Germany*
JEAN MAISONNEUVE . .	Paris	,,	*France*

AND

ALL BOOKSELLERS IN TOWN AND COUNTRY

CONSTABLE'S

ORIENTAL MISCELLANY

OF

ORIGINAL AND SELECTED PUBLICATIONS

VOL · IV

LETTERS

FROM

A MAHRATTA CAMP

DURING THE YEAR 1809

Westminster
ARCHIBALD CONSTABLE AND COMPANY
14 PARLIAMENT STREET S·W
MDCCCXCII

CONSTABLE'S ORIENTAL MISCELLANY

Volumes already published

VOL. I.—BERNIER'S TRAVELS IN THE MOGUL EMPIRE, A.D 1656–1668 . . . . 6s. nett

,, II.—POPULAR READINGS IN SCIENCE . . . 5s. ,,

,, III.—AURENG-ZEBE, A TRAGEDY, AND BOOK II. OF THE CHACE, A POEM . . . . 5s. ,,

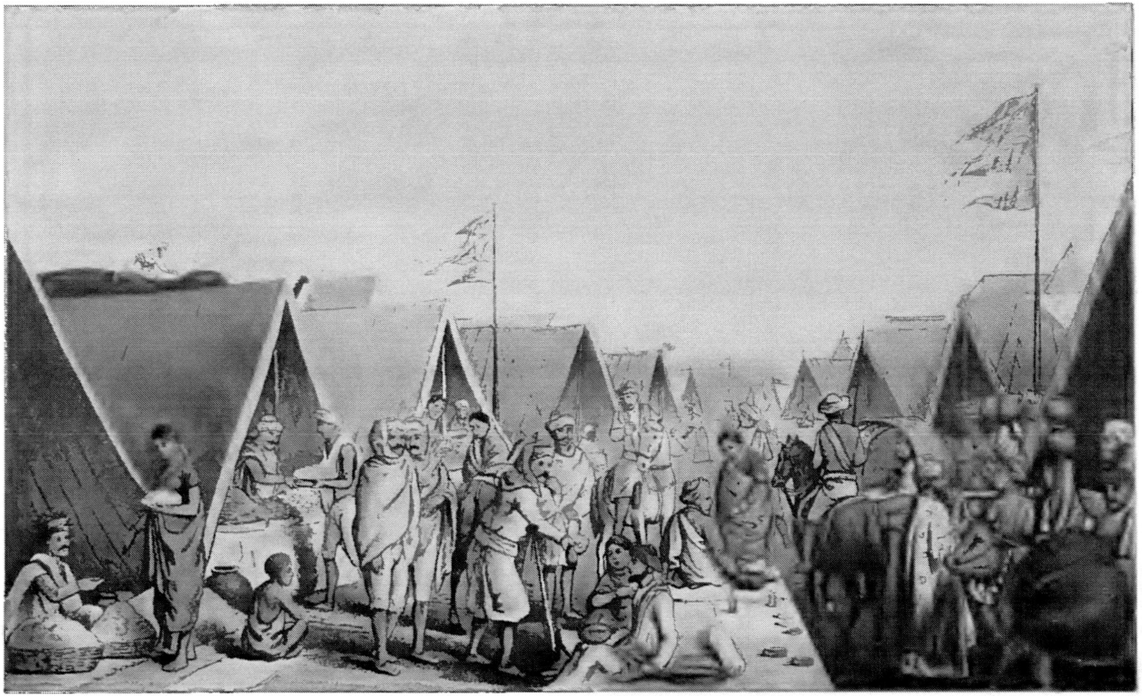

WG.

A BAZAR IN SEENDHIYA'S CAMP

LETTERS

WRITTEN IN

A MAHRATTA CAMP

DURING THE YEAR 1809

DESCRIPTIVE OF THE CHARACTER MANNERS DOMESTIC HABITS AND RELIGIOUS CEREMONIES OF THE MAHRATTAS

BY

THOMAS DUER BROUGHTON

FORMERLY COMMANDER OF THE RESIDENT'S ESCORT AT THE COURT OF SCINDIA

A NEW EDITION

WITH AN INTRODUCTION BY

THE RIGHT HONOURABLE

SIR M · E GRANT DUFF

G·C·S·I F·R·S

Westminster

ARCHIBALD CONSTABLE AND COMPANY

14 PARLIAMENT STREET S·W

MDCCCXCII

TO THE MOST NOBLE

THE MARQUES [*sic*] WELLESLEY, K.G.

&c. &c. &c.

THE ACUTE DETECTOR OF MAHRATTA WILES,
THE FIRM REPELLER OF THEIR INSOLENT PRETENSIONS,
AND THE FORMIDABLE BARRIER TO THEIR
AMBITIOUS PROJECTS;
THEIR VIGOROUS OPPONENT IN TIME OF WAR,
AND THEIR GENEROUS PACIFICATOR IN THE HOUR OF
VICTORY:

THESE LETTERS,
DESCRIPTIVE OF THE DOMESTIC HABITS AND PECULIAR
CUSTOMS OF THAT PEOPLE,
ARE OFFERED, AS A TRIBUTE OF GRATITUDE,
ADMIRATION AND ESTEEM,

BY HIS LORDSHIP'S
OBLIGED, FAITHFUL,
AND DEVOTED HUMBLE SERVANT,

THE AUTHOR.

[DEDICATION OF THE ORIGINAL EDITION
LONDON, JOHN MURRAY, 1813.]

LETTER IV

LETTER V

LETTER VI

LETTER VII

LETTER VIII

LETTER IX

LETTER X

LETTER XI

LETTER XII

LETTER XIII

LETTER XIV

LETTER XV

LETTER XVI

LETTER XVII

LETTER XVIII

LETTER XIX

LETTER XX

LETTER XXI

LETTER XXII

LETTER XXIII

LETTER XXIV

LETTER XXV

LETTER XXVI

LETTER XXVII

LETTER XXVIII

LETTER XXIX

LETTER XXX

LETTER XXXI

LETTER XXXII

LIST OF ILLUSTRATIONS

FIGS. 1–9 *from blocks supplied by Messrs. J. C. Drummond & Co., London*

INTRODUCTION

THE author of the book which Mr. Constable now reproduces in the series so intelligently planned and successfully commenced, was a great-grandson of Dr. Broughton, chaplain to the first Duke of Marlborough, and author of a sermon on the battle of Blenheim. He was educated at Eton, went out to India as a cadet in 1795, and ran a useful if not a very brilliant career. He was at the siege of Seringapatam in 1799, and for a short time before the restoration of Java to the Dutch commanded in that island. When he wrote the letters which are reprinted in this volume he held the rank of Captain. He married a Miss Chamier, a member of one of those Huguenot families which have in so many different ways distinguished themselves in the countries which afforded them hospitality.

A Chamier co-operated with Johnson, Reynolds, Burke, and four others, in founding "The Club." Another was a popular writer in the days of our grandfathers, and they have been for several generations closely connected both with Civil and Military affairs in the Presidency of Madras. The energy and ability of General Chamier, C.B., who is happily still alive, contributed not a little to the rapid success of the Burmese Expedition in 1885.

After Captain, later Colonel, Broughton's return home, he became Honorary Secretary to the Royal Asiatic Society, and filled that office while Colonel Tod, the author of the "Annals of Rajasthan," was Honorary Librarian. The two comrades and colleagues died, strange to say, within two days of each other, in November, 1835.

The only one of Colonel Broughton's writings which seems to have attracted any general attention was that which recorded his experiences in the Camp of Scindia, where he lived as commander of the escort of the British Minister, or, in Anglo-Indian phraseology, the Resident, deputed to keep up relations between our Government and that Potentate.

It is well, perhaps, that a narrative like this should have been left behind by a man for whom the scenes which he describes had no novelty, and who saw nothing very extraordinary either in the picturesqueness or the squalor of his surroundings in a Mahratta Camp. Here and there some display more brilliant than ordinary excites his admiration, or some peculiarly horrid atrocity is duly reprobated; but the dirt and the scampishness, and the absurdity and the impecuniosity, and the faithlessness and the mutiny, and the extortion and the superstition seem to him, so to speak, "all in the day's work."

If his rather matter-of-fact method of treatment detracts from the pleasure which the reader experiences, the truthfulness of the picture is brought better home to the mind than it could have been by a more brilliant presentation, and, after all, nothing much could have been made of the main story Colonel Broughton had to tell. Something no doubt might have been made of the accessories, but he does not seem to have had much interest in nature, or much acquaintance with the history of the country in which his lot was cast. His literary power was small, and he constantly forgot the maxim which he probably learnt at Eton, "the half is more than the whole;" but he was fortunate in the moment at which he served in India. Only a few years before, the Mahratta power, which seemed likely, up to its crushing defeat at Paniput in 1761, to overshadow the whole peninsula, and which even after that catastrophe was strong enough to give us a prodigious amount of trouble for nearly sixty years, received its deathblow on the field of Kirkee.

The existing generation in India, safe under the ægis of the British power, is apt to forget how hideous was the state of things which prevailed before we struck up the swords of all combatants, and commanded peace. Those who wish to know from what they have been saved, can hardly do better than to run through Colonel Broughton's pages.

The work is thrown into the form of a series of letters to the Author's brother, who seems to have represented to him that, since the war which was illustrated by the victory of Assaye, a considerable interest in the Mahrattas had been excited in England, and that the Commander of the Resident's escort was in a position to gratify the natural curiosity of the public.

The part of the country to which the letters almost exclusively relate is Rajpootana, which was eighty years ago like the Laigh of Moray in the 17th century, a place "where all men take their prey." Speaking generally, we may say that the theatre of the scenes described was the valley of the Chumbul and of the streams which feed it, more especially the Banas, together with the tangled hills through which they find their way; but the latest letters describe Ajmere and its neighbourhood—deal, that is, with the centre of the country, and not merely with that portion of it which is nearest to the territories still belonging to the House of Scindia.

Colonel Broughton begins by an account of his journey from Agra to Kerowli, whence the first letter is dated in the December of 1808, but there is little of much interest save an indication here and there of the terrible incubus laid on the country by the Mahratta raids, till we come to Letter III., which contains a full account of the disposition of a Mahratta camp. In the fourth there is a sketch of Scindia himself, who was by this time over thirty, and about as unlike as a man of his race well could be, to his vigorous and statesmanlike predecessor Madhoji Ráo, whose life has been so well described by Mr. Keene in the Rulers of India series which Sir William Hunter is now editing. In the same letter there is a description of sitting in "dharna," which was probably more interesting to European readers eighty years ago than it is now, when Mr. Whitley Stokes and Sir Henry Maine have shown that far from being peculiar to India, it was well known in Ireland many hundred years since. In the fifth letter there is a vigorous picture of crossing a ford on the Chumbul, and of the elephants forcing a way through a thick jungle, "pushing with their foreheads against the trees, till they had bent them low enough to place their fore-feet upon the trunks, when, with another effort, they broke them to the ground."

The following passage is highly characteristic of those evil times:—

"The road lay over a continued plain, covered with fields of young corn affording fine forage for the Mahrattas;

who were to be seen in every direction, men, women, and children, tearing it up by the roots; while their cattle were turned loose to graze at liberty, and make the most of such an abundant harvest."

While this agreeable state of things was of the order of the day in the region which fell a prey to Scindia, matters went even worse in the domains of Holkar. The head of the race, Jeswunt Rao, had, indeed, after a long course of atrocity, gone fairly out of his mind; the nominal ruler was a child of four years old, the son of one of his concubines, and the government was in the hands of a Regency controlled by the notorious Mussulman adventurer, Ameer Khan; but even he went off to pursue the designs which ended in the consolidation of his power in the small Principality of Tonk, leaving Indore and all that depended upon it to confusion worse confounded.

In the seventh letter there is an account of the great Shiah festival of the Mohurrum, which has been adopted by the Hindus in many parts of India, and was a special favourite with the Mahrattas. This is the celebration which has so puzzled the British private soldier, and has been christened by him Hobson-Jobson, that being the nearest imitation at which he could arrive of the cry which goes forth from the crowd of "Hassan, Hussein," the martyred sons of Ali. It is this confusion of his which has given its name to Sir Henry Yule's great Glossary of Oriental words which have come into use in English books or newspapers, a work abounding in facts of the most curious interest not elsewhere put together, and which ought to form part of every library of the smallest pretension, public or private.

In the ninth letter the even madder follies of the Hohlee, the vernal festival of the Hindus, are fully detailed, while the tenth contains a very edifying narrative of the feckless-ness with which the army of Scindia conducted the siege of Doonee, a small fort belonging to a near relation of the ruler of Jeypore. No one could be surprised to read, after studying it, the remark made to Colonel Broughton, or one of his party:—"Why don't you let your two companies come and take the fort for us? They could do it if they would; *we*, you know, *are Mahrattas!*"

Some readers will remember the words of the Rajpoot chief of the old school in Sir Alfred Lyall's Poems, which contain, in their too few pages, so much of the perfume of India:—

> "Eight months my grandsire held the keep,
> Against the fierce Mahratta hordes;
> It would not stand three Winter suns,
> Before the shattering English guns;"

The portrait of Scindia in Letter XI. is very lifelike, and the following passage in the fourteenth, which deals with the period immediately after the conclusion of peace between him and the Jeypore State, is quite of a piece with it:—

"Mark the consistency and good faith of this Durbar; in the evening, Seendhiya receives an entertainment from an Ambassador, upon the occasion of a peace being concluded; and the very next morning wantonly plunders a miserable little hamlet, for we are still in the Jypoor country, that chances to be in his road; then, to complete the farce, writes letters to Meer Khan (whose troops are playing the same game in the vicinity of Oojyn, Seendhiya's own capital) remonstrating upon the unfriendliness and impropriety of his conduct."

This hamlet was inhabited by Meenas, whose habits are related in Letters XIII. and XIV. That such ruffians should have their houses burnt over their heads by other ruffians is not a matter of much importance, but that it should happen just after the chief of the one set of ruffians had, after long and intricate negotiations, made a treaty with the chief of the other set, is sufficiently amusing and characteristic. It is true that the Jeypore authorities did not deserve any great amount of compassion, for here is the account of their proceedings with regard to treaty obligations in Letter XV. :—

"The mode in which the Jypoor Durbar is accustomed to execute such agreements is quite notorious. They pay one-half, and agree to pay a quarter, after a certain number of months; and the remainder after another lapse of time. The payment of the second instalment is generally delayed, upon various pretences, for about a year, and for the last, they fight again, and if worsted, enter into another treaty."

In the sixteenth letter there is an excellent account of a Nautch, a form of entertainment in which *l'ennui tombe du plus haut* than it does in any of those Western pleasures whose absence would, according to an eminent statesman of the last generation, render life endurable. The murder of the Minister Surjee Rao, Scindia's own father-in-law, in Letter XX., is racy of the soil of Maháráshtra, and no less so is the free fight described in Letter XXIII., between two parties of camp-followers, or the account of the gymnastic exercises in Letter XIX.

Letter XXIV. is remarkable as being almost the only one which contains a story creditable to human nature, while XXV. is interesting as fully redressing the balance by its account of the worthless prince who was then the head of the Lunar race, of the base conduct of Scindia to two Pindaree chiefs, themselves the most detestable of mankind, and of two separate attempts made to poison members of the House of Holkar.

A description of the festival of the Dussera in Letter XXVII. is well worth reading, and not less so is the account in Letter XXX. of the Mohammedan Fakir who was the spiritual adviser of Scindia, himself, of course, a Hindu. Interesting too are visits to the great Moslem shrine of Ajmere, and the Brahmin one a few miles off at Poshkur. Colonel Broughton was more impressed with the priests at the latter place than was a great Continental Sanskritist who visited me at Madras. I had been remarking to him that the ignorance of the Jain priests at Mount Aboo, with regard to the beautiful temples under their care, had somewhat surprised me. "Yes," he said, "but the priests who provoked me most were those at Poshkur, in the temple of Brahma. It is the only temple he has got in the whole of India, and they don't even know his name; they call him Barma!" Before Colonel Broughton had done his self-imposed task he was sick enough of it. His second last letter, which was meant to be his last, ends as follows:—

"But enough of Seendhiya and Mahrattas. Let me close my descriptions of them with a fervent wish that the coming year, and many successive ones, may rise upon my dear brother, not only rich in health and happiness, but in a mind more and more impressed with the blessings he enjoys as an Englishman; blessings which, I hope, may have been rendered more evident, and consequently more dear, by a perusal of my attempts to depict the manners and customs of a people as much separated from Englishmen by character, as they are by actual distance upon the face of the globe. Farewell!"

Two thoughts will arise in the minds of many persons acquainted with India who read these letters; first, how far away seem the scenes which they describe, which were nevertheless being enacted when the present Prime Minister of England was in long clothes, and, secondly, how soon they would come back if the power, which saved and saves India from tearing her own vitals, were to be withdrawn for a single lustrum. How different is the state of Rajpootana now from that which we here contemplate! It is now in many ways the most delightful portion of the peninsula, possessing all the charm of old India, with all the evils left out. Just compare the wretched ruler of Jeypore described in these pages with his successor who occupied the same position in 1875, and may not impossibly have suggested Sir Alfred Lyall's noble poem, "Meditations of a Hindu Prince."

Then look at the other side. Who can doubt that all the jealousies, all the passions, all the superstitions which are set forth in Colonel Broughton's narrative, are still there ready to break forth at any moment?

Very gradually, yet as fast as in any way possible, we are raising up barriers against their coming in as a flood. In every direction we are working; but a great many of the best things we set on foot are dependent for their continuance on the maintenance of British power in India for a quite indefinite period. The only influences which are working directly towards rendering it possible for India to govern herself, if Great Britain ever got tired of her Asiatic experiment, are the habit of peace and the habit of justice. Our army, our police, our codes, our fiscal system; these, and I think these only, are bringing at all nearer the end which some political philosophers have put before their mind—the abandonment of a regenerated India to its own devices. Many of our other useful and even admirable works have a very complex effect. Education, excellent as it is, has introduced many new elements of disintegration. Railways, telegraphs, and other facilities of intercourse could be used quite as frecly by the lawless as by the law-abiding if we were not there to look after them.

In many parts of the country they have not even yet quite realized that they are living under a settled government. Some years ago there was a dispute about the exact line of demarcation between one of our Madras districts and a tiny, extremely well-managed little State called Cochin, which is an *enclave* in Madras territory. The then Governor of the Presidency was about to pay a visit to the Anamalai hills, which lie close to the disputed boundary. A number of the perfectly harmless but wild people who inhabit those hills disappeared from their homes, "for," they said, "he is coming to make war on the Raja of Cochin, and we shall all be impressed to carry baggage for the army." That is to say, they conceived themselves still precisely in the position of the *Bégars* described in the twentieth of these Letters. Any one who is well acquainted with India could cap this anecdote by numbers of others, showing how very little way civilization has penetrated below the surface. One in a thousand we are scattered over the country, white grains, as has been said, "amongst the myriads of black ones, but each white grain linked to the next white grain by a slender line of steel!" So long as that organization continucs, all will go well enough; but if ever, by mistakes at home or, by what is far less likely, some shock from abroad, the delicate mechanism of our rule is broken up, then our descendants will see all over the land the same sort of "devil's delight" which Colonel Broughton has described in the work to which, with these few introductory remarks, I now invite attention.

I ought perhaps to mention that Colonel Broughton's very peculiar way of spelling Indian words has been carefully retained in the text of his letters, and that a map, which will be found very useful by the reader, has been specially compiled for this edition.

M. E. GRANT DUFF.

LETTERS

FROM

A MAHRATTA CAMP

LETTER I

Introduction—March from Agra—Ruins of Kumal Khan's palace—Kagarol—Sepou—Baree—Moohumedan tombs—Marauding chiefs—Hunting seat of Shah Jihan—Siree-Muttra—Dreary country—Visit of the Raja—Dholpoor Wukeel—March—Kiruolee—Bad weather—Halt.

KIRUOLEE, *Dec. 26th*, 1808.

MY DEAR BROTHER,

You have often urged me to give you some account of the people among whom I have been living for the last three years; and, when I have objected the dulness and uninteresting nature of the subject, you have replied, that those incidents, manners, and customs, which may, from habit, have lost all interest for myself, will at least possess the charm of novelty for you: especially as, since the late war[1] in India, the Mahratta name has become more commonly known in England, and, consequently, all which

[1] The second Maráthá War of 1803–4, in which General Wellesley defeated the armies of Sindhia and Raghují II. of Nagpúr, and Venkají, his brother, at Assaye (23rd Sept., 1803), and Argaum (28th Nov., 1803), in the south, while Lord Lake was victorious over Maráthá armies at Delhi (14th March), and Laswari (1st Nov.) in the north. On the 14th Nov., 1804, General Fraser defeated Holkar at Deeg, thus ending the campaign.

relates to it an object of more general inquiry and attention. I have now resolved to gratify your curiosity; and have only to express a hope, that you will not find my former objections too well founded.

Of the origin and early history of the Mahrattas so many accounts have been published, that it would be superfluous for me to dwell upon those points: and as a history of their empire[1] is now, I understand, about to proceed from hands every way better qualified than mine to elucidate the subject, I shall confine myself to a simple narration of their manners and customs such as they appear to me.

The end of my journey to the Company's provinces having been attained, I am now on my way back to resume my situation in the camp of Seend,hiya; and as I carry with me a numerous train of servants, and a large quantity of supplies for the use of the Residency, I shall consequently travel sufficiently at my leisure to detail all the incidents of the march. After my arrival in camp, I propose to note down events as they arise, together with such observations as may occur to me, for your amusement. I must, however, premise two things: first, that you expect no political secrets, not merely because I have little opportunity of procuring authentic information on such topics, but because, if I had, you would derive no pleasure from reading a dry narrative of measures, the offspring of systematic meanness, bad faith and constitutional cunning. As the intrigues and common politics of a Mahratta Durbar are, however, always matters of public notoriety and discussion, I shall be able to lay before you enough of each to convey a tolerably correct idea of that policy and faith, which have become as proverbial in modern India, as those of Carthage were among the ancient Romans. Secondly, I must beg you always to bear in mind, that when an English gentle-

[1] "A History of the Mahrattas," since published by Mr. Scott Waring. B. [" A History of the Mahrattas; to which is prefixed an Historical Sketch of the Deccan." London, 1810. 4to.]

man undertakes to give an account of Indian manners and habits of private life, he labours under many disadvantages. The obstacles which prevent our ever viewing the natives of India in their domestic circles are great and insuperable; such as the restrictions of caste on their side, rank and situation on ours, &c. We do not intermarry with them, as the Portuguese did; nor do we ever mix with them, in the common duties of social life on terms of equality. What knowledge we have acquired of their domestic arrangements has been gained chiefly by inquiry; and hence we are often led to describe customs and institutions unfavourably, because our own prejudices render us incompetent to feel their propriety, or correctly to judge of their effects. These observations apply more particularly to the Mahrattas, with whom neither we ourselves, nor our Indian fellow subjects, have little else than merely a political intercourse. As it is probable, therefore, that I may often view things in an imperfect light, or perhaps with a prejudiced eye, I shall confine myself as much as possible to plain matters of fact, and leave you to draw your own conclusions. These two provisos being made, I now proceed to my narrative.

On the 20th inst. I marched from Agra to a small village named Kagarol, a distance of about fourteen miles; the country flat and open, and pretty well cultivated; but with very few trees, except in the vicinity of three or four large villages which lay on either side of the road. I saw no tanks, nor any *nalas* or rivulets, which had water in them at this season; but several wells, from which alone the country seemed to be watered. About two miles from the cantonments at Agra are the ruins of a palace built by Kumul Khan, a nobleman of the Emperor Acbar's court. The buildings are all of a fine red stone; and some of them are still very perfect; especially a spacious *boulee*, or well, surrounded by a handsome circular building consisting of two tiers of arches, in each of which a pair of bullocks used to be employed to draw the water.

On the 21st I marched about fifteen miles to Sepou, a village belonging to the Rana of Dholpoor, situated on the bank of the river Parbuttee. The villagers pointed out to me the remains of a mud fort called Roshungurh, which, they said, was once a place of considerable strength. They were civil and attentive, and willingly supplied me with wood, straw, and such other necessaries as I required for the use of my little camp. On this day's march I passed the boundary which separates the territories of the Company from those of the Rana of Dholpoor.

On the 22nd I reached Baree, fourteen miles from Sepou, the second town, in point of consequence, in the Rana's dominions. The streets are narrow; but many of the houses, which are built of the red stone found in the neighbourhood, are two stories high, and have a greater appearance of comfort than is usual in Indian habitations. The town is surrounded by gardens, and groves of mango and tamarind trees. The Rana sometimes resides here; and has a good house within an inclosure, dignified with the appellation of the Fort, but which is nothing more than an open square space surrounded by a wall of red stone, and having round towers at each angle and centre. Baree has for many years been chiefly inhabited by Pithans; and some handsome Moohumedan tombs are still to be seen in the environs. The country on this side of Sepou is not so well cultivated as on the other; neither did I observe so many or so large villages. Provisions, however, are cheap for this part of the country; wheat flour selling at eighteen *seers*, and gram, a grain with which we feed our cattle, at twenty-four *seers* for the rupee: a *seer* is very nearly two pounds. An officer of the Rana's, who was himself at Dholpoor, waited upon me by desire of his master, and took care that I was plentifully supplied with every thing which I stood in need of. He informed me that an attack had been made upon the town a short time before by a party of plunderers in the service of Ram Pal and Bukhshee Goojur, two notorious marauding chieftains; and that they had been beaten off, with some loss, but were still encamped in the neighbourhood. In the afternoon I rode out to see a hunting seat built by the Emperor Shah Jihan. It is situated in the midst of an extensive plain, about two miles from the town. The palace is built upon the borders of a fine piece of water, formed by strong embankments faced with stone, along the top of which runs a wide and well paved terrace. At three angles of the embankment are as many handsome pavilions, each containing a complete suite of apartments; and on the northern bank is an enclosure, about a hundred and fifty yards square, which was formerly a garden surrounding the apartments allotted to the ladies. The whole of the buildings are faced with massy slabs of red stone, and are in very good repair.

On the 23rd we had a tedious and disagreeable march of eighteen miles to Siree-Muttra; the residence of a petty Raja, a tributary of the Rana of Dholpoor. The road lay over rocks of the red stone, so common in this part of the country, covered only in a few places by shallow strata of mould. Near a cluster of little hamlets I saw some spots cultivated with inferior kinds of grain, a little sugar cane, castor, and cotton: the rest of the country was a perfect desert. Siree-Muttra is a pretty large town, built on a naked rock of red stone; of which material all the houses are constructed: so that, at a little distance, it is not easy to distinguish that there is any town at all. The houses are mean, and the streets so narrow, that it was with difficulty my elephant passed through without injuring the roofs. The chief occupation of the inhabitants seemed to be working the red stone into slabs, with which the whole country around is covered in such abundance, that it was some time before I could find a spot to pitch my tent upon. The Raja was very civil, and gave immediate orders for furnishing me with whatever I required. In the afternoon he came to wait upon me, attended by his Deewan or minister, and a

Wukeel or envoy, of the Rana's. The Raja himself is a fat good-looking man, middle aged, and apparently not marked with any striking character: but his minister is a lively sensible old man, very inquisitive, and talked a great deal. He examined every thing about the tent; and seemed particularly pleased with a printed book, which lay upon the table; an art of which he appeared to have had before no conception. It happened to contain a portrait of Marquis Wellesley, which I showed to him: he instantly inquired if it was he who beat the Mahrattas; and when I told him it was, "it makes my heart quake to look at him," cried he, and shut the book. The Wukeel was going on a mission to Seend,hiya's camp; and the main object of his visit to me was to ask permission to proceed under my protection. He had halted at Siree-Muttra for seven days, from a fear of falling in with the marauding chiefs: to one of whom, Bukhshee Goojur, he was particularly an object of hatred; having been the adviser of his dismissal from the Rana's service, and since placed in the very situation which the Bukhshee had filled. As I was aware of this, and had been informed that the Goojur was awaiting his arrival at Kiruolee, I did not at all relish the idea of this addition to my party. I told him, therefore, as politely as I could, that I should be most happy in his company; but as I had a large quantity of baggage, upwards of fifty camels and three elephants, and a numerous train of followers with me, and scarcely fifty Sipahees to protect them, it was important that I should become as little an object of jealousy to these people as possible; and therefore I recommended that we should move separately, and that he should wait for a more favourable opportunity of prosecuting his journey. He acquiesced; but seemed, I thought, still to harbour an idea of joining me at the next stage. You may judge in what estimation British soldiers are held here, when I tell you that this Wukeel, who wanted protection from my little detachment, had with him upwards of two hundred armed men. While my visitors stayed with me, they all expressed themselves in terms of high admiration of the prowess, humanity, and justice of the British Government; which alone, the Deewan said, seemed to understand and to practise the true art of ruling. Above all things they commended our having crushed the intolerable power of the Mahrattas; and launched forth in unqualified praise of Lord Wellesley; whose character seems, amongst these rescued states, to have secured that veneration and esteem which his splendid talents and distinguished services so eminently entitled him to.

On the 24th the road was so bad, that I with difficulty reached a small village on the Siree-Muttra territory, a distance of only eight miles, where I encamped for the day; and had the satisfaction to find that the Wukeel had given up his intention of joining me. Yesterday I reached this place [Kiruolee], after a march of fourteen miles. Soon after we started in the morning it began to rain, and continued to do so throughout the remainder of the day: in consequence of which, and the badness of the road, I did not get to the ground till past one o'clock, wet to the skin, cold and tired. The baggage did not arrive till two hours after; and, as the tents were by that time completely wetted, the people fatigued, and the cattle jaded, I resolved to halt to-day. Our supplies did not come from the town till late in the evening; and altogether it was the most comfortless Christmas Day I ever passed. No people suffer more from cold and wet than the natives of India; at this season, they dress in clothes stuffed with cotton, and wrap themselves in shawls or quilts, according to their means. The poorer sort throw a coarse blanket over their shoulders, and, with their lower extremities always exposed, go about shivering and shaking in the most lamentable manner. They never dream of keeping themselves warm by exercise; but cower round the embers of a few burnt sticks, with more eagerness than we crowd about a fire in the severest weather: and should a shower of rain chance to fall, it renders them absolutely helpless.

I shall take the opportunity of a messenger's going off to camp, to send this account of my journey thus far. Wishing you many happy returns of the season, and a much merrier Christmas than I am likely to pass,

I am,

My dear brother,

&c. &c.

LETTER II

Account of Kiruolee—Interview with the Daroghu—March to Harutee—The Bunas—Difficulties respecting remainder of the route—Hirkarus—March down the Bunas—Goojurs—Arrival at Kund,har—Difficulties of encamping—Kund,har—Qiludars—Runtambor—Nuya Shuhur—Buniyas—March to Palee—Crossing the Chumbul—Arrival in Camp.

SEEND,HIYA'S CAMP, SOOPOOR, *Jan.* 1, 1809.

SOON after I had despatched my last letter from Kiruolee, I received a message from the Raja, intimating that he intended me the honour of a visit, and also that he expected to see me at his own house: at the same time he gave orders for supplying my camp with every thing that I could require. The present Raja, whose name is Hurree Bukhsh Pal, succeeded, a few years ago, to his brother, who is said to have been a most promising young man; and of whom his people still speak with enthusiastic admiration. He was particularly fond of conversing with Europeans, and informing himself of their manners and customs. The natural timidity of the present Raja, who is represented as a youth of very limited capacity, prevents his imitating his brother in this respect. As the hour appointed for visiting me drew near, his courage failed: some of his people had told him that I had brought with me a battalion of infantry, a whole corps of cavalry and some guns; and though he might so easily have ascertained the truth, his apprehensions were too strong to be overcome, and he sent to excuse himself. His family, which is of the Rajpoot tribe of *Jado*, is among the most ancient of the country: they reigned formerly at

Biana,[1] and possessed extensive territories. Like most of the petty chiefs, however, in this part of Hindoostan, they have been stript from time to time of their best possessions by the Mahrattas, who have risen upon their ruin: and about sixty years ago, Raja Gopal Sing,h, wishing to preserve for his family what was yet left to him, quitted the venerable residence of his ancestors and retired to Kiruolee, where he built the present town and fort. The revenue of this little state does not exceed a lakh and a quarter of rupees, or about £15,000 sterling; out of which the Peshwah claims a tribute of twenty thousand rupees: and its affairs are conducted by the foster-father of the Raja, and one of his relations who has the title of Deewan: these two persons possess the entire confidence of their master, and exercise unlimited control over his country, while he himself is exclusively occupied in the sports of the field.

My tents were about two miles from the town, and in the afternoon I rode towards it. The situation is a strong one; having the *Puchperee*, a river with high and perpendicular banks, and which during the rainy season swells to a tremendous torrent, running close under the wall on the south side; while on the others it is almost entirely surrounded by deep and extensive ravines. The fort is in the centre of the town, which is also strengthened by a good stone wall with bastions. Returning from my ride I met the foster-father of the Raja, who sent to beg I would stop, and favour him with an interview. I alighted of course; and horse-cloths being spread upon the ground, the usual manner of conducting such meetings, we sat down. This man, who has the rank of *Daroghu*, or superintendent, is about forty years of age, and is pleasing in his manners and appearance. He mentioned his master's youth and inexperience as an apology for his not having seen me; but

[1] The fort at Biána was once regarded as one of the strongest in India. It was taken in 1004 A.D. by Sayyid Sálar Masáúd, a nephew of the great Mahmúd of Ghazní, when held by the Jadun Rájá, Bijai Pál.

offered to introduce me the next day, if I would put off my departure. In return, I begged him to assure the Raja how anxious I was to offer my personal thanks for the attention I had received in his country; but that it was necessary for me to reach camp as expeditiously as possible. We continued our *moolaqat*, as these interviews are termed, for about half an hour, and then parted; the Daroghu having furnished me with some useful information respecting the remainder of my route. While I continued with him, I saw a battalion of Sipahees at exercise near the gate of the town, disciplined and dressed, though somewhat in an outré style, after the European manner: this, with a corps of *nujeebs*, or infantry with match-locks, a body of about a thousand horse, and one of *pueks*, or footmen irregularly armed and chiefly employed in collecting the revenue, completes the military establishment of Kiruolee.

On the 27th and 28th our route lay over a narrow tract of land between two ridges of hills and scarcely exceeding a mile in breadth, till we reached the Bunas river, at a distance of about thirty miles from Kiruolee. This valley is almost the only part of the Kiruolee territory from which the Raja derives any revenue: it is cultivated throughout; and has several small villages scattered over it. On the second day our camp was pitched on an island in the bed of the Bunas, which is here nearly two miles from bank to bank; though at this season of the year it has but a small stream of fine clear water running through the sand. Our supplies were furnished from a village on the left bank called Haruotee, from which this *ghat*, or passage over the river, takes its name. The road from Kiruolee is good, till within four miles of the Bunas, where the country becomes so completely intersected by ravines, that the remaining actual distance is more than doubled by the winding of the road. About this point too the valley widens into an extensive plain, and opens a fine view of the hills about Mularna to the right, and those near the town of Rampoora in front. On this day I was met by two *Hirkarus*, or messengers, from camp; who brought letters advising me to avoid the road by the city of Nuya Shuhur, as it was supposed that Seend,hiya himself meant to proceed against it; and recommending me to take a circuit by Mularna, and endeavour to cross the Chumbul at some ferry higher up the river. As I had now got so near my journey's end, and hoped to conclude it before New-year's-day, I did not at all relish the idea of extending it so much as I necessarily must, if I followed so circuitous a route. I held a consultation therefore with the Hirkarus, whom the Kiruolee Raja had sent with me, and whom I had found smart and intelligent fellows, and learnt from them that there was a road, shorter even than that by Nuya Shuhur, which passed under the fortress of Kund,har; and by this route, as it was very little known, they thought I might proceed without any fear of molestation. These Hirkarus are a most active and useful set of men: their business is to obtain information, to act as guides, and convey letters or messages: they are always well acquainted with the country, its roads, passes through hills, or across rivers; and are so generally useful, that, like the ancient heralds, they are looked upon as privileged, and allowed to pass unmolested where other travellers would be in the utmost danger. They are often sent to great distances, and are absent for many months; when they must necessarily be subjected to the greatest hardships, in a country where there are no inns, and where the inhabitants of many provinces subsist entirely by plunder.

On the morning of the 29th I accordingly started for Kund,har: the first part of the road ran along the right bank of the river, and then directly down its bed; which being of fine sand, rendered this part of our journey very tedious and fatiguing to the cattle. The river passes through an opening in a ridge of high hills to the southward, washing their bases on either side. On the left hand the ridge continues to a hill fort, called Bariur, belonging to Jypoor; on the right, it turns off to the S.W. and forms part of the still larger range called *Arrabaree*, in the midst of which is situated the celebrated fortress of Runtambor, and the city of Madoopor or Nuya Shuhur. After marching about four miles down the bed of the river, we turned off to the right, and entered a narrow defile between two high ranges of hills, which rose almost perpendicular on either hand: the intermediate space, not much more than half a mile in breadth, was covered with an impenetrable jungle of trees and underwood, through which ran a narrow sandy road, or rather pathway, apparently formed by the torrents which rush from the hills in the rainy season. Soon after entering this defile, we were stopped by a party of *Goojurs*, a race of plunderers who inhabit the hills. At first they assured us there was no road that way; but finding us resolved to go on, they said that their orders from the *Qiludar*, or commandant, of Runtambor were positive, to allow no one to pass, and declared, if we persisted, that they would, by firing a few matchlocks, quickly bring all the parties in the neighbourhood to oppose our progress. The Hirkarus at length contrived to pacify them, by asserting that I had passports from the Qiludar himself, who would be highly displeased, should they presume to stop me; one of them adding, aside to me, that they were mere *gunwars*, boors, and that it was always lawful to outwit such fellows by any means. At the further end of the defile we were hailed by another party of Goojurs half way up the mountain, who, not hearing, or not understanding, the answer which my witty conductors made to them, fired at us; they were, however, too far off for their balls to reach us, and we proceeded on towards Kund,har, over a plain which extends from the mouth of the defile to the foot of the hill upon which the fort is situated. As we approached, the inhabitants of some little hamlets, scattered about the base of the hill, came out to stare at us; and soon spread the alarm around the country: and when you recollect that this passage through the hills was supposed to be almost unknown, you will not wonder that some alarm should be experienced at seeing, issuing from it, such a party as I had with me; and which appeared more formidable than it really was, from the narrowness of the road having obliged the followers and baggage to extend to an amazing length. Signal guns were now fired from the fort; whose report reverberated through the mountains, and produced a tremendous effect. The *Nuqqaru*, a species of large kettle-drum, was beaten from post to post along the hills, as signals of alarm to the country, and the neighbouring forts; the peasants came flocking in from all quarters, with their families, herds, &c., and before night the garrison was reinforced by a thousand men. I confess that I did not feel quite easy, at such *warm* preparations for my reception; and now began to suspect that I had been led into an act of great imprudence, in penetrating, without permission, by so unfrequented a route. It was now, however, too late to retreat; and the only plan left was to put a good face upon the matter, and go boldly on. When I came near the town, which is at the foot of the hill on the south side, I found the inhabitants assembled, and the military drawn up outside the walls. I had previously sent on an Hirkaru and one of my own servants, with a complimentary message to the Qiludar; informing him who I was, whence I came, and whither I was going: and added a request that I might be permitted to encamp there for the night, and proceed quietly on my way in the morning to Palee, where I proposed to cross the Chumbul. The *Amil*, the chief civil power, who resided in the lower town, would not admit my messengers within the gates; but said that he would make known my request to the Qiludar, who resided above, and transmit his answer to me; and that in the meantime I must remove to a little distance from the town and await the event. I accordingly alighted under the shade of some trees about a mile from the walls, where there was a well; and ordered all the baggage to be collected together, and the cattle to be watered, but not unloaded. As it was now past two o'clock, and the next stage full nine miles further on, I began to be exceedingly anxious for the return of my messengers: two had arrived from the Qiludar, to learn every thing respecting me: to whom I delivered a passport in Persian signed by the British resident with Seend,hiya (though they frankly told me their master could not read it), as a voucher, and repeated my former request, adding, that I also hoped the Qiludar would send some of his people with me the next day, to show the road and assist in procuring boats to cross the river. By this time a vast number of people from the town, all armed, and soldiers with their matches lighted, had assembled to view the *Firingee*, the generic term by which Europeans are distinguished all over India. They formed a circle round me and sat down, and we entered into conversation: they asking innumerable questions, and I answering in such a manner as I thought most likely to please them. They all agreed in assuring me that I must not hope to remain there for the night; for that such a thing had never before been heard of as a *Qafilu*, or caravan, passing that way. They were, however, mistaken; for, after waiting till near sunset, an Hirkaru at length arrived from the Qiludar, with permission to encamp, and assurances that *Buniyas*, or merchants, should be sent to supply the people with all that they wanted: he added, however, that he could afford me no assistance in crossing the river, as the ferry was under the superintendence of the commandant of Nuya Shuhur, to whom he advised me to write immediately. As I was now completely in their power, I thought the safest way was to follow this advice, and had just finished my letter, when a servant introduced a very respectable looking man, who informed me that he was himself the Zumeendar, or renter, of Palee; that the boats were under his direction; and that he would very willingly accompany me the next morning, and be answerable for my crossing, without putting me to the trouble of sending any message to Nuya Shuhur. You may guess how agreeable this unexpected offer was to me: I felt my mind relieved from much anxiety, and returned most sincere thanks to Natoo

Sing,h, which was the Zumeendar's name, for his politeness.

The fort of Kund,har belongs to Jypoor, and was built about eighty years ago by one of the Rajas of that country. It is deemed impregnable by its possessors · and I was seriously asked by some of the people who crowded about me, if I thought that a ball fired from a gun on the plain would reach the top. The fort, however, appeared to me to be little more than a stone wall, with turrets and round towers at certain distances, built round the brow of the hill, which may be about half a mile in length, of an oval form, and its acclivity, in which I imagine the chief strength of the place consists, very great : it is besides rugged with projecting rocks, and covered to the top with low jungle. There are seven gateways, through which it is necessary to pass before one reaches the main body of the fortress on the top of the hill : the gates are under the charge of as many Qiludars, each independent of the others ; though one has the nominal rank of supreme commander. The whole are under the orders of the commandant of Runtambor, who is generally a *Takoor*, or lord, of the highest rank, and one of the most confidential servants of the Raja. This last fortress is about five miles from Kund,har, in the centre of the Arrabaree hills. It was built by Raja Ameer Sing,h, in the reign of the Emperor Alo-oo-deen ; and is esteemed the strongest as well as largest fortress in Hindoostan. When the Jypoorians talk of it, they call it the work of giants : and should any one betray such ignorance as to ask if it could be taken, they would laugh him to scorn. As no European, however, has yet seen it, we have no adequate means of judging of its real strength ; and may therefore doubt a little its impregnability : though there can be no doubt of its being a stupendous fabric. It was represented to me as situated upon seven hills, which are on all sides completely scarped, and accessible only by one path ; which path, like that of Kund,har, is defended by seven gates, also under the direction of seven Qiludars, without whose signatures and seals no *purwanu*, or passport, is valid, either to or from the fort. The avenues leading to it are strictly guarded, and access prohibited to all except those belonging either to the garrison or the town. The name of the latter is Tuletee; and it is so called from the Hindoostanee word *tule*, beneath, the town being built at the bottom of the hill: it is said to be extensive, commodious and well inhabited. The city of Madoopoor, or Nuya Shuhur (which last appellation only means the new city), built in later days by Raja Madoo Sing,h, is at the distance of two or three miles from Runtambor; and is second only to Jypoor itself in size and consequence: the approaches to it, however, being guarded with as much jealousy as those to Runtambor, all the accounts we have obtained of it are from hearsay only. Two roads lead to it through the hills; and both are strongly fortified and carefully guarded. Soon after the tents were pitched, Buniyas came from the town, plentifully furnished with meal and other articles requisite to afford the people a good supper after their fatigue: our purchases, however, were scarcely completed, before the Buniyas were seized by the servants of one of the Qiludars, whose permission for their coming to us had not been procured; and who in consequence had made no bargain as to what share of their profit was to accrue to himself. I heard next morning that they had all been thrown into confinement, and a good round sum extorted from them before they were again released.

On the 30th I marched about nine miles to Palee, a village on the left bank of the Chumbul, where there is a ferry. Natoo Sing,h, according to his promise, accompanied me; and exerted himself greatly to get the things across: owing, however, to the smallness of the boats, and the unskilfulness of the boatman, it was past nine o'clock at night before the whole detachment was on the other side; and then not a pound of grain was to be procured for either men or cattle. Luckily it had been so late before the camp was pitched on the preceding evening, that many of the people had brought on their day's provisions: the rest were obliged to fast—an hardship to which the prospect of finishing their journey on the next morning made them submit without repining. The road from Kund,har to Palee, which is a small insignificant village, is good; and the country open and well cultivated.

Yesterday we had an easy march of eight miles to camp, across a fine country which appeared to have been lately well inhabited and highly cultivated; but from which the approach of Seend,hiya's army had driven the inhabitants, and made ruins of all their villages.

LETTER III

Description of a Mahratta camp—The Bazars—Tents—Mode of life —Liquors—Huts—The Jinsee and Brigades—Want of cleanliness—The Baruh B,haees and Pindaras—The Shohdahs—Baboo Khan—Misery of the poor people—Children sold—Khuburdars —Soopoor; the Raja a Sukee Buo—Cold weather.

CAMP AT SOOPOOR, *Jan.* 14, 1809.

NOTHING, having any claim to the appellation of a regular encampment, can well be less so than that of a Mahratta army. On marching days, the *Beenee Wala*, or quarter-master general, moves off at an early hour; and upon reaching the ground where the army is to encamp, he plants a small white flag, to mark the spot where the tents of the Muha Raj (the title by which any Hindoo prince is commonly designated), are to be pitched; and which collectively are termed the *Deooree.* The flags of the different *Bazars*, or markets, are then fixed as they arrive; always in the same relative situation to each other, and generally in as straight a line as the ground will admit of. The shops, called *Dokans*, are pitched in two lines running parallel to each other; and thus form one grand street from the front to the rear of the army. This street often extends from three to four miles; the *Deooree* being situated about three-fourths of the whole length from the front, having only the market called the *Chuoree Bazar* in its rear. The different chiefs encamp to the right and left of the principal street; generally, however, in the neighbourhood of some particular *Bazar.* Their respective encampments are made without the smallest attention to regularity, cleanliness or convenience: men, horses, camels, and bullocks are all

C 2

jumbled together in a mass; which mass is surrounded on all sides by others of a similar nature, in a continued series of comfortless confusion. This forms what is termed the *Bura Lushkur*, or main army; and is generally about as many hundred yards in breadth, that is from flank to flank, as it is miles in length from front to rear; thus exactly reversing the order of encampment which obtains in the disciplined armies of Europe.

The shops, which compose the *Bazars*, are mostly formed of blankets or coarse cloth stretched over a bamboo, or some other stick for a ridge pole, supported at either end by a forked stick fixed in the ground. These habitations are called *Pals*: and are of all sizes, from three to eight or nine feet high, and proportionally wide and long according to the circumstances of the owner. Under these miserable coverings not only are the goods exposed for sale, but the family of the shopkeeper resides throughout the year, and for many years together. The wealthiest merchants of the *Bazars* use these *Pals*: but the military men, and others attached to the camp, generally possess a dwelling of somewhat a more comfortable description, regularly made of two or three folds of cloth in thickness, closed at one end, and having a flap to keep out the wind and rain at the opposite one: these are dignified with the name of *Ruotees*, and come nearer to our ideas of a tent. The *Ruotees*, like the *Pals*, are of all descriptions and sizes; and most of the chiefs of the highest rank inhabit them. I do not believe that there are, throughout the camp, ten tents fashioned like our European marquees, even including those of the Muha Raj himself.

After this account of the common dwellings of the Mahrattas, it will scarcely be necessary to add that they are total strangers to the comforts of domestic life. The Dii Penates are not among the deities whom they worship. The cheerful fire, and the clean hearth surrounded by smiling faces, are as much unknown to them as the brilliant drawing-room or the crowded theatre. They never feel even the solid and cheap comforts of a snug room, or the light of a candle: but, in the cold weather, huddle round a miserable fire made of horse or cow dung, or dirty straw collected about their tents; and wrapping themselves up in a coarse blanket or cotton quilt, contrive, with the aid of a pipe of bad tobacco, to while away a few hours in listless indolence; when tired of smoking and chatting, they creep into their *Pals*, and are quickly in a state in which, at last, they need not envy the luxurious and refined European. In this manner do the more sober of them pass their evenings: but such as think that life is bestowed for superior enjoyments, and have a taste for more spirited modes of whiling it away, retire, at the approach of evening, to the arrack shop, or the tent of the prostitute; and revel through the night in a state of low debauchery, which could hardly be envied by the keenest votary of Comus and his beastly crew. Even these scenes of mirth and jollity are enacted in such tents as have already been described, and are exhibited to the eye through the medium only of half a dozen wicks immersed in thick gross oil, arranged in a dirty brass cruise, and which together scarcely afford as much light as a common English rushlight. The liquor sold in the shops is distilled from the fruit of a tree called *Mouah*: it is about as strong as common gin, and is impregnated with a smell and flavour that would turn the stomach of the stoutest porter in London. In this state it is termed *Daroo*: and when distilled over again, with a little care for the use of such as can afford it, *Phool*: four quarts of the former and two of the latter are sold for a rupee; and it is now common to see it exposed for sale in English bottles. An inferior kind of rum is also sometimes to be purchased in these shops at the same rate.

At the door of every tent is a fire, such as I have before described; the smoke of which being too heavy to ascend into the air, spreads throughout the whole camp; where it serves to keep the people warm, to drive the flies away from the cattle, and to put out the eyes of all those who are unused to so gross an element.

Such is the general picture of a Mahratta camp. Sometimes, indeed, when it is known that the army is to halt for any length of time, and there happens to be abundance of grass or trees in the neighbourhood, the people construct little huts for themselves; and enjoy, comparatively, a degree of comfort. This was the case during the rainy season of 1807, when Seend,hiya lay for seven months before the fort of Rutgurh. The whole army then presented the appearance rather of a rustic city than a camp; and reminded us of that which is described by Gibbon as the residence of Attila in the wilds of Germany.

The *Jinsee*, or park, forms a separate encampment, as do the brigades of regular infantry: these last always pitch in a square; or, as they term it here, a *qilu*: literally meaning a fort. Our station is in the rear of the whole; and we generally contrive to keep at the distance of about a mile from the army; their disgusting want of cleanliness rendering them most disagreeable neighbours. It is impossible to take a ride in the vicinity of the great camp without being poisoned by the stench arising from the carcases of horses, bullocks and camels, which no one takes the trouble to remove, and a variety of other nuisances; besides being interrupted by the crowds of people and cattle that go out every morning to forage, and return again in the evening.

One of the most noted corps in the Muha Raj's army is a *Risalu*, or troop, called the *Baruh B,haees*, or twelve brothers; from that number of leaders which originally headed them. It is composed entirely of Mahrattas, or at least of inhabitants of the original territories of the Mahrattas in the *Duk,hun*. and is reckoned the most unruly and licentious crew in the army, hardly even excepting the Pindaras themselves. The only difference between the two corps is, that the latter receive no pay whatever, supporting themselves entirely by plunder; while the *Baruh B,haees* do receive a small monthly stipend, which is supposed to render them more amenable to the control of the prince in whose service they may be enlisted, and to keep their acts of violence and rapine within some bounds. This is, however, little else than a nominal distinction ; for nothing in the shape of plunder was ever known to come amiss to a *Baruh B,haee.* They had taken offence at some delay in issuing their salary about the time I went to the provinces last May, and quitted camp in a body ; to which they only returned a few months ago. During their absence they supported themselves by plundering and laying under contribution the country wherever they went : and since their return, were so little able to throw off these congenial habits, that they became a source of terror and alarm to the whole country around, and even to the people of their own camp. At length the Muha Raj found it necessary to take some steps to reduce them to order : and accordingly, about three weeks ago, surrounded them by some corps of cavalry, two or three battalions and some guns ; and declared his resolution to order a general attack to be made upon them. This threat would probably have been carried into execution, if they had not, in the most humble manner, implored his mercy, and solemnly promised a reformation of their manners—a promise which they most likely cannot, if they ever intended to keep. One of our Sipahees returning from leave of absence and several of the Hirkarus attached to the *Dak*, or Post, have been plundered by them since their reform. Such infringements of diplomatic rights pass unnoticed here ; forbearance, sometimes to the most mortifying degree, being the general rule by which our conduct is squared in these cases.

Another very distinguished corps in this motley camp, though not strictly speaking a military one, is that of the *Shohdas :* literally the scoundrels. They form a regularly organized body under a chief named Fazil Khan ; to whose orders they pay implicit obedience. They are the licensed thieves and robbers of the camp ; and from the fruits of their industry their principal derives a very considerable revenue.

On marching days they are assembled under their leader, and act as porters for the Muha Raj's baggage. At sieges they dig the trenches, erect the batteries, and carry the scaling ladders. But their grand concern is the gambling houses, which are placed under their immediate control and superintendence; and where they practise all the refinements of accomplished villany to decoy and impose upon the unwary, which you perhaps fondly flatter yourself are the distinguishing excellencies of these establishments in Europe. Baboo Khan, a Mahratta chief of some rank and consideration, is an avowed patron of this curious society; and is in fact, though in a higher sphere, as accomplished a *Shohda* as any of the band. About a year ago, a merchant came to the camp with horses for sale: the Khan chose out some of the most valuable, and paid down the merchant's own price for them on the spot; desiring him, at the same time, to bring more, as he was about to increase the numbers of his own *Risalu*. Such unheard-of honesty and liberality induced other merchants to bring their horses also for sale: the Mahratta took them all at the prices demanded; but when the owners came for payment, he scoffed at them for their credulity, and had them actually beaten away from his tent by the rascally crew who always attend upon him. The merchants carried their complaint to the Muha Raj; and after waiting for several months in expectation of justice being done them, were paid at the rate of seven *annas* in the rupee; besides a deduction for the *Buniyas*, with whom the unfortunate fellows had been obliged to run in debt for subsistence during their stay in camp. The whole transaction lasted about a twelvemonth; at the end of which time they were obliged to decamp with less than one-third of what was strictly their due.

Where such acts of injustice and oppression are committed with impunity, it is not wonderful that there should be much misery among the poorer orders of the community. When grain is dear, hundreds of poor families are driven to the most distressing shifts to obtain a bare subsistence.

At such times I have often seen women and children employed in picking out the undigested grains of corn from the dung of the different animals about the camp. Even now, when grain is by no means at a high price (wheat being sold in the market for thirteen *seers* for the rupee), it is scarcely possible to move out of the limits of our own camp without witnessing the most shocking proofs of poverty and wretchedness. I was returning from a ride the other morning, when two miserable looking women followed me for charity: each had a little infant in her arms; and one of them repeatedly offered to sell hers for the trifling sum of two rupees. Many of our Sipahees and servants have children whom they have either purchased in this manner, or picked up begging among our tents. In adopting these little wretches, however, they have so often been taken in, that they are now more cautious in indulging their charitable propensities. The poor people of the army finding that a child, who told a piteous tale and appeared to be starving, was sure to find a protector in our camp, used, in hard times, to send their children out to beg; and when better able to support them themselves, would pretend to discover their lost infants, and reclaim them.

There is a strange custom, which prevails at all Indian courts, of having a servant called a *Khubur-dar*, or newsman, who is an admitted spy upon the chief, about whose person he is employed; and whose business it is faithfully to report all his actions, of whatever nature, to his employer. Seend,hiya has such an one in our camp; and we of course another in his. This latter is a perfect original. He has been in the service of the British residents for more than forty years; and in the course of so long a period has, as may be supposed, picked up a collection of anecdotes of the most extraordinary nature: most of them are entertaining enough; but many not over delicate, and perhaps not always restrained within the strict line of truth.

Soopoor, near which place we are encamped, is the capital of a small principality belonging to Jypoor, and now possessed by a relation of the prince of that country. The present Raja has acquired the title of *Sukee Buo*, or the Dancing Lord; from his dancing, on particular festivals, before the image in the temple. This appellation is not peculiar to himself; but is always conferred upon such Hindoo princes as distinguish themselves by performing so laudable a piece of religious ceremony.

The weather is becoming very cold; the thermometer having stood, at sunrise, for some days past at 31°. We cannot, as you do, fly for warmth to the cheerful blaze of a fire; but we substitute for it, in the evening, a large chafingdish of live coals; over which we enjoy a bottle of old port with as keen a relish as you can do in the more northern climate. Adieu!

LETTER IV

March to Kutolee—Raja of Kota—Zalim Sing,h—Visit the Durbar—Seendhiya—The Surdars—Gopal Rao Buo—The Mamma—Familiar appellatives of Mahratta chiefs—Seendhiya's encampment—His pecuniary difficulties—Sitting D'hurna—Quarterly payments—Elephant fights—Duk,hunee horses—The Bukree Eed—Moohumedan feasts for the dead—The Sunkrat—Feeding Brahmuns—The Busunt, or spring—Mode of grinding corn—A Busunt song—Foragers.

CAMP AT KUTOLEE, *Jan.* 31.

WE marched eleven miles to this ground yesterday; and encamped on the right bank of the river *Parbuttee*, opposite to Kutolee, a town belonging to the Raja of Kota. The road lay over a fine flat country interspersed with several villages, and everywhere well cultivated; though, until we had almost reached our new ground, scarcely a particle of the crop was to be seen; the whole having been destroyed and the villages unroofed by the Mahrattas. Our tents are pitched in a garden filled with orange and lime, tamarind and mango trees. Immediately opposite to us, across the river, is the palace of the Raja of Kutolee, a handsome old building after the Hindoo fashion, very lofty, and built upon the bank of the river. The *Zunanu*, or women's apartment, occupies one wing; and we could plainly see the ladies yesterday afternoon, seated in an open turret, enjoying the fresh air and a view of the camp. Soon after our tents were pitched, a message was brought from the Muha Raj, requesting us to take great care of the trees, as the garden was held in high estimation by the town's people: and the only difficulty we found throughout the day was to prevent his own people from cutting them down to forage his elephants and camels.

The *Parbuttee* here forms the boundary of the Kota territory; the garden being the only spot belonging to Kutolee on this side of the river. The legitimate Raja of Kota is, with his family, kept in close confinement by a person named *Zalim Sing,h*, who has long usurped the entire management of public affairs; and is indeed recognized as ruler by all the states of Hindoostan. He is a man of very considerable talents; and, though not governing a very extensive territory, has yet contrived to render himself feared and respected by all his neighbours. He was lately nominated by Seendhiya to the office of Soobu, or governor, of the province of Mewar; and paid a lakh and a half of rupees, about eighteen thousand pounds, for the appointment. The Muha Raj, however, soon after changed his mind; and continued the celebrated *Ambajee* in that situation: though he did not think it at all necessary to return his money to *Zalim Sing,h*.

A few days before we left Soopoor, I accompanied the acting Resident to the Durbar. We were received in a small tent, lined with scarlet cloth fantastically embroidered with coloured silks. Seendhiya was seated nearly in the centre, on a large square cushion covered with gold brocade; his back supported by a round bolster, and his arms resting upon two flat cushions; all covered with the same costly material, and forming together a kind of throne, called a *Musnud*, or *Guddee*. He is turned of thirty; about five feet five inches in height; and inclined to be fat, but not largely made. His complexion is rather dark, and his features agreeable: but his whole appearance strongly indicates a debauchee; and in so doing, does not most certainly belie him. He was dressed very plainly, in a purple turban, an old yellow silk robe, called *Ilkalik*, and a faded lilac shawl thrown carelessly over his shoulders. He wore several strings of valuable pearls and uncut emeralds round his neck: of the former he is particularly vain; and even affects to be styled *Motee Wala*, or the "Man of Pearls." Some horse-cloths were spread upon the floor to the right and left of the *Guddee*, which on great occasions are exchanged for carpets: and on these were seated the Surdars, or chiefs, and others who had business to transact at the Durbar. It is contrary to etiquette for the Muha Raj to speak often himself; but when he does, his voice is soft, and his address pleasing: indeed he is universally allowed to be naturally a mild and good-natured man. Some Surdars of the highest rank sat close around the *Guddee*, and occasionally addressed the Muha Raj, to state what was going on and receive his orders. Our place was on his left: and immediately in front sat *Atmaram*, a Pundit who resides in our camp on the part of the Muha Raj, and is the general medium of communication with the Durbar. The Surdars were all dressed in the plainest manner: they affect a great simplicity in all their actions; though they are probably the haughtiest and most ignorant race of nobles of any country on the face of the globe. Many inquiries were made after Mr. M.,[1] the Resident, as to his health, where he was, when we expected him, &c., but when his arrival at Moorshedabad, the capital of Bengal, was mentioned, there was not an individual in the Durbar who seemed to have any idea where that city was situated. Of all the chiefs now in camp, after the Muha Raj's own family, one named *Gopal Rao Buo* is the most distinguished for rank and character. He is a Brahmun; and is generally acknowledged to be possessed of more information, honour and integrity than any of his compeers. His countenance is handsome, and his deportment dignified; though his manners are tinctured with rather too much

[1] Charles Theophilus Metcalfe, born in 1785. His Indian career began in 1801, and after filling various high appointments he was nominated "Provisional Governor-General," on the resignation of Lord William Bentinck in 1835. He resigned office in 1838 and returned to England in the early part of that year.

hauteur to be agreeable. With all these advantages, however, he is sometimes guilty of littlenesses, which betray the race to which he belongs. In the year 1803, after Colonel Collins[1] the British envoy, had left Seendhiya's camp, an officer, Lieutenant Simpson, attached to his escort, who had strayed to some distance from the tents, was seized and carried off by a party of *Pindaras*. The Colonel wrote to *Gopal Rao* to demand his restitution. It was refused : and in his answer, the *Buo* childishly observed, that as the colonel himself had forced the war, he had no right to claim exemption from its consequences, of which he now seemed, though too late, to feel the effects : and added, that what had now happened was but a trifle to that which was about to follow. Mr. Simpson was treated with every indignity and cruelty, till after the battle of Assye ; when he was delivered into the charge of Colonel Soleure, a French officer in the service of the *Begum* Sumroo ; who released him from his close confinement, furnished him with clothes and other necessaries, and in fine did all that lay in his power to make his situation as comfortable as circumstances admitted of.

Before we quitted the Durbar, the representative of the family of *Ingria*,[2] whose piratical depredations were formerly so formidable on the coast of Malabar, arrived. He is a little man ; full fifty years of age, very short and very black ; but possessed of an intelligent countenance, and, unlike

[1] Colonel John Collins was appointed by Sir John Shore in 1795 to be resident at the Court of Daulat Ráo Sindhia, where he remained until 1803. In 1804 he was appointed Resident at Lucknow, where he died on 11th June, 1807. The principal tomb in the old Christian cemetery near the Aminabad Bazar is his, hence the vernacular name of the place "Kallan-ka-lat." *See* a "List of Christian Tombs of Historical and Other Interest in the N.-W. Provinces and Oudh," issued in 1888.

[2] Or more correctly, Angria, whose piratical fleet dominated the entire coast of the west of India from Bombay downwards, until the power of this "Maráthá pirate dynasty" was broken in 1756, by the expedition sent from England under the joint command of Admiral Watson, and Clive.

the other Surdars, was dressed magnificently in cloth of gold, and wore several strings of pearls about his neck. His sister was the Muha Raj's mother: and he is in consequence known throughout the camp by the familiar appellation of the *Mamma*, or uncle. The Mahrattas are particularly fond of distinguishing their chiefs by such terms. Most of them have the words *Dada*, *Appa*, or *Baba* added to their names; which are familiar designations of Father, Grandfather, Uncle, &c. Such appellations are generally bestowed upon them, while children, by their relations and attendants; and they afterwards retain them through life. When we rose to depart, *uttur* and *pan* were presented; and *Gopal Rao*, who had met us at the entrance of the enclosure, conducted us so far, and took his leave.

The Muha Raj's tents are all pitched in an enclosure of canvas walls about one hundred and fifty feet long, and half as many broad; in which the spaces allotted for the public tents, his own private ones, and those of the *Zunanu*, are all parted off by other walls of the same description. Around this enclosure the *Khas Paega*, or body guard, is encamped; as is the numerous train of servants and attendants attached to the Muha Raj's establishment.

The pecuniary distresses into which Seendhiya is plunged, and which, no doubt, I shall have many opportunities of recounting to you, sometimes place him in the most ridiculous situations, for a reigning prince, that it is possible to conceive. A few days ago a man called upon me on the part of two *Khans*, with whom I had some acquaintance, and who command a large *Risalu* in the Muha Raj's service. He informed me that, as usual, his masters were in the utmost distress for money; being driven to the necessity of borrowing it, for their daily expenses, at the ruinous rate of *five per cent.* per month! He stated their claims upon the Muha Raj to amount to nearly seven lakhs of rupees: and added, that if they could not get their accounts settled immediately, they meant to go the next day and sit *dhurna* at his tents. This curious mode of enforcing a demand is in universal practice among the Mahrattas: Seendhiya himself not being exempt from it. The man who sits the *dhurna*, goes to the house or tent of him whom he wishes to bring to terms; and remains there till the affair is settled: during which time the one under restraint is confined to his apartment, and not suffered to communicate with any persons but those whom the other may approve of. The laws by which the *dhurna* is regulated are as well defined and understood as those of any other custom whatever. When it is meant to be very strict, the claimant carries a number of his followers, who surround the tent, sometimes even the bed, of his adversary, and deprive him altogether of food; in which case, however, etiquette prescribes the same abstinence to himself: the strongest stomach of course carries the day. A custom of this kind was once so prevalent in the province and city of Benares, that Brahmuns were trained to remain a long time without food. They were sent to the door of some rich individual; where they made a vow to remain without eating, till they should obtain a certain sum of money. To preserve the life of a Brahmun is so absolutely a duty, that the money was generally paid; but never till a good struggle had taken place to ascertain whether the man was staunch or not: for money is the life and soul of all Hindoos. In this camp there are many Brahmuns, who hire themselves out to sit *dhurna*[1] for those, who do not like to expose themselves to so great an inconvenience.

[1] Under the Indian Penal Code the practice of *dharnā* is an offence punishable "with imprisonment of either description for a term which may extend to one year, or with fine, or with both." Marco Polo (Vol. II., p. 327,) describes a variety of the practice in Southern India as follows:—"If a debtor shall have been several times asked by his creditor for payment, and shall have put him off from day to day with promises, then if the creditor can once meet the debtor and succeed in drawing a circle round him, the latter must not pass out of the circle until he shall have satisfied the claim or given security for its discharge. If he in any other case presume to pass the circle he is punished with death as a transgressor against right and justice. And the said Messer Marco, when in this kingdom [Province of Maabar] on

The Khan's servant wanted to ascertain how many of the quarterly payments, made by our government to Seendhiya, were forestalled; as a report was prevalent, that a Mahratta banker of great wealth had bought them up for the next eighteen months. These quarterly payments amount to upwards of a lakh and a half of rupees; one lakh being paid to Seendhiya himself, and eighty thousand nominally to some of the principal chiefs of the Durbar: I say nominally, because, in fact, the Muha Raj appropriates the whole sum to his own use. To this is now added seventy-five thousand rupees, in lieu of the *Jagheer* settled upon *Bueza*[1] *Baee*, Seendhiya's favourite wife, at the peace of 1805; the Muha Raj preferring the receipt of this sum in cash to the possession of the estate itself, subjected to the regulations of a court of judicature: an active and impartial administration of justice conveying the most unusual and disagreeable ideas to the mind of a Mahratta prince. When he wants to raise a sum of money, or to satisfy any very clamorous creditor, he signs receipts for these instalments; they being the only stock that will fetch a reasonable price in the market: and these receipts are generally sold again, at a discount of from eighteen to thirty per cent.; the latter being the usual rate when they have a year to run. The Khan's servant told me that his master has taken one of these receipts, for a payment to be made two years and a half from the present time. For such an acknowledgment he would probably not be able to realize twenty per cent.!

his return home, did himself witness a case of this. It was the king, who owed a foreign merchant a certain sum of money, and though the claim had often been presented, he always put it off with promises. Now one day when the king was riding through the city, the merchant found his opportunity, and drew a circle round both king and horse. The king, on seeing this, halted, and would ride no further; nor did he stir from the spot until the merchant was satisfied. And when the bystanders saw this they marvelled greatly, saying that the king was a most just king indeed, having thus submitted to justice."

[1] Bija, or Bájí.

In spite, however, of all his difficulties, the Muha Raj seldom loses his gaiety and good humour: nor does he regard the strictest *dhurna*. unless he should chance to be informed, while it lasts, of a tiger having been discovered in the neighbourhood. Tiger hunting is one of his favourite amusements: another is fighting elephants; and in this he indulges four or five times a week, especially during the cold weather. The largest elephants are selected for the purpose; and are pampered with hot spices, and other stimulants, to make them vicious. There is but little sport in the combat; though there is doubtless something grand in the concussion of two such enormous creatures. It is often a matter of difficulty to bring them near to each other; but when the drivers have succeeded in urging them within a certain distance, they rush forward at once, entwine their trunks and tusks, and push with all their might, till one gives way and runs. The conqueror pursues, belabouring his adversary with his trunk, and endeavouring to throw him down; and so eager is he in following up his victory, that it is sometimes necessary to let off fireworks to intimidate him and make him desist from the pursuit. On these occasions Seendhiya is attended by large bodies of cavalry: and there is a fine display of *Duk,hunee* horses. This is a breed peculiar to the *Duk,hun*, or Deccan as you term it, and held in the highest estimation by the Mahrattas. They are bred from Arabians with the original mares of the country, which are very small. The *Duk,hunees* themselves are seldom above fourteen hands and a half high; and the most valuable ones are often much less. They are short in the barrel and neck; have small well-shaped heads, and slim, though remarkably well formed, limbs: they have generous tempers, and are full of spirit; and are said to be capable of undergoing more fatigue and hard fare than any other horses in India. The sum of three, and even four thousand rupees, is often paid for a *Duk,hunee* whose pedigree is well known: and so fond are the Mahrattas of these beautiful and valuable favourites, that, when they can afford it, they will feed them on wheaten cakes, boiled rice, sugar, butter, and other similar dainties.

The Moosulmans in camp have just been celebrating the *Bukree Eed;* a festival in commemoration of Abraham's offering up his son Isaac. On this occasion every good Moslem, who has the means to do it, sacrifices a goat; and the poorer sort bring one among several. Princes, and men of the highest rank, substitute a camel, and sometimes a cow; which they spear with their own hands, and send about pieces of the flesh in presents to their friends: this festival is on the tenth of the month Zilhij. You know that the Moohumedan month commences on the appearance of the new moon; at which time they discharge cannon, matchlocks, &c., and sound their drums and trumpets; saluting each other, and sending complimentary messages to their friends. A very large proportion of the people who compose this camp are Moosulmans. The servant of the Khans, whom I before mentioned, assured me that at the customary feast, which his masters had lately given upon the tenth day subsequent to the death of their elder brother, five thousand persons sat down to dinner. The fare provided consisted of a hundred maunds of wheat flour (a maund being eighty pounds), sixty maunds of rice, and sixty goats. What was not eaten by the guests invited was distributed among the *fuqeers*, and poor people of all descriptions, who swarm about the camp. Other entertainments, though not upon quite so extensive a scale, are to take place on the twentieth and fortieth days.

The Hindoos have also been celebrating a feast, called *Sunkrat:*[1] when parcels of a small black seed, called *Til*,

[1] The festival which in Upper India is celebrated as the Uttaráyana or Makara Sankránti, or sun's entrance into the sign Capricornus. "The observances enjoined on this occasion are partly of a private, partly of a public character. The first consists of offerings to the Pitris, or progenitors, whether general, as of all mankind; or special, as of

are sent in presents to those whom they wish to compliment. The Muha Raj sends them to the British resident, and to the principal Surdars in camp. Poor people carry about quantities of it, and present it to such as are rich enough to bestow a rupee or two in return. A rich banker gave a dinner upon this occasion to a number of Brahmuns, at which he exhibited a good specimen of Mahratta delicacy and management. A most plentiful meal was prepared; and when each guest had eaten as much as he could possibly contrive to swallow, he arose, and was presented with a new *dotee*, or cloth to wrap about the loins, a blanket, and a coarse linen jacket quilted with cotton: he was then conducted to a small ruined fort in the neighbourhood of the camp, where he was locked in, to prevent his offering himself a second time, and appropriating an undue portion of the benefaction. In this confinement the guests were kept throughout the night; and on the following morning were all let out together, arrayed in their new habiliments. To feed Brahmuns is an act of religious duty, sedulously inculcated upon the minds of all Hindoos: and on such occasions the greater the quantity of victuals that is devoured by these holy men, the greater the merit and honour accruing to the entertainer. Brahmuns, after eating till they are ready to burst, will sometimes consent, at the earnest entreaty of their host, to cram down a little more; receiving for each successive mouthful an increasing number of rupees, till nature revolts at the oppressive load: and instances have not infrequently occurred of this being repeated, till the poor gorged wretch tempted by, perhaps, some hundred rupees, has forced another morsel into his mouth, and expired on the spot. In this case no kind of blame attaches to the feeder; while the fed goes straight to heaven, *ex officio*.

This is the season of the *Busunt*, or spring of the

the family of the worshipper; to the Vastu devas, the Dii Lares, or domestic genii; the guardians of the dwelling, or the site on which it is erected; and to the Viswa devas, or universal gods."

Hindoos. The word signifies joy: and at this time all are accordingly joyful and happy. They present little bunches of green corn or flowers to their friends, and wear them in their turbans, which they dye yellow, as being the gayest of all colours: many dress themselves in full suits of yellow; songs and music are heard in all quarters: and every one feeds Brahmuns and distributes alms according to his means. The general gladness diffuses itself even among the poor women who grind the corn, and who now always lighten their labour by a song. The whole of the corn consumed in camp is ground by women: who for this purpose use a very simple mill, consisting of two flat circular stones about fifteen inches in diameter; the upper one of which is turned by a handle upon a pivot fixed in the lower one. The woman sits on the ground with the mill, which is called a *chukkee*, before her; and if she works hard, may grind from forty to fifty seers of corn in the day. Servants and others of the poorer sort, who have their wives in camp, earn something in addition to their wages, by employing them in this manner at their hours of leisure. An industrious woman, when not inclined to sleep, will arise at any hour of the night and busy herself with the mill: and any person lying awake, would be sure to hear two or three women so employed, singing over their work in a strain which, if not positively beautiful, is far from being unpleasing, and accords well with the stillness of the hour. Some of these songs, those especially which allude to the *Busunt*, possess no inconsiderable share of merit. I send you the literal translation of one, which I think will please you: it is supposed to be sung by a woman who pines for the absence of her husband, and can take no share in the general festivities of the season. It must be recollected that the term *Busunt* not only implies the season itself, but also the little presents of flowers, &c, which I before mentioned, and which are presented by the women to the objects of their affections.

FIG. I.—A MAHRATTA SURDAR ENTERTAINING BRAHMUNS.

A BUSUNT SONG

The lively drum is heard around;
The tamborine and cymbals sound:
But I of lengthen'd absence plain,
And perish by a parching flame.

The women all around me sing,
And own th' inspiring joys of spring;
While I, from darts of ruthless Love,
Never ending torments prove.

The amorous *Kokil* [1] strains his throat,
And pours a plaintive pleasing note:
My breast responsive heaves with grief,
Hopeless and reckless of relief.

When *he* again shall glad my hours,
Then, girl, I'll take thy blooming flowers;
But now my love is far away,
Where should I place thy *Busunt* gay.

The foragers are scattered all over the country; and are to be seen at all hours returning to camp with their *tuthoos*, a hardy species of pony, or bullocks groaning under their loads of green wheat or barley. Such depredations necessarily cause the greatest distress among the unfortunate peasants; who are driven from their dwellings, and forced to seek a shelter in *Kota*, or some other territory which is not threatened with a visit from a Mahratta camp. I have myself met several families emigrating in this manner; who one and all raised their voices, to call down curses upon Seendhiya and his horde of ravagers. In some cases they have avenged themselves, by carrying off cattle from the foraging parties, when there has not been a detachment sufficiently strong to protect them. Many of the Muha Raj's people have been wounded in these skirmishes.

[1] The *Kokil* is the Ring-dove of Hindoo poetry. It is a small green bird, whose note is peculiarly melodious in the spring, and is supposed to be a great inciter to the tender passion. The cry uttered by this bird, the Koel of Northern India (*Endynamys orientalis*, Lin.), *ku-il*, *ku-il*, is familiar to all.

LETTER V

March to the Chumbul—Ford of the Parbuttee—Destruction of the young corn—Bunjaras—March to Babue—Confusion in the ravines—Cross the Arrabaree Hills—Elephants forcing a passage through the woods—Moisture of the soil—Goojurs—Grupchat—Surjee Rao—The Muha Raj in d,hurna—Holkar's villages—The Hohlee and Moohurrum—B,hanmittees—Fruit merchant.

CAMP AT BABUE, *February* 12.

WE have made two marches since I wrote last; and from their direction it would appear that the Muha Raj means to pursue his plans of hostility against the Raja of Jypoor. Our first march was on the 2nd inst. to Deepree, a village upon the right bank of the Chumbul. Its distance from Kutolee is not more than thirteen miles; but Zalim Sing,h knew the Mahrattas too well to let them cross the river at that place, where the ford is a tolerably good one, and pass through the skirts of the town. We were obliged, therefore, to march four miles along the bank of the Parbuttee to gain another ford, and a most abominable one it was, at a place called Balohpa. The bed of the river is a mass of large fragments of rock; and the banks, especially the left one, are very steep and difficult of ascent.

We observed several fine villages on the Kota side of the river, situated upon level spots among the ravines which intersect the country for a mile from the bank. By the route we went, our march was protracted to nearly twenty-two miles: the road lay over a continued plain, covered with fields of young corn affording fine forage for the Mahrattas; who were to be seen in every direction, men, women, and children, tearing it up by the roots; while their cattle were turned loose to graze at liberty, and make the most of such an abundant harvest. We also fell in with large ricks of *Kurbee*, the dried stalks of *Bajiru* and *Jooar*, two inferior kinds of grain; an excellent fodder for the camels. To each of these three or four horsemen immediately attached themselves, and appropriated it to their own use: so that when our cattle went out for forage after the march, there was as much difficulty in procuring it as if we had halted near the spot for a month. In the neighbourhood of our new ground we passed through some fields of peas, of which we secured a share: quieting our consciences with the conviction that if we spared them, they who came after us would certainly not be so abstemious: at dinner we found them excellent. Although we started at day-break, we did not reach our ground till past twelve o'clock; and it was full two hours more before any of the servants made their appearance with the tents and breakfast things: upon inquiry, we found that they also had passed among the peas, which offered too tempting a regale to be resisted after the fatigue of so long a march. The Chumbul at this place is neither wide nor deep; the current flows smoothly over a bed of find sand, and on the left washes the base of a range of the Arrabaree hills.

On the 3rd we halted; and many of our people, who had been detained by the crowd at the ford of the Parbuttee, joined us. They had put up, during the night, with some *Bunjaras* encamped upon the road. These are a race of people whose employment it is to transport grain from place to place. They commonly move in large bodies under the guidance of a chief; and attach themselves to particular armies or places. They travel with their wives and children; and incommode themselves with very little baggage: the only tent they ever use being a coarse red canvas sheet spread across a ridge pole, which affords shelter not only to themselves, but to their grain, when the weather is bad. When they encamp for the night, they fasten their bullocks in two rows to a long rope; and, in fair weather, pile their loads and saddles in such a manner round the encampment, as to defend themselves from the depredations of jackals, wolves, &c. ; and even to afford some protection against the attacks of thieves. The *Bunjaras* are generally *Goojurs*, *Jats*, or of other low castes of Hindoos ; and very rarely Moosulmans. They are a decent, well-behaved people ; and so much reliance is placed on their honesty, that large sums are often paid to them in advance, by the merchants who employ them, to make their purchases of grain. In consequence of being so generally useful, their persons and property are always respected, even in times of war.

On the 4th we made a march of thirteen miles to this place ; during which we crossed both the Chumbul and the Arrabaree hills. The ford over the river is good, and the water not more than three and a half feet deep : but the ground on this side, like most of that which lies along its banks, is very much intersected by ravines.

The infantry brigades, the park, and some of the bazars, had passed over the preceding day, and encamped upon such spots as they could find among this broken ground : and the scene of confusion that ensued in the morning, occasioned by the narrowness of the path they had left through their encampment, the press of people coming across the river on foot and on horseback, together with animals of all kinds, mixed with guns, tumbrils, and carts, all indiscriminately pushing to get through, exceeds the powers of description. The horses of our cavalry, which are always vicious, made their way through the crowd, by dint of fighting and kicking, better than any other animals I saw : but it was sorely to the annoyance, and often to the imminent danger, of the by-standers ; who, naturally enough, revenged themselves by uttering execrations against us for our intrusion.

The hill over which we passed was very rugged, and covered with trees to the top ; through which, as the only road was occupied by the guns, the elephants were of great use in opening a way for us. It was really astonishing to see with what ease and sagacity these docile creatures effected their purpose; pushing with their foreheads against the trees, till they had bent them low enough to place their fore-feet upon the trunks, when, with another effort, they broke them to the ground, and bore us safely through the cracking branches.

After getting clear of the *Ghata*, as such passes over hills are called, we came upon a fine level country: and before we reached the camp, had a good view of the fort of Indra Gurh, belonging to a petty Raja, a tributary of Kota. I had observed that neither on this march, nor on that from Kutolee to the Chumbul, we crossed any *nalas*, or saw a single well; although the country everywhere displayed a luxuriant cultivation; and, upon inquiry, I was assured that the soil hereabouts is so moist as scarcely ever to require irrigation, and hardly even to feel an occasional drought in the rainy season.

The *Goojurs*, who inhabit the hills, reaped a fine harvest during this march: every straggler from the main body was plundered; several men were killed and wounded; and a number of bullocks, horses, and camels carried off. Five *Suwar* (a common appellation for all horsemen), who went with the hope of booty to a little village near the camp, which they supposed to be deserted, were attacked by the villagers; four of them were killed, and the fifth came running into our camp, with a bullet through his body. Some of the people of the *Jinsee*, which could not be brought up in consequence of an immense gun, called *Grupchat*, sticking fast in the jungle, were killed by the Goojurs; and many of the cattle belonging to the train were carried away. The name of this gun is peculiarly appropriate: it is a Mahratta word, and signifies *the remover of difficulties*, and whencver any difficulties occur in consequence of a bad road, the passage of a river, &c., it is sure to be left behind, and detain the army for a day or two.

Our present encampment is not above ten miles from the city of Nuya Shuhur; near to the gates of which a party of our Sipahees went a few days ago to forage: they were fired upon by the *Goojurs*, and two men, who had strayed from the party, were wounded; but no further injury was done.

The Muha Raj went yesterday evening to meet his father-in-law, the famous, or, to speak more correctly, the infamous *Surjee Rao Gooatkia*, who has lately returned from Mewar, and is encamped about five miles off. This man was excluded from taking any part in the councils of Seendhiya by the treaty of 1805, as his sentiments were supposed to be particularly hostile to the British interests: but that prohibition has since been taken off; and it is conjectured that he is now returning to camp, with a view of being reinstated in power. The meeting was to have taken place the day before; but Seendhiya was detained by the Khans, whom I have before mentioned, sitting *dhurna* upon him till he came to some settlement about their accounts. An agreement was patched up between them at a late hour of the night; and the Muha Raj gave them receipts upon our government for payments which will become due in July, 1811!

Holkar owns some villages in this neighbourhood; and a general order has been given to prohibit foraging parties from visiting them. It is no weak proof of the apprehensions universally entertained of that chieftain, that his villages, though close to the camp, should alone be exempted from the visits of these general plunderers.

The Hindoos have already begun to sing their Hohlee songs; and the Moosulmans to prepare their *Taziyas* for the Moohurrum; these two most opposite festivals happening this year to fall together.

A set of jugglers, called *Bhanmittees*, came into our camp this morning, and exhibited some surprising feats of activity. One woman in particular astonished me: she rested on her head and feet, with her back toward the earth;

two swords, with their blades inwards, were crossed upon her chin, and two others, the blades also inwards, under her neck: she then traversed round in a circle, with great rapidity; keeping her head always fixed in the centre and leaping over the points of the swords, whenever her breast chanced to be downwards. The *Bhanmittees* are of the lowest classes of the people; and support themselves by travelling about, and exhibiting their feats in the towns and villages through which they pass. We had at the same time a much more welcome visitor in the person of a fruit merchant from the Punjab, with an assortment of pears, apples, grapes, apricots, &c., who having before experienced the protection of a Mahratta camp, has wisely taken up his quarters, this time, in ours. The fruits are packed in small round boxes between layers of cotton, and are generally brought in a very good state of preservation.

LETTER VI

March to Choroo and Puchala—Ooniara and Rampoora—Circuitous route—Great inconvenience from heat—March to the Bunas—Rejoin the army—Bad encampment—Commencement of the Moohurrum.

CAMP ON THE BUNAS, *Feb.* 16.

WE left Babue on the thirteenth, and had a most disagreeable march of twenty-two miles to the villages of Choroo and Puchala; although the direct distance is certainly not above ten miles. The line was at first led towards Ooniara, the residence of a Raja related to the Jypoor family: but, after approaching to within three miles of the place, we turned off to the right, nearly retracing our steps; and did not reach our ground till one o'clock. We passed a little to the right of Rampoora, a fort belonging to Holkar; which was gallantly stormed by a detachment under Lieut.-Colonel Don, in 1804, and restored to that chieftain at the peace. It would be difficult, with any other army than a Mahratta one, to assign a reason for this circuitous route; the whole country being one continued plain, presenting neither ravines, *nalas*, nor any other obstacles to the movement of troops in any direction that might be required. But here the thing is clearly understood: certain villagers having joined in bribing the *Beenee Wala* to avoid their lands, and lead the army by another route. As the order for marching was not given till late the preceding night, the camp was not struck at so early an hour as usual: in consequence of which, and the day proving very hot, and there being little or no water to be found upon the road, the people and cattle suffered great inconvenience: cups of water were sold by the *Bihishtees*, or water-carriers, for several pice each (the name of a small copper coin), which on ordinary marches would have been bought for half a dozen cowries.

Seendhiya marched again the following day: but as his intention was not intimated to us till past seven in the morning, it was resolved that we should halt, and join him the next day. This we accordingly did, after a march of eighteen miles, upon the right bank of the Bunas, and about three miles beyond the town of Bugwuntpoor. The road lay over the same kind of flat country which we have everywhere seen since we crossed the Parbuttee; was well cultivated, and covered with flourishing villages. As most of these belong to Holkar they and their inhabitants were protected from pillage and insult.

We found the Muha Raj's army preparing to cross the Bunas, and encamp a little higher up, on the opposite bank. As we had already made a long march, however, we determined to remain for that day where we were; and pitched our tents near the ford where Colonel Monson's detachment crossed the river, on the unfortunate retreat before Holkar's army in 1804; and on the very spot where the brave first battalion of the second regiment of Bengal infantry, commanded by Lieut.-Colonel St. Clair, which was left as a rear guard, was cut to pieces by overwhelming numbers,[1] after having gallantly stormed and possessed themselves of a battery of the enemy's guns.

This morning we rejoined the army; the greatest part of which is encamped along the bank of the river, and the remainder in its bed: there not being sufficient ground for the whole among the numerous and deep ravines by which the bank is intersected. We are ourselves in the same predicament; being encamped on the sandy bed, in an uncomfortable situation, between the rear of the main army and one of the brigades of infantry. What little stream there is at present in the river runs under the opposite bank, at

[1] On the 24th August, when the twelve European officers fell with their commander.

the distance of three-quarters of a mile from us ; and we are supplied with water from small wells only, dug in the sand around our tents. Report says that we are to halt here for some time : if so, I trust we shall be able to find some other ground for our encampment, as, in addition to these inconveniences, the ceremonies of the Moohurrum are commenced, and we are annoyed from the close to the break of day with the discordant noises of drums, trumpets, and matchlocks, mixed with the beating of breasts, loud sobbing, and half frantic exclamations of the devout Moslems about us.

LETTER VII

Change of ground—Insolence of the Infantry Sipahees—Aleegols—Change of Ministry—Surjee Rao—Raja Ambajee—The Resident visits the new Minister—The Moohurrum—Alarm among the merchants—The country laid waste.

CAMP ON THE BUNAS, *February* 26.

WE have been fortunate enough to find a good spot of ground, about a mile higher up the river, and have removed our camp to it. Returning from a ride I had taken to look out for this situation, I passed along the sentries of the brigade near us, who could not let the opportunity slip of being insolent with impunity: they called to us to keep off: and warned the trooper who accompanied me, that if he came that way again they would fire at him. I had heard in the morning that the same men had abused the whole troop, while going out to water, in the most gross manner. These Sipahees are all inhabitants of the Company's provinces, or of Oude; and are, I think, as insolent a set of fellows as any in the whole camp. Whether this is to be attributed to the pleasure which the vulgar are apt to find in abusing their superiors, when they can do it with impunity, or merely to the relaxed state of discipline which prevails in these brigades, I do not know; but am inclined to believe the latter: for no class of people can be more orderly and respectful than the same men are in the character of British soldiers. It was evening as I passed their camp; and there I again saw a number of tricoloured flags, which I had before observed carried along the line of march: they were now planted in a row, with a quantity of small lamps burning about them; and a number of people were seated round with drums and trumpets. It is usual with such of the native troops, as are still regulated by their own customs, to do honour to their colours, on particular occasions, by observing similar ceremonies. Upon inquiry, I was informed that these were French colours, belonging to a corps of *Aleegols* attached to the brigade, which had been presented to them under Monsieur Perron's government, and had not since been changed. The *Aleegols* are bodies of irregular foot; armed according to the fancy of each individual, and without any sort of discipline: they consist principally of Moosulmans; and have acquired their name from their habit of charging the enemy in a *gol*, or mass, and invoking the aid of *Alee* in their onset. Their pay is trifling; but, by way of compensation, they are allowed to plunder at discretion.

While our tents were pitching in the new position, a servant of Seendhiya's came up, and desired that they might be removed to another spot; as *that* was reserved for the convenience of the Muha Raj's fishing and shooting. We accordingly moved them a little further on; and are at length comfortably settled, quite out of the reach of all the nuisances of the army.

A great revolution in the politics of this Durbar has taken place since I wrote last: Surjee Rao has completely re-established his influence; and on the 23rd, when we visited the Muha Raj, the new administration was formally announced. It consists of Surjee Rao himself as *Premier*; the *Mamma*; and Raja Ambajee, who arrived in camp only a few days ago. The Minister is a stout square-built man, not more than five feet high; his features coarse and large, especially his eyes, which are grey, and uncommonly penetrating. His countenance is just what his character would lead one to expect; strongly marked, and expressing, in legible characters, cunning, cruelty, and daring ferocity: yet there is a certain quickness in his address and manner of speaking that indicates talents and genius. His complexion is fair; and what little hair he has is quite grey.

He wore a plain muslin *Dotee* hanging, in the Mahratta fashion, below the calves of his legs : a short white jacket ; and a gauze shawl, called a *Sela*, thrown over his shoulders. On his head he had a small skull-cap, with a narrow strip of gold brocade twisted round the bottom of it ; the ends of which hung fantastically upon his left shoulder. His whole appearance conveyed the idea of a man quite crazy : and that idea was not a little aided by a small string of sandal-wood beads, which he held in his hands, and told over and over again with unceasing perseverance and rapidity.

Ambajee is a tall, hale-looking man for his age, which is said to be upwards of eighty : his complexion is dark ; and there is much good humour and intelligence in his countenance. His dress was remarkably plain, almost amounting to meanness ; consisting of a common chintz jacket, quilted with cotton, a coarse red shawl, and a white turban.

After we quitted the Durbar, at which not one of the old set of courtiers was present, we visited Surjee Rao at his own tents. He was exceedingly civil ; talked a great deal : and, which came oddly enough from him, made many protestations of his regard and esteem for the English character ; and of his wish to cement the friendly relations which now subsist between the two governments : he added, that his former actions, which certainly spoke another language, were to be attributed solely to *Holkar*, with whom he had intimately connected himself, and under whose influence he had acted.

It is usual on such visits of ceremony for the company to be entertained by a *Nach* . but on this occasion there was none, in consequence of its being the *Moohurrum*. This is a general mourning, observed by the Moohumedans, to commemorate the death of the Imam Hoosen, the grandson of the prophet : and the universal ardour with which the Mahrattas, who are Hindoos, participate in its ceremonies, is curious enough. Every one turns *Fuqeer ;* that is, he wears some green rags ; with a string of green and red cotton yarn, tied up like beads, across his shoulders; and goes about begging from such of his acquaintance as are foolish enough to give him anything; the term *Fuqeer* implying a religious beggar. Groups of such grotesque figures are to be seen in all directions, wandering about the camp, asking for alms, and calling upon the names of Moohumed, Alee, and Hoosen. The Muha Raj himself even gives into this ridiculous custom; and is a Fuqeer during the whole of the *Moohurrum*. At the Durbar the other day he was dressed entirely in green, the mourning of the Moosulmans, with no other ornament than eight or nine strings of beautiful emeralds round his neck. In this garb, accompanied by a few of his confidential servants, he roams about at night, and visits the different *Taziyas* throughout the camp. These are light frames of split bamboo, made in the form of Mausoleums; covered with gilt and coloured paper, foil, talk, &c., and sometimes ornamented with valuable jewels. They are supposed to represent the tomb of Hoosen: in the inside is laid a clean white cloth for the shroud, with a few flowers; and sometimes a turban is added. Around the *Taziya* a number of long poles are placed, fixed in the ground; to which are attached extended bands (emblematic of the five holy personages of the prophet's family); red and green flags (the first, types of the blood of *Hoosen*, who was slain in battle; the other, of the poison by which his brother *Hussun* was treacherously destroyed); and naked scymitars, representing *Zoolfikar*, the victorious sword of Alee. In front of the *Taziya* a large white cloth is spread; around which the Moosulmans assemble in the evening, and seat themselves. A *Moolla*, or one learned in the laws of Islam, takes his place in the centre, and reads a passage from the *Qoran*: he and his assistant then alternately repeat elegiac stanzas, called *Mursiyas*, descriptive of, or alluding to the events which attended the death of Hoosen. Some of these verses are simple and affecting; but the effect they produce upon the audience is wonderful. The stoutest and most rude of the party are often melted into tears; and deep sobs and groans are heard from all around. At the conclusion of this part of the ceremony, they all rise, and, gathering round the *Moolla*, uncover their breasts, which they smite with the right hand, and call upon Hoosen at every blow. At first, the strokes are repeated gently; and the invocations made in an under voice: but by degrees they increase the force of both; till at length they work themselves up to a state of enthusiasm, in which they inflict their blows and raise their exclamations with such violence, that they appear quite frantic. The effect produced is impressive in the highest degree; almost indeed terrific. I ought to have said that they who repeat the *Mursiyas* are not necessarily *Moollas;* other people make it a study; and, if they have attained to any perfection, are hired for the purpose of reciting them during the celebration of the *Moohurrum*.

On the anniversary of the battle of Kurbulla, the tenth of the month, in which Hoosen was killed, the *Taziyas* are conveyed in great pomp, and thrown into the river, if it be sufficiently deep; if not, large pits are dug for the purpose of receiving them. The night previous to this final ceremony, it is the custom here for all the *Taziyas* of the camp to be carried in procession to the Muha Raj's tents: I put on an Hindoostanee dress, and accompanied that which our people had constructed, upon one of the elephants which the Resident permitted to go with the procession: and though I did not get home again till past three in the morning, I must acknowledge that I was well recompensed for my trouble. There were more than a hundred *Taziyas*, each followed by a long train of *Fuqeers*, dressed in the most extravagant manner, beating their breasts, and loudly calling upon the prophet and his grandson. The flaming of torches, firing of matchlocks, and the harsh and discordant sounds of Mahratta drums and trumpets, united with the strange but animated groups passing on all sides,

FIG. 2.—PROCESSION OF THE TAZIYA.

to produce the most extraordinary scene I ever beheld. Such of the Mahratta Surdars as are not Brahmuns frequently construct *Taziyas* at their own tents, and expend large sums of money upon them: many of these were very handsome; and some were accompanied by a kind of platform, on which were placed three figures, designed to represent the ass *Borak*, upon which Moohumed rode to heaven, and two of the Hoorees of Paradise: the first was an animal with four legs, a woman's face, and a peacock's neck and tail, covered with gold and green foil: the latter were frightful dolls, tricked out in tawdry silk and gold brocade. Some of the processions were attended by elephants painted for the occasion, and richly caparisoned; on which were borne large green and red standards: they occasionally halted to give an opportunity for *Mursiyas* being repeated, and the devotees to collect in a circle and beat their breasts: most of them were attended by a camel laden with wheaten cakes, which were distributed among the poor who flocked about them; and at every place, where a *Taziya* had been constructed, large pitchers of sherbet and cold water were prepared, which were also served out to such as chose to partake of them. After passing from front to rear of the *Deooree*, the processions came to a small tent, erected for the accommodation of the Muha Raj's wife. A kind of blind formed of split canes, called a *chik*, was let down before the door; and there being no light within the tent, the lady and her attendants remained perfectly concealed, while they could distinctly see every thing that took place outside. In front of this tent a circle was formed, where a number of men exhibited their skill in flourishing swords, or long poles with lighted flambeaux at each end; sometimes singly, and sometimes in mock combat with each other. Another kind of exhibition was made, which I never witnessed anywhere but in this camp: a man stood up with a flag in his hand, and immediately about a hundred others formed a circle, three or four deep, about him, and kept prancing round and round in a strange measured step, brandishing their naked scymitars, and every now and then calling out the names of Moohumed, Alee, and Hoosen. After this long account of the Moohurrum, I must in justice add, that the more enlightened among the Moosulmans look upon the whole as little else than Paganism ; and only join in the ceremony to avoid giving offence to the rest. The *Soonees*, or orthodox Moohumedans in particular, are greatly scandalized at it, although they admit the propriety of weeping in secret over the fate of their prophet's martyred family.

The late change of ministers is as acceptable to the troops, among whom Surjee Rao is popular, as it is alarming to the *Buniyas* (the merchants) of the Bazar. The enormities he was guilty of when he was before in power have naturally rendered him an object of terror and suspicion ; and they are now waiting in trembling anxiety for the moment when he may choose to begin breaking some of their heads, the common mode of execution among the Mahrattas ; and which is done with a large wooden mallet, preserved with great care for the purpose. A day or two after his arrival in camp he made the tour of the Bazars, and visited the shops of all the principal merchants ; who vied with each other in the attentions they paid to him, and the presents with which they hoped to propitiate the good will of the new minister. He has also secured his popularity, for the present at least, with the troops, by distributing among them a large sum on account ; and by holding out flattering promises of a speedy settlement of their arrears.

Within a short distance of our camp are two fine hill forts, *Sursot* and *Sowar*, belonging to a distant branch of the Jypoor Raja's family ; one of the *B,haee Betas*, brothers and children as they are termed, of the reigning prince. This chief has already made the Muha Raj sensible that he is not to march through the Jypoor territories unmolested ;

having carried off a great number of the bullocks belonging to the train of artillery. A general order for plundering and laying waste has in consequence been issued; and at this moment a dozen villages are smoking in ruins within sight of our camp.

LETTER VIII

March to Issurdu—Jamdars—March to Kakorh—Scarcity of water—March towards Tod,ha—Face of the country—Cavalry moving in advance—Mahrattas destroying the crops—Remonstrance of the Takoor of Issurdu—Detachment sent to Kurera and Doonee—Ana Siknuvees dismissed from camp—His nephew poisoned—Quicksands of the Bunas—Villages laid waste—The Rangras retaliate—The Muha Raj plays the Hohlee—A sally from Doonee.

CAMP ON THE BUNAS, *March* 8, 1809.

WE have made three marches since I last wrote to you: the first, to a spot about seven miles from our old ground, higher up the river; whose course is here admirably adapted to the accommodation of an army. The ground on both banks is level, and unbroken by ravines; and the stream, even in the driest season, affords plenty of water of an excellent quality. The man who usually goes on to select our encamping ground was this day prevented from pitching the tents close upon the bank, by a scrupulous *Jamdar* posted to protect a small field of gram, a species of grain now just in pod, from injury. *Jamdars* are soldiers, generally horsemen, detached to villages and spots of cultivation, to prevent their being spoiled by the troops or camp followers. The one in question, who evinced towards us so lively a sense of his duty, did not however think it incumbent upon him to oppose whole droves of camels, horses, and bullocks, which wandered over his field and in less than half an hour totally destroyed the crop he was so assiduous to preserve. Unless the villagers are bold enough to defend their property, or sufficiently rich to bribe their protector, the *Jamdar*, as a matter in course, remunerates himself for his trouble in keeping off the mob, by appropriating such little matters as he can lay his hands upon to his own use; and winking at the depredations of such of his immediate friends as may choose to avail themselves of his acquaintance for the same purpose. On that day's march we passed by the town of *Issurdu*, and encamped about four miles from it. It belongs to a *Takoor*, or lord, of the Jypoor family; is surrounded by a strong wall and ditch; and has a citadel in the centre of the place: and is, apparently, by much the handsomest and most commodious town that I have seen in this part of India.

On the following day, the 28th, we made a march of seventeen miles to *Kakorh*, a large town belonging to the Raja of *Ooniara;* with a fort, or castle, in a most romantic situation upon the southern extremity of a range of hills; at the northern point of which is another fort called *Boneto.* No information was given of this march till near eight o'clock; so that the day was far advanced when we reached our new ground. The weather was very hot; and the clouds of dust, raised by the line of baggage, rendered the march one of the most disagreeable ones I have experienced for a long time. Two or three small wells afforded the only water, and that bad, which we met with on the road, after quitting the *Bunas.* Unfortunately, too, after pitching the tents, there was such a scarcity of this necessary article, owing to a large *jeel*, or piece of water, at *Kakorh* being dried up, that the Mahrattas were obliged to come for it to our camp, upon the banks of a small pond nearly three miles from the grand army. We did not discover this precious supply till after having wandered about for a long time in absolute despair of finding any water near which we might encamp; at that time it was perfectly clear and sweet: and covered with flocks of the finest water-fowl I ever saw: but before evening it became little better than a mass of mud, from the numbers of people and droves of cattle that thronged to it from the great camp.

It was evidently impossible to remain at such a place:

accordingly we marched on the following morning about fourteen miles; and encamped again upon the left bank of the *Bunas*, on a spot eight miles to the eastward of the town of *Tod,ha*. The country over which we passed was a continued level plain; with ranges of rocky hills, from one to six miles and upwards in length, and decreasing gradually to a sharp ridge at their summits, rising abruptly from the surface, and scattered over it in such a manner as to give one the idea of their having been placed there after the plain itself was formed. Upon this march I saw, for the first time since I have been in camp, several *Risalus* moving at the head of the line; which on common occasions consists almost entirely of baggage and followers, with here and there a few horsemen riding slowly along at their own pleasure. Both Surjee Rao and Ambajee were also in front with their respective corps; and the wide extent of plain being favourable for the display of cavalry, each *Risalu* forming a separate body and proceeding distinct from the rest, the whole made a grand appearance. I counted five different corps; which might together have amounted to about twelve hundred men; though, from their loose and undisciplined mode of moving, they might have easily been mistaken for a much greater number. When the ground admits of it, as on this day, they generally form an irregular line, three or four deep: the chief marches in front of the centre, preceded by colours, kettle-drums and trumpets, *Hirkarus*, &c., &c.: and individuals of the corps are to be seen on all sides, galloping about and flourishing their arms, to display the excellence of their steeds and horsemanship; both of which, it must be allowed, are often well worthy of such an exhibition. One of these *Risalus*, which was attached to the brigade commanded by a Portuguese, named *Baptiste*, evinced, comparatively, a certain degree of discipline: it was divided into three troops, each troop having a different coloured dress; and marched in files, with a small gun in front. We passed over large fields of wheat and barley, where the ear was just ripening, with no more remorse than if it had been a desert; the Mahrattas tearing up the corn, and loading themselves and their cattle with it, and the *Risalus* occasionally halting in the midst of a particularly flourishing spot to allow their horses to get a good feed. The riper ears the people reserved for themselves; and parties were to be seen under every tree which could afford them shade, beating large bundles of wheat and barley with sticks, to separate the grain from the husk. The grain they usually throw upon a few brambles or dry sticks, to which they set fire; they then rub the roasted pods between their hands, and cast them into the air, that the wind may blow away the burncd chaff: the grain, parched in this manner, is very palatable, and bears some resemblance in flavour to roasted chestnuts. The sudden march from *Issurdu*, I have since learned, was occasioned by a spirited remonstrance from the *Takoor* against our remaining in his neighbourhood, after he had complied with the Muha Raj's demands, and paid him forty thousand rupees on condition of his marching away immediately. The reasonableness of this remonstrance cannot be questioned; but that it should be attended to is rather extraordinary.

The troops, which I described to you as having been in front upon the last march, proceeded directly to a fortified village called *Kurera*, about three miles from camp, which they invested. I rode yesterday to see how they managed these matters; and found that they had completely surrounded the place, which is by no means extensive, with strong parties, chiefly of horse, at regular intervals of about a quarter of a mile. There are no guns within the place; and the inhabitants, finding themselves unable to oppose such a force, have since agreed to pay ten thousand rupees. Another strong detachment under Bala Rao, the brother of Ambajee, has been set against a fort eight miles off, called *Doonee*, where they expect to raise a much larger contribution.

The new administration have already evinced their

strength in procuring the dismission from camp of a Surdar, named Ram Chundur Baskur, commonly called Ana Siknuvees; who was their predecessor in office, and is the principal leader of the party which opposed their being called to power. This respectable person has attained to an advanced period of life; the greatest part of which he has ably and faithfully devoted to the service of the Muha Raj; and has now been driven from camp in disgrace, under a small escort of two hundred horse, without even an audience of leave, or any the smallest token of approbation and esteem from his ungrateful and capricious master. It is however boldly asserted that his having been hurried off at only two hours' notice is, in itself, a proof of Seendhiya's regard for him; who felt, that if he had continued in camp, his own authority would not have been sufficient to protect an old servant from the malice and revenge of his now powerful rival. If this assertion be true, what an enviable state of sovereign authority must Seendhiya be possessed of!

Anajee (for it is by this familiar appellation only that he is called) lost a nephew some months ago, to whom he was exceedingly attached, and whom he strongly suspected to have been poisoned. A paper, containing a portion of some medicine which had been administered to him, was privately shown to Captain C——, and his opinion asked of its nature; he of course declined giving any, and pleaded ignorance of the subject. The powder was afterwards given to Mr. M——, who found it to be composed of a preparation of mercury, and the coarse ore of arsenic, called *Hurtal*. I must, however, state that this last mineral is sometimes used by Hindoos, in small quantities, under the idea of its tending greatly to strengthen and invigorate their constitutions.

The bed of the Bunas, in the neighbourhood of our camp, is full of quicksands. I crossed it on an elephant yesterday evening; and the animal, with much difficulty, extricated himself from one, into which he had sunk nearly up to the belly. On the opposite side of the river the crops are all laid waste, and most of the villages in ruins: I rode through some of them, and everywhere saw traces of recent pillage: the beams and thatch of the houses carried away; the doors and door-posts broken down; and the little enclosures, which produced a few vegetables or flowers for the inhabitants, trampled under foot. The houses are all built of mud, with gavel ends, and seldom contain more than one room, of which the door is the only opening. When the family is large, the number, not the size, of the houses is increased; and the habitations of one family often occupy the four sides of a pretty large square, into which the cattle are driven for protection during the night. The *Rangras*, a general name for the peasantry in this part of India, have retaliated some of the evils they experienced from the neighbourhood of the camp, by carrying off cattle, whenever they can find them: I met several horsemen, belonging to the army, galloping over the plain in search of their lost cows and buffaloes, and vowing vengeance against the thieves who had robbed them of their property.

These marches have been a sad interruption to our Sipahees, in playing the *Hohlee*, which ended, according to the calendar of the Hindoos of Hindoostan proper, with the new moon, on the first instant. The Mahrattas, however, keep this festival many days longer than our people; and the Muha Raj is gone this afternoon to play it with the Mamma, in tents pitched for the occasion about a mile in the rear of the army. We shall probably be invited to take a share in these extraordinary festivities, of which I shall accordingly defer giving you an account till the visit is over.

We have just heard that the garrison of Doonee have made a vigorous sally upon the detachment under Bala Rao; and that the reduction of the place will prove a much more serious matter than was at first supposed. We shall, therefore, in all probability move nearer to the scene of action.

LETTER IX

Orders for a march—Uncertainty respecting it—March towards Doonee—Wandering Gosaeens—Visit to the Muha Raj—Playing the Hohlee—Arrangements for the purpose—Extraordinary scene—Account of the Hohlee—Sports and songs of the season—Concluding ceremony—Dancing boys—Bengal Sipahees—Surjee Rao returns the Resident's visit—Khiluts—Trait of Ambajee's character—Destruction of the cornfields—Attack upon the garrison of Doonee—Positions taken up for the siege—Butkees—Management of them.

CAMP AT DOONEE, *March* 15, 1809.

ON the morning after I closed my last letter we received intimation of a march. Orders were accordingly given for striking our camp; and the breakfast tents, &c. were sent on. We had scarcely, however, crossed the Bunas ourselves, when we found the whole line halted: it being undetermined whether the camp was to be pitched again, or whether the army was to proceed further on. After a full hour's delay, the line moved on, and we marched about six miles; when another halt took place, and fresh doubts were started as to where the camp was intended to be pitched. At this moment Balo Rao, with a numerous train of attendants, passed by, to rejoin his detachment before Doonee; and everybody followed him. We had not advanced, however, above a mile, when some camel Hirkarus overtook us, and assured us that the camp was then pitching in the rear. We judged it prudent to make a third halt, although most of the army went on; and presently one of our own people came galloping up to us, with information that our tents were actually pitched a good way to the rear. We traced back our steps; recrossed the river; and found our camp not two miles from the spot we had quitted in the morning. Such is the regularity and decision with which military matters are conducted in this army. As I was recrossing the river, some horsemen wished to prevent my taking the straight road to our tents on the opposite bank, because I must have passed within a hundred and fifty yards of the Muha Raj's wife; who had taken post in the middle of the bed, seated in her *Ruth*, a carriage drawn by bullocks, to enjoy the refreshing coolness of the breeze; and did not scruple, merely for her own gratification, to put the whole army to the utmost inconvenience, which had then been exposed to the sun for upwards of seven hours.

On the following day we effected a march of about nine miles, and encamped again on the banks of the Bunas, at a spot where the river is full a mile in breadth, and where there was, at that time, abundance of water. Bala Rao's detachment was not above two miles off and Doonee within sight: the garrison of which place this movement was intended to intimidate. While our tents were pitching we seated ourselves beneath a large banian tree, and were highly entertained by listening to the narrations of four wandering Gosaeens, or Hindoo Fuqeers, who had also taken refuge under its shady branches. One of them held a long walking-staff in his hands, which, when another expressed a wish to smoke, he instantly converted into a pipe, by placing the *chillum*, or little earthenware pan for receiving the tobacco and embers, in a small hole at the bottom of the stick, which was hollow, and applying the other end to the mouth.

While we remained on that ground, we paid the Muha Raj the customary visit at the Hohlee.[1] Everything was prepared for playing; but, at Captain C.'s particular request,

[1] Holi, a vernal festival originally designed to typify the genial influence of spring upon both the inanimate and animate creation, and to express the passionate feelings inspired by the season, and the delight which the revival of nature diffused. The carnival of the Hindoos.

that part of the ceremony was dispensed with. Playing the Hohlee consists in throwing about a quantity of flour, made from a water-nut, called *singara*, and dyed with red sanders; it is called *abeer*, and the principal sport is to cast it into the eyes, mouth, and nose of the players, and to splash them all over with water, tinged of an orange colour with the flowers of the *dak* tree. The *abeer* is often mixed with the powdered talc, to make it glitter; and then, if it gets into the eyes, it causes a great deal of pain. It is sometimes also enclosed in little globes, made of some congealed gelatinous fluid, about the size of an egg, with which a good aim can be taken at those whom you wish to attack; but they require to be dextrously handled, as they yield to the slightest touch.

When we visited Seendhiya last year, to partake of this curious amusement, he received us in a tent, erected for the purpose, about a hundred and fifty feet in length. He himself was seated at the upper end, on a kind of platform; upon which were also ranged the Surdars, and others who were entitled, from their rank or situation, to the honour of playing with him. Before him rose a temporary fountain, in which certain courtiers were immersed, for the amusement of the company, who enjoy substantial privileges at the trifling price of exhibiting themselves as butts for the Muha Raj's practical jokes and manual wit. In front were assembled all the dancing girls in camp; and to the right and left, the tent was filled with a motley rabble of all such as had any employment about the *Deooree*, or interest enough to gain admission. We went dressed for the occasion, in white linen jackets and pantaloons; and were told, upon entering, that no one was expected to quit the tent till the playing should be over. In a few minutes after we had taken our seats, large brazen trays, filled with *abeer* and the little balls I have already described, were brought in and placed before the company; together with a vase of yellow-coloured water, and a large silver squirt, for each individual. The Muha Raj himself began the amusements of the day, by sprinkling a little red and yellow water upon us from *goolabdans*, which are small silver vessels kept for the purpose of sprinkling rose-water at visits of ceremony. Every one then began to throw about the *abeer*, and squirt at his neighbours as he pleased. It is contrary to the etiquette of the Durbar for anybody to throw at the Muha Raj: he had however been told that we had declared our resolutions to pelt every one who pelted us, and good-humouredly replied, "with all his heart; he was ready for us, and would try which could pelt best." We soon found, however, that we had not the slightest chance with him; for, besides a cloth which his attendants held before his face he had in a few minutes the pipe of a large fire-engine put into his hands, filled with yellow water, and worked by half a dozen men: and with this he played about him with such effect, that in a short time there was not a man in the whole tent who had a dry suit upon his back. Sometimes he directed it against those who sat near him with such force, that it was not an easy matter to keep one's seat. All opposition to this formidable engine was futile; whole shovelfuls of *abeer* were cast about, and instantly followed by a shower of the yellow water: and thus we were alternately powdered and drenched, till the floor on which we sat was covered some inches in depth with a kind of pink and orange-coloured mud. Such a scene I never witnessed in my life. Figure to yourself successive groups of dancing girls, bedecked with gold and silver lace; their tawdry trappings stained with patches of *abeer*, and dripping, like so many Naiads, with orange-coloured water; now chaunting the Hohlee songs with all the airs of practised libertinism, and now shrinking with affected screams beneath a fresh shower from the Muha Raj's engine: the discord of drums, trumpets, fiddles, and cymbals, sounding as if only to drown the other noises that arose around them; the triumph of those who successfully threw the *abeer*, and the clamours of others who suffered from their attacks; the loud shouts of laughter and applause which burst on all sides from the

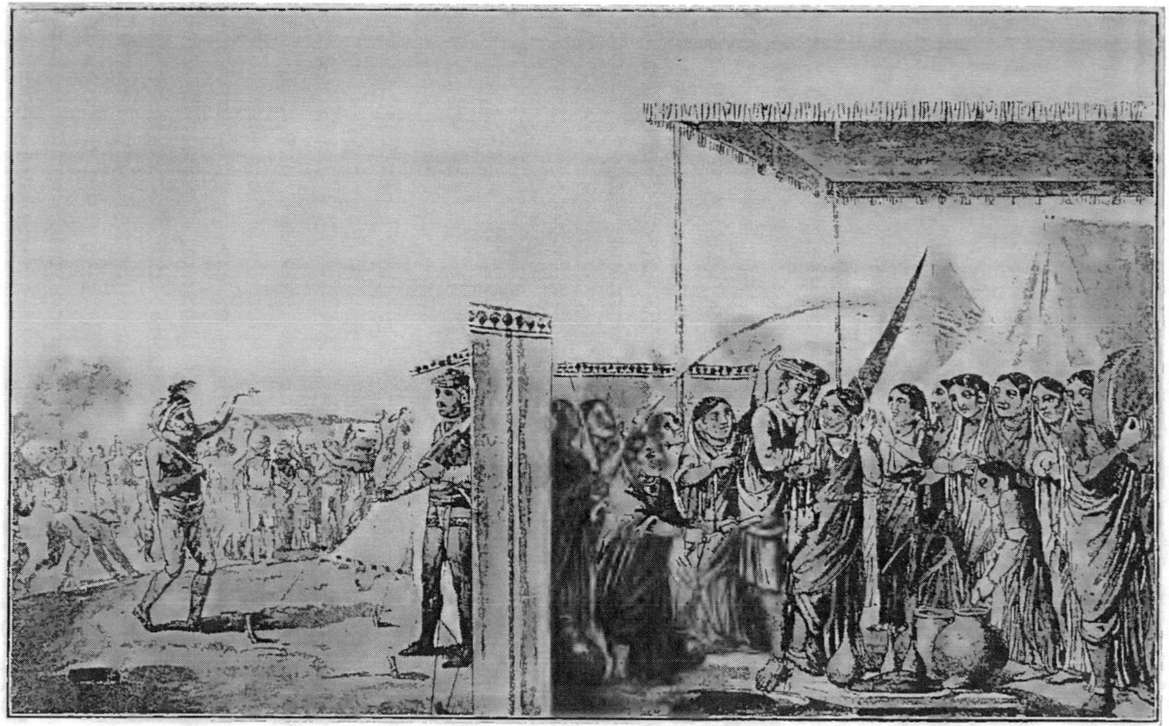

FIG. 3.—PLAYING THE HOHLEE.

joyous crowd: figure to yourself, if you can, such an assemblage of extraordinary objects; then paint them all in two glowing tints of pink and yellow, and you will have formed some conception of a scene which absolutely beggars all description. To have participated in it once, however, is sufficient; and I was not sorry to be exempted from undergoing a similar ordeal this year: though, had we played at all, it was to have been in a much more private manner, and before a more select audience.

The festival of the Hohlee is observed by all classes throughout Hindoostan: it is the season of universal merriment and joy; and the sports that take place at its celebration bear some resemblance to those which were allowed in Rome during the Saturnalia. The utmost licence is permitted to all ranks; the men, old and young, parade about the streets, or the camp, in large groups, singing *Kuveers*, or extemporary stanzas, full of the grossest indelicacy, into which they freely introduce the names of their superiors, coupled with the most abominable allusions; the whole party joining in the chorus, and expressing their delight by loud peals of laughter, hallooing, and almost frantic gestures. An individual sometimes exhibits himself dressed in a most grotesque and indecent manner, as a personification of the Hohlee, and is followed by crowds throwing about the *abeer* and singing the *P,hagoon* songs, to the great annoyance of such women as they may happen to meet, whom they delight to attack with the coarsest ribaldry. The ladies, however, are not without their share of the festivities of the season: they make parties at each other's tents or houses; sit up at *Naches* all night; and play the Hohlee with as much spirit as their male relations. No men, however, are admitted to these select parties, except their husbands; or sometimes their brothers, if they happen to be of a very tender age. These joyous parties begin with the month of *P,hagoon*, the last of the Hindoo year, and the commencement of the spring. The words *P,hagoon* and *P,hag* are also used to denote the little presents of flowers, fruits, or sweet-meats, which lovers are accustomed to make to their mistresses, as well as the sports and songs peculiar to the season: and when these last are marked with more than ordinary licence, they are termed *Dhumaree.* But the Hohlee songs are not necessarily indelicate: in the following one, Krishna,[1] in his youthful character of *Kunneya*, or the beloved, is described as attacked by a party of the *Gopees*, or maids, of Muttra, during the time of the Hohlee. As it pourtrays, with much accuracy and spirit, the peculiar customs of that festival, I have translated it for your amusement.

HOHLEE SONG

While some his loosen'd turban seize,
And ask for *P,hag*, and laughing teaze;
Others approach with roguish leer,
And softly whisper in his ear.
With many a scoff, and many a taunt,
The *P,hagoon* some fair Gopees chaunt;
While others, as he bends his way,
Sing at their doors *Dhumaree* gay.
One boldly strikes a loving slap;
One brings the powder in her lap;
And clouds of crimson dust arise
About the youth with lotus-eyes.
Then all the colour'd water pour,
And whelm him in a saffron shower;
And crowding round him bid him stand,
With wands of flowers in every hand.

The term *P,hagoon* is compounded of two Sunskreet words—*P,hal*, which signifies faults or slight errors; and *Goon*, admissible or venial—and implies, that little irregularities, such as talking indecently, rallying the women, or innocently romping with them, are allowable at this joyous season; when Nature herself sets the example, and smiles voluptuously on all the world. The Hohlee, however, strictly speaking, does not commence till the 23rd of

[1] The Indian Hercules and Apollo combined, the eighth incarnation of Vishnu.

the month; which day is the anniversary of a goddess named *Hohlika*, in whose honour the festival is held. On the last night of the month, the ceremony of burning the Hohlee concludes the festivities. A quantity of wood having been collected for the purpose, a lucky moment is fixed upon for setting fire to the pile. Every family has a small one within their own premises, where they burn little balls of cow-dung strung upon a rope, called *Bulha* , and a larger one is burned in every street or market place, around which all the neighbours assemble. In the morning, when the fire has burned out, they who have watched it through the night cast the ashes upon one another, and throw them into the air; laughing and hallooing, and repeating for the last time their favourite *Kuveers*. This concluding ceremony is allusive to the demise of the old year now just expired, and expressive of their joy at the approach of the new one now commencing. The riotous crew then bathe themselves, put on clean clothes, and go about to compliment their friends.

During the Hohlee, the Hindoos are fond of seeing exhibitions of dancing boys: they are called *Kuthiks*, and are, as well as the attendant musicians, always Brahmuns. Their dress is nearly the same as that of the Nach girls, but their dancing and singing are in general much better. The Sipahees are so fond of these exhibitions, that they will often sit up for many successive nights to enjoy them; and I have known a favourite set collect so large a sum as five hundred rupees from one company. The whole festival indeed is to them a season of mirth and relaxation, in which they delight to see their European officers participate, being highly gratified when any of them attend their Naches; and still more so if they join with them, as they often do, in playing on the last day of the Hohlee. They delight also in introducing their officers' names, European as well as native, into their Hohlee songs; and the greater the indecency attributed to each individual, the louder the burst of laughter and applause which is sure to attend the facetious effusion. It is perhaps a peculiar, and certainly a pleasing trait in the Hindoo character, that such licence is never known to produce any real relaxation in the respect for their officers, and obedience to orders, for which the Bengal Sipahees are so justly celebrated: on the contrary, they who can occasionally relax, and join with them in such innocent amusements, are commonly the officers to whom the men are most evidently and warmly attached.

Surjee Rao returned the Resident's visit two days ago; he was accompanied by Ambajee, and some other Surdars of his own party, but by none of those whom we had been accustomed to see upon such occasions. He was entertained with a Nach; after which the usual *Khiluts*, or dresses, were presented. There is something very repugnant to European ideas of delicacy in the mode of conducting this part of an entertainment; especially at a Mahratta Durbar, where it is considered more as a matter of bargain and sale than as a compliment. When a great number of *Khiluts* are to be presented, several are often brought in together, with labels attached to each, upon which is written the name of the individual for whom it is designed. The person who superintends the distribution holds in his hand a list of all those who are to receive the *Khiluts*, made out according to their respective ranks; and has often to search over the bundle before he can find the one he wants. It is then placed on a shield, and laid before the person who is to receive it; who nods to his servant to take it away, but makes not the slightest salutation to the giver, or any acknowledgment of the favour conferred. The value of the *Khilut* is adjusted by the rank of the person to whom it is presented: those most commonly given are termed *panch parchu*, or five pieces, and consist of a pair of shawls (reckoned always as one article), a piece of brocade, two of white cloth, and a turban. To these an ornament of jewelry, generally false and of very trifling value, is added on particular occasions; and to Princes, Ambassadors, and persons of the highest rank, an elephant and a horse are also presented. At this court the *Khiluts* are notoriously bad, the different kinds of cloth are of the coarsest quality; and the Muha Raj always seizes the opportunity to get rid of a lame horse or a foundered elephant. I have nevertheless known some of his Surdars return a pair of shawls which they did not like, and desire that they might be changed, with as little delicacy as if they had purchased them at a shop; and Raja Desmookh, the Muha Raj's cousin, and heir to his dominions, once did the same with an elephant, which had no blemish or fault whatever, but which he did not think handsome enough for him.

At this visit Ambajee displayed an instance of gratitude and attention which pleased us all: when as he perceived Mr. M. sitting in the circle, who had cured him of a wound in his side, inflicted by himself about two years ago (in consequence of his having been thrown into confinement by Seendhiya), he got up, and went towards him, and cordially embraced him; at the same time explaining to Surjee Rao who Mr. M. was, and how greatly he esteemed himself to be indebted to him.

All descriptions of people belonging to the army are employed throughout the day foraging in the corn-fields, which are abundant and very luxuriant in the neighbourhood of the camp. The whole plain is covered with them, loading their cattle, which are allowed to graze about at leisure while their masters are employed in tearing up and destroying: what they do not require for their own use, they hawk about the camp for sale. You will not wonder that the peasants should evince the utmost inveteracy towards such spoilers: they attack and fire upon them whenever they have an opportunity; and annoy them so much, that they do not venture, except in very large bodies, to any distance from camp. A horseman was brought to Mr. M. a few days ago, who had been wounded in the eye with an arrow: his own friends had pulled away the shaft, but left the point buried in the head: it was extracted, and measured nearly five inches in length: but the eye was entirely destroyed. As we have not yet so thoroughly acquired Mahratta habits as to be reconciled to the idea of foraging in green corn, we send out our cattle in search of something else; but the inhabitants of the country, confounding us with the bad company we keep, fire upon our parties; and we are obliged to take what we want by force.

The affair of Doonee appears to be wearing a much more serious aspect than was at first expected. The Qiludar received orders from Jypoor to offer Seendhiya fifty thousand rupees to march away; and the Muha Raj, confident in his own strength, demanded *five Lakhs;* but subsequently agreed to take three, provided they were speedily disbursed. The demand was instantly rejected; and a grand attack in consequence resolved upon. It took place yesterday morning, under the personal inspection of Muha Raj and the new ministers; and was made upon the garrison, entrenched without the walls, by all the troops in camp, backed by the whole of the artillery. It failed, however, completely; and with a heavy loss on the part of the Muha Raj, who is severely mortified at this repulse, and now conceives his reputation to be interested in the capture of the place. The whole army moved in consequence this morning closer to the town: the garrison have retired within the walls, and the Mahratta troops taken up positions for a regular siege. On the march we passed within a quarter of a mile of the town: it is not large, but appears to be filled with houses to the very wall, which is only a common one of mud. There is a small stone fort at the south-east corner, commanding an extensive piece of water; but the general appearance of the place is nothing less than strong, though there is said to be a good ditch all round the walls.

As I was sitting in my tent a few mornings ago, I was not a little surprised by an irruption of half a dozen women with large brazen trays of *pan* in their hands. They said they were *Butkees*, or slave girls, of the Mamma; and were come for a present. They were both old and ugly; yet indignantly refused a couple of rupees, and would hardly condescend to take four. They told me that they were brought up in a family of the Mamma, where they led a very easy life; their only employments, during the day, being to attend upon his wives, of whom he had three in camp, and to rub the old gentleman's legs when he lay down to repose; and at night they were at liberty to dispose of themselves as they pleased. This is the custom in Mahratta families of the highest rank, even in that of the *Baee* herself; a title common to all Mahratta ladies, but emphatically used to designate the Muha Raj's favourite wife. She has a number of these girls about her, from every part of India, who receive their daily food and two suits of clothes annually, and are allowed to earn as much more as they can, and in any way that they may think proper. Accordingly four of their number are regularly warned to be in waiting during the night; and the rest are instantly on the wing to their gallants. Of these they make no scruple to talk, even in their mistress's presence, and to boast of the fine things which they receive from them; calling them *Shuohur*, husband, and vaunting of the number whom they hold enslaved in their chains. The *Butkees* remain attached to the family during their lives. When they die, their jewels and other ornaments become the property of their mistress; who, if there are any children, generally bestows them upon them as marriage portions: if not, she divides them among the favourite little girls who are bringing up in the family to run a similar course. You will, I am sure, admire the simplicity, economy, and morality of this domestic arrangement.

LETTER X

Siege of Doonee continued—Two classes of Mahrattas—Brahmuns—Inferior classes—Their want of public attachments—Personal peculiarities—Moral qualities—Progress of the siege—Fanatic Fuqeer—Guns taken from the battery—Reinforcement to Doonee—The Muha Raj displeased with his ministers—Surjee Rao's drunkenness and debaucheries—His passion for Juwahir—Distress from want of water and forage—Thieves—Distress of the country—Requisitions on the merchants—Mankurrees—Meenas of Jypoor—Of Kota and Boondee—Ladkunnees—The small-pox appears in camp—The Muha Raj applies for vaccine matter—Raja Ambajee dying—Doonee, Tod,ha, and Malpoora—Raja of Boondee's present—Charge and use of Grupchat.

CAMP, DOONEE, *April* 7.

THIS famous siege is still going on, and appears to me as little likely to be brought to a happy conclusion as when we first arrived before the place. A detail of its progress will afford you a pretty just idea of Seendhiya's present power, and the mode in which military operations are conducted in his camp. But before I proceed to this, let me give you some more particulars of the manners, customs, and characters of this strange people. The Mahrattas may be divided into two grand classes: the first consisting entirely of Brahmuns; the second comprehending almost all the inferior *castes* of the Hindoos, but composed chiefly of *Aheers* or shepherds, and *Koormees* or tillers of the earth. The Brahmuns are all *Byshnoos*, or of the sect of Bishn; and consequently eat no flesh. They are distinguished by their turbans, which are generally white, and plaited, in a particular fashion, high above the head; they wear long muslin *dotees*, hanging down to the feet, except on state occasions, when it is the custom of this Durbar for them to appear in trowsers, commonly made of gold brocade; a plain white gown reaching to the knees, called *Unga;* and a shawl, or in warm weather a scarf of gauze or muslin called a *Sela,* thrown loosely across the shoulders; the Mahrattas of all classes agreeing in never girding the loins, and being, I believe, the only exception in India to this assimilation with the general costume of the ancients. The various *castes* of the second class are freer from religious prejudice, as to eating, than any other Hindoos; and abstain, with the single exception of beef, from no kind of flesh, whenever they can procure it. They highly esteem fowls and onions, both of which are abominations to other Hindoos; but their common food consists of cakes of coarse grain, called *Bajru,*[1] baked on an iron plate; with which they eat *Dal* (a name given indiscriminately to several kinds of split-peas), boiled with salt and pepper; or *Kurhee,* a mixture of pea-flour with sour curds. Their usual dress is a turban bound flat on the head, a *sela* thrown over the shoulders, and a pair of short breeches reaching just to the knees and made very tight, called *gootinnas:* if they wear a jacket, which they do but seldom, except in the cold season, it is short and coarse, and generally dyed of an olive colour. They are fond of ornamenting their ears with small gold rings; and such as can afford it have silver chains, twisted like ropes, fastened round their necks. Every one wears a sword and commonly a shield; and, when on horseback, carries either a matchlock or a long spear called a *Bala.* I have before mentioned that the Mahrattas are strangers to the comforts of domestic society. They seem to be equally so to public attachment: quarrelling to-day with their chief, and always about their pay; to-morrow, with the utmost indifference, ranging themselves on the side of his adversary; and the next day returning to their former master, if he is fool enough to send a deputation, and make a few false pro-

[1] Bájra (*Penicillaria spicata. Willd.*) or bulrush millet.

FIG. 4.—A MAHRATTA PUNDIT AND HIS FAMILY.

mises to lure them back to their duty. This may perhaps be the effect of the wandering and unsettled kind of life they lead: they have no home but a camp; no hope but for pay and plunder: of course that chief who can hold out the fairest prospect of both, will have the best chance of assembling them around his standard. To the same cause must be attributed their power of sustaining deprivations and fatigue; and their apparent cheerfulness and content under a system of domestic arrangement and economy that would be intolerable to any other set of people throughout India.

The two classes of Mahrattas are as much distinguished by personal peculiarities as by *caste* and dress: the Brahmuns are fair, have prominent features, and comely persons; the rest are dark, with broad flat faces, small features, and short square persons, but are very seldom, if ever, stout. I have never been able to discover any quality or propensity they possess which might be construed into a fitness for the enjoyment of social life. They are deceitful, treacherous, narrow-minded, rapacious, and notorious liars: the only quality they are endowed with, which could, according to our systems of ethics, be placed to the credit side of the account, being candour: for there is not one of the propensities I have enumerated to which a Mahratta would not immediately plead guilty: in his idea of things, they are requisite to form a perfect character: and to all accusations of falsehood, treachery, extortion, &c., he has one common answer:—"*Mahratta durbar hue*" ('tis a Mahratta court)!

Seendhiya seems to have called up all his might to crush this little place. A line of posts is established within musket-shot entirely round the walls, with batteries upon three sides: one of these is erected on a rock which overlooks the place, and from which a six-pounder well managed would easily lay the whole town in ruins. The garrison, however, do not appear to be at all intimidated: a flag of truce was sent on the 16th to endeavour to prevail upon them to accede to the Muha Raj's terms; they returned for answer, that "they defied the Muha Raj; they were but earth themselves, like their walls, and they were resolved to stand or fall with them." You will admire this spirited reply the more, when informed that there is not a gun in the place. Throughout the whole of that night the firing from the Mahratta batteries was kept up briskly; on the following day it continued, but slackened towards evening. On the 18th they began a mine; but Baptiste, to whom the operations of the siege were principally entrusted, was obliged to quit camp, for the purpose of quelling a mutiny which had broken out among his own *regulars* detached, under a Mahratta chieftain, in the neighbourhood of Jypoor. Up to the 22nd, the firing on the fort continued at intervals, but no apparent progress was made in the siege; the garrison plastering up, during the night, the mud which had been knocked down the preceding day. On that day the garrison in their turn sent out a flag of truce, but nothing of consequence ensued. Mounted patroles were ordered to parade round the army during the night; a reinforcement to the garrison being expected from Jypoor. A strong detachment for this purpose had actually marched from the capital; but, finding it impracticable to throw themselves into the place, they took refuge in another fort, about eight miles off, from whence they have continued to annoy the foragers. Some nights ago, three or four horses were carried off from one of these patroles, while their leaders were fast asleep, by thieves, who commit nightly depredations on the camp. On the 23rd a fanatic *Fuqeer* went to Surjee Rao in the trenches, and offered to take the fort for a certain reward. The reward was promised in the event of success; and the man advanced towards the walls, calling loudly upon his prophet for assistance; an unlucky ball, however, struck him on the leg, and broke it; and the man was brought back to camp, exclaiming that his blood lay on the head of Surjee Rao. The minister, alarmed at such a burden, had a tent pitched directly for his accommodation; and gave instructions that he should be served with everything he wished for, and attended with the utmost care. The *Fuqeer* makes the best of his situation; orders the richest dinners; and summons to his presence the choicest sets of dancing girls, whenever he feels an inclination for such amusements.

On the night of the 28th the garrison made a sally upon a new battery erected opposite to the gateway, drove away the troops which guarded it, and carried off two guns; but succeeded in conveying only one of them safe into the fort. This they mounted upon the walls; and opened next morning with such effect on a part of the army encamped near the piece of water, that it obliged them to strike their tents and fall back with the utmost precipitation. On the night of the 30th an attempt was made to advance the batteries nearer to the walls; but the garrison again sallied out upon the troops, and drove them back with some loss. On the following night the garrison became the assailants, and made two separate attacks upon the trenches; with no other effect, however, than greatly annoying the besiegers. About this time ten men disguised as *Bihishtees*, or water-carriers, were detected in endeavouring to carry powder to the garrison in their water-bags. For three or four days the fire upon the place slackened; and a report prevailed, that negotiations between the garrison and the Muha Raj were going on; as well as that an envoy was on his way from Jypoor, with power to settle all matters in dispute between the two states. On the night of the 5th, however, the garrison made another sally upon the trenches, and killed and wounded about twenty of the besiegers. On the preceding evening they had received a most acceptable reinforcement of a hundred men, who contrived to enter the place, notwithstanding it was so closely invested, each carrying a quantity of powder and ball, and opium; the latter being as indispensably necessary as the two former articles to the comfort and efficiency of Rajpoot soldiers.

Such is the progress made by a powerful chieftain, during twenty-five days, in the siege of a place which four companies of Sipahees with one six-pounder would have taken easily in as many hours. The Muha Raj is greatly vexed at the whole affair, which he justly considers as disgraceful to his arms; and is so angry with both Surjee Rao and the Mamma, that neither of them have appeared at the Durbar during the last three or four days. It was from a battery under the direction of the latter that the gun was taken on the 28th; though Surjee Rao was more in fault than him, and was indeed the immediate cause of the attack. He had gone down to the trenches in a state of intoxication, and advanced, with only a few attendants, so close to the walls, that he was perceived by the garrison, who sallied out upon his party, and followed them as they retreated to the battery. The minister is notoriously addicted to the bottle, and is said to be frequently drunk: like most other great men, too, of Hindoostan, he indulges freely with women; and has so much injured his constitution by excess, that he has constant recourse to provocatives to excite his appetite and stimulate his failing powers: dishes of young pigeons, and goat's flesh stewed down to rich jellies, are daily served up at his table; and the female, or, as she is generally termed, the queen, of the white ants, a sovereign remedy in cases of exhausted vigour, is carefully sought after and preserved for his use. One of Surjee Rao's, or, as he is now familiarly styled in camp, Bapoo Sahib's whims, is to dress entirely in European clothes, without excepting even the hat, and thus equipped to appear at the head of his troops. This eccentric minister is at present under the all-powerful sway of a common Nach girl, named Juwahir; who has so completely captivated his affections, that he is miserable when separated from her, even for the shortest space of time: she lives at his tents; accompanies him in a palanquin whenever he goes abroad; and is herself attended by a far more numerous train than that of her venerable lover. To render the whole arrangement more strikingly correct, the same lady was, but a short time ago, the favourite mistress of the Muha Raj; to whose notice she was introduced by his moral father-in-law himself.

All descriptions of people are anxious for the conclusion of this siege. The camp is very ill supplied with water, which is only to be gotten by digging wells in the sand, and then but in small quantities. This is a serious evil at all seasons; but particularly so now, when the hot winds have set in, and we are obliged to make use of *tattees*, a kind of screens made of the roots of a coarse grass called Kus, which retain the water poured upon them, and cause evaporation as the hot wind passes through. The foragers are constantly attacked by the Meenas, or hill people, without the camp; and the Bazars almost every night by thieves within it. A wealthy merchant was robbed a few nights ago of a chest containing jewels and other valuables, to the amount of 70,000 rupees: this theft, however, has been traced to the *Shohdas*, thirteen of whom have been seized and confined; and Fazil Khan has actually restored 19,000 rupees; with a promise to make strict inquiries for the rest of the things, which are shrewdly suspected to be safe in his own keeping. The merchant, who is one of the sect called *Gosaeens*, is in the habit of occasionally accommodating the Muha Raj with loans: he might otherwise have bemoaned his loss for ever, without any steps being taken to discover the offenders. These repeated attacks of the Meenas have taught discipline, or at least caution, to the Mahrattas: a large body of horse, with two or three guns, now parades regularly every morning on the skirts of the camp, for the protection of the foragers, who assemble together, and go out in a body. Leaves, coarse grass, and old thatch is the only fodder they can now produce: the *kurbee* is almost exhausted; and what little remains has been removed into the villages, where it is fiercely defended by the peasants. The new crop has been entirely destroyed for miles around; the consequence of which will probably be a famine throughout this part of the country: at any rate, the deepest distress will fall upon a large portion of it. Had the declaratory articles not been affixed to the treaty of 1805–6, by which originally Seendhiya was prohibited from crossing the Chumbul in these parts, the British government would have had the glory of rescuing, with a single stroke of the pen, these fine and populous plains from such ravages as I am now describing; and which, recurring as they do almost every year, must in the end produce their total ruin.

Another class of people who are heartily tired of this protracted siege, are the merchants of the Bazars; upon whom the whole expense of the trenches, batteries, &c., falls. A requisition of four *tukhas*, or eight *pice*, is made upon each shop; the owner of which has, however, the option of substituting a *coolee*, or labourer, for the day. The collection is made daily throughout the different Bazars in rotation; and such shopkeepers as cannot afford to pay their proportion, are called upon to work themselves. When wood is required to form trenches, or construct batteries, every *buniya* sends a camel to fetch it; and a guard is allowed for the protection of the whole. The Shohdas too, as I mentioned before, become useful members of the community during a siege, when they perform all the duties of pioneers. The collection from the merchants is entrusted to their chief Fazel Khan, and its expenditure is made under his control; for which privilege, however, he pays a handsome fee to government. I formerly noticed their patron Baboo Khan; he has been lately created a *Mankurree*, a title conferred by the Peshwa, which gives the rare privilege of being received by the Durbar standing, and not saluting the prince if he happens to pass by on an elephant; though should he be in a palanquin, or on horseback, the *Mankurree* condescends to bow to him. The Meenas, whom I have two or three times mentioned in this letter, are, in the Jypoor territories, the tillers of the land; one half of the profit of which goes to the *Sirkar*, or government. They are of the *Chutree* tribe ; but are not styled Rajpoots : these last thinking it derogatory, except in cases of extreme poverty, to follow any other vocation than that of arms. Many of the Rajpoots, however, rent large Zumeendarees, or farms, on which the Meenas are employed to work. These Meenas were assembled some years ago in large bodies, by Seoo Sing,h, a natural son of Raja Man Sing,h of Jypoor, and employed by him in robbing and plundering. Seoo Sing,h was afterwards seized by the present Raja Jugut Sing,h, and trodden to death under the feet of an elephant ; when the Meenas returned to their former occupation. In the districts of Kota and Boondee the Meenas inhabit the hills and jungles, and are exclusively employed in thieving. With them, however, the Meenas of Jypoor hold no kind of communication : the former eat meat and drink spirits whenever they can get them ; the latter do neither. It is these last-mentioned Meenas, those of Boondee, who have committed such depredations on the army ; attacking the foragers, intercepting the Bunjaras, and plundering every one who is unfortunate enough to fall into their hands. Seendhiya has at last resolved to put a stop to these ravages, by taking a large body of them into his service, and employing them in protecting the foraging parties. A treaty has accordingly been made with the Zumeendar of Shursa, a district about twenty miles from camp, and reckoned the principal of the Meena villages, for a corps of five hundred. He came to camp for this purpose, and left it again yesterday to collect his people.

Their depredations had become so audacious, that a detachment of two thousand men was formed a week ago for the purpose of avenging the Mahrattas, and plundering a couple of Meena villages not very far from camp : a service so congenial to Mahratta feelings, that Raja Desmookh, the heir of the state, marched himself at its head. Another set of robbers, called *Ladkunnees*, have also been very active in cutting off supplies coming to the army ; they are Moohum medans, and inhabit a tract of country bordering upon the Sambur lake.

In addition to its other evils, the small-pox has lately made its appearance in camp; and the Muha Raj, alarmed for his daughter Chunna Baee, sent to the Resident to request that some vaccine matter might be procured with all possible haste. Lancets were accordingly brought by the post from Agra; and their arrival intimated to Seendhiya. In the true spirit of Mahratta apathy and suspicion, however, he took no notice of it for several days, and at length it was discovered that the little Baee had caught the infection. This is the second time he has made the same demand, and evinced the same indifference, since we have been with him.

Poor old Raja Ambajee is said to be dying: he was taken ill some days ago, and sent to request Mr. M. to come and see him once more. He found him in a wretched little tent, in the rear of the batteries, with very few attendants, and no kind of comfort, about him. Mr. M. returned two days after by appointment; and was informed that the Raja had quitted camp that morning, and was gone to a spot about eight miles off, on the banks of the Bunas; partly for change of air, and partly to meet his wife and family. At his advanced age the annoyance of public business, and the state of continual apprehension in which he is kept by his formidable colleague, will probably soon tend to bring his days to a close. He is said still to be possessed of immense wealth; though Seendhiya contrived, during Surjee Rao's former administration, to extort from him several lakhs of rupees, by setting fire to oiled cotton tied upon his fingers, and various other ingenious and similar contrivances. To a European mind it will appear inexplicable that a man so completely independent, who had experienced in his own person such indignities, and who is fully aware what reliance can be placed on Mahratta faith, could, by any offers of influence or wealth, be induced a second time to put himself in their power.

This place, which is likely to become celebrated in Mahratta annals, is one of nine forts attached to the *Purgunu*, or district of Tod,ha, farmed by Chand Sing,h, a near relation of the Jypoor Raja. It contains one hundred and thirty towns and villages: in all the open ones Seendhiya has established his *thanas*, or parties; but none in one of the fortified places, which are by far the most numerous. The revenue paid into the treasury by this *Purgunu* amounts to four lakhs: the neighbouring one of Malpoora is of equal extent and value, and was entirely taken possession of by Bapoo Seendhiya two years ago, when he was sent from this camp to *assist* the Raja of Jypoor in his expedition against Juodpoor. The Ooniara Raja, another relation of the Jypoor Prince, has paid to the Muha Raj a lakh of rupees, on the condition of his not entering his country. The Raja of Boondee, a branch of the same family, and on the borders of whose country we are now encamped, has endeavoured to conciliate the Muha Raj, by sending him a present of two hundred camels to compensate for the depredations of his Meenas. The Wukeel who brought them was attended by a large body of these people, without whose protection even the Raja himself would not have ventured to travel through his own country.

I mentioned to you in one of my former letters[1] a large unwieldy gun called *Grupchat*: the other morning I rode to a small rocky hill, from whence I had a complete view of the fort of Doonee, the trenches, &c., and observed several people, belonging to the park, loading a small cart with loose round stones, which, upon inquiry, I found were designed as a load for *Grupchat*. Two cart-loads are put into the gun at once, with eighteen pounds of powder; and it is then fired at an angle of about seventy degrees, and thus rains down a shower of stones upon the heads of the besieged and the roofs of their houses: a very adequate remuneration for the expense and trouble of dragging about

[1] *See* p. 43.

such an unwieldy machine in all the seasons of the year. These people were by no means backward in venting sarcasms upon the operations of the siege; and added, half jokingly, half in earnest, "Why don't you let your two companies come and take the fort for us? they could do it if they would: *we*, you know, *are Mahrattas!*"

LETTER XI

Siege of Doonee continued—Surdars sent to meet the Jypoor Ambassador—Mahratta claims upon the Rajpoot states—Character of the Rajpoots—Battle of Jypoor—Koosallee Ram—Presents brought for the Muha Raj—Seendhiya's employments and companions—His wives—Old Mogulanee attendant of the Baee—Divisions among the ministers—Distress throughout the camp—Baboo Khan—Detachments in the Jypoor country—Gosaeens—Change of officers—Remarkably dry weather.

CAMP AT DOONEE, *April 25th.*

I WILL now resume my journal of this memorable siege, of which there is at length some prospect of a conclusion. On the night of the 7th another sally was made upon the trenches, and several men were killed on both sides. The garrison began to feel the effect of the cannonade upon the town and the wall; such large portions of which fell daily, that they were unable to build them up again during the night; and the besiegers expected to make a practicable breach in a day or two more. To render this of as little avail as possible, if it should be effected, the garrison employed themselves throughout the whole of the 8th in digging a ditch along that face of the fort which was most battered. Seendhiya inspected the trenches in person that evening; and was much enraged at the officers of the batteries, who could not bring their guns to bear so as to interrupt this work. Ever since the unfortunate business of the 28th ult. the guns have regularly been removed from the batteries at night, and carried back again at break of day. On the morning of the 13th the garrison again sallied out, and succeeded in burning the batteries and trenches on the north side of the place; which being constructed of branches, now become quite dry, were easily consumed. After this misfortune the exertions of the besiegers slackened more and more, and on the morning of the 16th the firing from their batteries ceased; in consequence, as it was said, of the Jypoor ambassador having arrived at Nasurdu, a town about twelve miles off, where he had had an interview, though merely a ceremonious one, with Raja Ambajee. On the following morning, however, the batteries opened again with more spirit than ever, and even continued to fire during two heavy showers of rain; an exertion very unusual in this camp. On the 19th a requisition was made of all the flag-staffs in the army, to be used as scaling ladders: though it was pretty well understood to be nothing more than a bravado, with a view to influence the approaching negotiations. Since yesterday, however, all firing has ceased on both sides; though the troops and guns are still kept in the trenches. Friendly communications take place between the garrison and camp; and the former occasionally come into the Bazars to purchase provisions. Bala Rao, the brother of Ambajee, accompanied by another Surdar of high rank, went yesterday to Nasurdu to compliment Koosallee Ram, the name of the Jypoor ambassador; and this morning Surjee Rao himself, attended by Gopal Rao Buo and a splendid retinue, set out to meet him and escort him to camp, where he is expected to-morrow.

During the whole of these proceedings it is impossible not to admire the spirit and firmness displayed by the garrison of Doonee. What apology, however, can be made for a people who are capable of such exertions, and yet submit, without a struggle, to the insults and ruinous demands made upon them by the different Mahratta chiefs? Seendhiya claims as his right a tribute from Juodpoor, and Holkar the same from Jypoor; claims founded upon grants made to their families by the Peshwa, when the Mahratta empire, acting in a united body under one head, had established its influence and power in all the states of Hindoostan. At present, however, the case is very different; nor do I think that either of these chieftains could make good their demands against any one of the Rajpoot Princes singly; certainly not, if they were wise enough to lay aside the jealousies and distrust perpetually kindling among them, and join hand and heart in opposing their common enemies the Mahrattas. It may fairly be doubted, however, whether such an union, though so evidently tending to their mutual advantage, could by any means be effected. That chivalrous courage and high sense of honour, by which the Rajpoots were formerly so eminently distinguished, seems to have quite deserted them, and to have degenerated into tameness and apathy, and a despicable love of intrigue and domestic squabbles. Of the spirit which formerly animated them, let me give you a striking instance. While the *Jats* were in the plenitude of their power, Juwahir Sing,h, the son of Sooruj Mul, their chief, went on a pilgrimage to the celebrated temples at Pokur, in the neighbourhood of Ajmeer, escorted by a considerable force. On his return, he passed with great pomp under the walls of Jypoor, beating the *Nuqaru*, a large kettle-drum, the distinguishing appendage of sovereign rank. The sound reached the Durbar, where the Raja was seated surrounded by his nobles. Amongst them were several individuals of his own family, who, starting indignantly at the sound, drew their swords, and swore to chastise the insolent upstart who dared thus to flout them at their very doors: the *Jats* having been, a very short time before, but Zumeendars of the Jypoor state. In vain the Raja endeavoured to pacify them: they sallied forth, calling upon all true Rajpoots to join them; and, followed by such troops as could hastily be collected in the city, attacked Juwahir Sing,h, surrounded by his army; with which was a large body of disciplined Sipahees, and some brigades of guns, commanded by the famous, or more properly infamous, Sumroo. The conflict was dreadful; and report, no doubt greatly exaggerated, states forty thousand Rajpoots to have been left dead upon the field. The few, however, that survived had the satisfaction of forcing Juwahir Sing,h to retreat, surrounded by Sumroo's troops; to whose artillery alone he owed his safety and his life. Bukht Sing,h, a young Prince of the Juodpoor family, headed the attack, and with the flower of the Rajpoot nobles, fell in this fatal and romantic combat.

Koosallee Ram, now coming as Ambassador to this court, and who is commonly distinguished by the appellation of *Buhora*, or "the merchant," is a veteran who has often distinguished himself in the service of the Raja of Jypoor. He has had of course many enemies; the principal of whom, a Takoor named Raee Chund, Deewan of the state, effected the overthrow of his rival upon the following occasion. At the battle of Malpoora, fought against Lakwa Dada, one of Madoojee Seendhiya's best generals, the Rajpoots were completely defeated, and, with the Raja himself, fled in confusion towards the capital; leaving everything, even the ladies of the prince's family, to the mercy of the victorious Mahrattas. Koosallee Ram at that critical moment rallied the corps under his immediate command, gallantly surrounded the carriages in which the ladies were seated, and successfully defended them till they reached the city. The Deewan, jealous of this act of heroism, insinuated to his master, that if Koosallee Ram had not been secretly connected with the Mahratta general, it would have been impossible for him to have maintained his ground against such a host, or have performed so distinguished a feat. These insinuations had the desired effect; and the Buhora was instantly thrown into confinement by his weak and ungrateful master. From this confinement he has only now been liberated; when his enemies themselves have discovered that his acknowledged talents are requisite to the support of their tottering state.

He is said to have brought a variety of rich presents for the Muha Raj; amongst the rest, four horses and two elephants, caparisoned in the most superb manner; and, far more acceptable, two sets of Nach girls, the most beautiful and accomplished that Jypoor could produce ; and which will be more effectual in accomplishing his purpose with Seendhiya than the strongest pleas of justice or expediency. This light-hearted prince is by no means insensible to the embarrassment of his affairs, or the consequent failure and disgrace which almost always attends his undertakings. But these things affect him but for an hour ; a tiger or a pretty face, an elephant fight or a new supply of paper kites, have each sufficient attraction to divert his chagrin, and restore him to his wonted thoughtlessness and good humour. It is only, however, upon such occasions as the siege of Doonee that he tastes of almost unalloyed happiness. Under the pretence of attending to the operations of the siege, he directed a small suite of tents to be pitched for him in a garden in the rear of the trenches, and there, surrounded by a set of parasites and buffoons, he passed his time in one constant round of the grossest debaucheries. Emancipated from his two greatest plagues, his wife and his ministers, he refused to listen to any business ; and seemed to think of nothing but fresh modes of wiling away his hours, and indulging his own profligate propensities. Women and low company have been his bane ; and appear to have quite corrupted a heart and mind originally meant for better things. Virgin charms have been diligently sought for, and almost daily sacrificed upon the altar of his lusts ; and in the conclave of his wretched minions, scenes are said to be enacted for his amusement, so gross, and at the same time so ridiculous, as would stagger belief, and call a blush into the cheeks of the most depraved European. These miscreants are systematic in their infamy, their sports are regularly classed and organized ; but as common language is inadequate to their description, fancy is called in to their aid, and to every new diversion is given a new and unheard-of designation. Yet Seendhiya has no less than three wives with him in camp ; all of them young and eminently handsome.

To one only, however, the daughter of Surjee Rao, does he ever dispense his favours. The others pass their time in a wretched state of penury and neglect; objects at once of aversion to their husband, and of scorn and contempt to their favoured rival, emphatically called, as I before observed, *the Baee*. This title, which is literally a term of respect applied to mothers and sisters, or any other near female relatives, has been adopted by the Mahrattas, amongst whom the ladies of the prince's family are always persons of much political weight and consequence, as one by which they might be frequently mentioned by the multitude without the slightest impropriety; for they conceive that no man could possibly even think of a woman, whom he called mother or sister, but with the utmost purity and respect: no bad elucidation, by the by, of the principles of Asiatic delicacy with regard to woman. My information respecting the Baees was obtained from an old woman in the family of *the Baee*, who was turned a few evenings ago at once out of her service and the camp. She took refuge in our Bazar; and the following morning I received a message from Atmaram, the Muha Raj's agent, requesting that she might not be allowed to remain; as both the Muha Raj himself, and the Baee, were highly incensed against her. I sent for her to inform her of this message; and found she was a Mogul, very old and very plain. She told me that she had been three years in the service of the Baee; for whom, and for the ladies of her family, she worked bodices and veils: that she had incurred her mistress's displeasure in consequence of some aspersions, quite false she declared, thrown out against her reputation by a Pithan horseman in the service of Surjee Rao, who had long sued for her favour, and had become her bitterest enemy when he found that he could not triumph over her virtue. The poor old lady inveighed bitterly, and, it must be confessed, with some justice, against the cruelty of turning her out of the camp, in a country overrun with enemies, and at a time when no

Qafilu, or caravan, was likely to quit the army for Delhi, her native city.

The new ministry do not appear to coalesce heartily; old Ambajee—who, by the by, is so much recovered as to be negotiating a new matrimonial connexion for himself—is said to be so dissatisfied with his situation, as to express an intention of retiring to his government at Ajmeer, and even to threaten to put himself to death if his wishes should be thwarted. The attack upon Doonee was, it seems, a measure of his recommending; and the negotiations with the Jypoor Wukeel are entrusted to his management; and the little prospect that exists of bringing either to a propitious termination, is a source of perpetual uneasiness to the old man: for the demands on one side, and the offers on the other, are reported to be so incompatible with each other, that the negotiations will in all probability be protracted to an indefinite length.

The Mamma too has not been without his share of vexation. A party of his cavalry went to him, a few days ago, in a clamorous manner, to demand their pay; he refused it of course, for, in truth, he had none to give them: and to revenge himself for the insult, he seized upon their tents, arms, and whatever else he could lay his hands upon, and drove them out of camp; telling them that they might, if they chose, take advantage of a *Qafilu* proceeding to Oojyn to return to their own houses. They were brought back on the following day by the Muha Raj, who undertook to accommodate matters with their master. Upwards of three hundred horsemen have joined themselves to this *Qafilu*, weary of a starving service, and seeking for something better. Great distress prevails throughout the camp, owing to a total want of forage, the dearness of grain, and the scarcity of cash; and numbers of people are quitting it by every opportunity that offers. About ten days ago Baboo Khan, whom I have before mentioned to you, attempted to rid himself of the importunities of some merchants, who had incautiously sold him horses and other goods, in the usual way; and, in addition to other acts of violence, fired upon them. The men went in a body to complain to Surjee Rao; who instantly gave orders for the Khan's tents to be surrounded and plundered, and himself to quit the army that very afternoon. Seendhiya, however, again interposed as a mediator; and took upon himself the adjustment of the debt.

Two detachments under Bapoo Seendhiya and Jugoo Bapoo, Mahratta chiefs of some consequence, are now employed in levying contributions in different parts of the Jypoor country. Such detachments are called *churee fuoj*, they are generally equipped very lightly, with but little artillery, and are equally formidable in their progress to friend and foe. The former of these leaders has even gone the length of levying contributions upon Kanuon and Narnuol; two petty districts upon the borders between the Jypoor and the Company's territories, and held immediately of the British government: another instance of the benefit derived from the *safe policy* which dictated the explanatory articles. Such proceedings are of course not countenanced, and perhaps not approved of, by the Durbar; and orders have been sent to Bapoo Seendhiya to quit that part of the country immediately, and even to refund whatever he may have taken from the districts in question. As it is notorious, however, that he will never venture himself within the clutches of Surjee Rao, it is probable he may enlist himself and his troops in the service of some of the chieftains of that neighbourhood; and in the meantime will assuredly not let any opportunity slip of enriching himself as much as circumstances will allow. The army has received a considerable reinforcement, since my last letter, by the arrival of a body of Gosaeens under Kumpta Gir. This chief succeeded to the command of the corps, which consists of nearly 1,500 men, chiefly horse, upon the death of Ram Gir, who died about a month ago. They were both *Chelas*, or disciples, of Kunchun Gir, the Chela of Himmut Bahadoor, a celebrated Gosaeen in the service of Shumsheer

FIG. 5.—A MUHUNT AND GOSAEENS.

Buhadoor, one of the chiefs of Boondelkund. The Gosaeens are a religious order of Hindoo mendicants who attach themselves to the service of particular chiefs; and frequently, as in the case of Himmut Buhadoor, amass great wealth, and raise themselves into consequence. They then adopt Chelas; and are themselves styled *Gooroos*, or teachers. Upon the death of the Gooroo, the eldest Chela succeeds to his honours; and after him, the others, according to the dates of their adoption, before the Chelas of the second Gooroo. When they become numerous and wealthy, and enrol themselves as a military band in the service of some Prince, their leader is termed *Muhunt*: they then retain but little of their original manner and appearance, distinguishing themselves alone by the *jutta*, or long matted hair folded like a turban on the head, and having some portion of their dress dyed of a kind of orange colour, called *Geroo*, peculiar to their sect. As soldiers, they are accounted brave and faithful; and they are the only *Hindoos* who bury their dead. When one of the order dies, he is interred in a sitting posture, with his staff and *tombree*, a small kind of calabash, the emblems of his mendicity, placed before him in the grave; and if the band be rich enough, a small monument is erected to mark the spot.

Almost all the old officers of the Sirkar have been turned out, and their places filled by creatures of the new minister. Among others, Atmaram has been removed from his situation in our camp; and two others sent in his room. They delivered their credentials three days ago; in which they were described, one, as residing with us, to be the immediate organ of communication between the resident and the minister; the other, for the purpose only of picking up information. Such is the terror with which Surjee Rao is regarded throughout the army, that Atmaram quitted our camp without taking leave; and when Seendhiya expressed his astonishment at his having done so, he attributed it to his fears of the construction which Surjee Rao might have put upon such a step; and at the same time entreated the Muha Raj to solicit the minister's sanction to his making the usual farewell visit. This was accordingly done; and Atmaram was permitted to take leave in due form, and to receive the customary *Khilut* upon the occasion. The weather has for some days past been extremely hot and dry: I awoke last night, and was surprised at observing faint gleams of light about my bed; I rubbed my eyes, to convince myself that it was not the moonlight; and found, that whenever I ran my hand along the upper sheet, small pencils of light were emitted from each side of my fingers. I called up a servant, who slept near the wall of the tent, to bear witness to this phenomenon; which, however, I could not produce by rubbing the counterpane, or the sheet upon which I lay.

LETTER XII

Arrival of the Jypoor Ambassador—Extravagant demands of the Durbar—Demands of Jypoor—Strength of the Jypoor country—Disaffection of the Rajpoot Generals—Differences respecting Doonee—Visit to the Durbar—Surjee Rao's cruelties—His influence over the Muha Raj lessened—Revolution in Holkar's camp—Mutiny in Appa Kandra's camp—Corps of Meenas—Account of them—Increasing distress of the camp—Surdars quit it—Others sit D,hurna—Rajah Bawanee Purshad—Seendhiya's privy purse—Flying kites—Eclipse of the moon.

CAMP AT DOONEE, *May* 4.

THE Jypoor ambassador arrived on the 26th ult. He was met in the neighbourhood of the camp by the Muha Raj in person, who on such occasions appears with great state and pomp. The whole of his cavalry attend, and generally form a street, through which the procession passes. The immense number of attendants, the various and gaudy banners floating in the air, the fine horses and elephants richly caparisoned, and exhibited to the greatest advantage, all unite to form a gay and striking spectacle. Several conferences and communications have already taken place between the Buhora and the minister; but the former has found the demands of this Durbar so far exceeding what he has power to grant, that he has been obliged to send to his court for further instructions. Neither has he been backward in bringing forward demands; but is said to have presented a schedule of damages, done to his master's country by various detachments during the last two years, amounting to forty lakhs of rupees. This is probably a most exaggerated statement; but were it, on the contrary, below the real injury sustained, I could find but little pity for a people who, possessing so many advantages, voluntarily bend their necks to one of the most galling yokes in the world.

The territory of Jypoor is compact and populous, and contains some of the strongest fortresses in Hindoostan: those which defend the capital and Runtambor, are deemed impregnable. There are besides a number of forts of inferior strength scattered over the country; and every second village is surrounded by walls and a ditch, and defended by a race of men, who have shown at Doonee how capable they are of opposing an invading foe. Seendhiya has advanced thus far into the country, leaving the fortress of Runtambor and the city of Nuya Shuhur, the second in the state, in his rear; without any attempt to reduce them, or, which is more extraordinary, receiving any check from the troops which compose their garrisons. Such a military error, however, is accounted for by the very prevalent suspicion of a good understanding being established between the Muha Raj and Jeewun Chela, the governor of those places. Disaffection and treason are crimes of such luxuriant growth in these countries, that such a charge excites neither abhorrence, nor even astonishment, in the breast of any one who hears it. Seendhiya's demands on the Jypoor state are for seventeen lakhs; a sum promised him for his assistance in the famous expedition against Juodpoor, which the Raja undertook about two years ago. The *Churee-fuoj*, now under Bapoo Seendhiya, was sent for that purpose; but did not arrive till the Raja had returned from Juodpoor, completely foiled: and then remunerated itself, by seizing upon his villages, and laying waste his country. Koosallee Ram, however, is authorized to offer twelve lakhs; making a reasonable deduction from that sum for *Paemalee*, or devastation done to the country, since the grand army entered it. Another cause of difference between the parties is Doonee; respecting which the Muha Raj conceives his honour to be implicated; and insists upon treating for it separately: a proposition which the Buhora as firmly resists.

We went to the Durbar a few days ago, where we hoped to have seen the Jypoor Wukeel, who had, however, departed about a quarter of an hour before we arrived. He was described to me as a tall venerable old man, with an interesting countenance, and his hair and beard as white as snow. We found the Muha Raj seated in the open air, under the shade of a clump of trees, enclosed by *Qunats*, or screens of cloth. Surjee Rao was present, but not one of the old set of courtiers. He is said to have lost almost entirely the ascendancy which he once held over the mind of his son-in-law. During the last administration, this power was so unbounded, that he daily committed the most horrid enormities with impunity; men of rank or of wealth, if obnoxious to him, were continually put to death without ceremony by the halter or by poison; or by blowing them into the air, fastened to rockets made of the trunks of small trees. The Muha Raj's sanction to these acts was certainly implied; but if it was ever obtained, it was doubtless during a fit of intoxication, for he is by no means of a cruel disposition. A man, who was lately detected in some petty theft, was condemned by Surjee Rao to have his hands and ears cut off: which being reported to the Muha Raj, he countermanded the order, and directed that some less severe and more adequate punishment should be inflicted upon him. The control, so evidently evinced by the Prince over the so-much-dreaded minister, has inspired confidence into all ranks of people throughout the army. Surjee Rao succeeded, however, another day, in cropping the ear of one of his own servants; who was suspected of too great an intimacy with his beloved Juwahir: the order was given for hands, nose and ears; but the man, who was entrusted with the execution, had the temerity to let the poor wretch off with the loss of only one ear: an act of mercy for which he was immediately rewarded with a good

FIG. 6.—A MEENA OF JAJGURH.

flogging by a leathern martingale, the instrument always used by the Mahrattas on such occasions.

Accounts have been received of a revolution in Holkar's camp, in consequence of Meer Khan's seizing upon the persons of that chieftain and his principal ministers. The *regular* infantry pretended to mutiny; and pointing their guns on the main army, the ministers fled for protection to Meer Khan, who was encamped in the neighbourhood, and by whom they have been retained in safety ever since. At the same time we heard that a mutiny had broken out in the camp of Appa Kandra, one of Seendhiya's principal favourites, who commands a detachment in the neighbourhood of Sagur. He had called in a party of Pindaris to assist him against his infantry, who were clamorous for pay; but on their arrival in camp, they joined the mutineers, and seized the person of Appa Kandra; whom they tied to a gun, and kept there till he agreed to issue a sum of money for their use. He afterwards found means, however, to strengthen his own party so much, that he was enabled to punish some of the ringleaders with death, and drive the rest out of his camp.

The corps of Meenas from Jajgurh has been some time in camp, and as I was anxious to see and converse with them, I sent a servant to ask some of them to come to my tent. Accordingly a party of thirteen or fourteen waited upon me. They were all stout, good-looking fellows, and entered cheerfully into conversation respecting their own manners and customs. They were armed with a bow and quiver of arrows, and a dagger, at the use of which they are particularly expert; and wore their turbans very high, ornamented on the top with a bunch of feathers of a species of curlew called *Bojha*. From them I learnt the following particulars: Jajgurh was wrested by Zalim Sing,h of Kota from the Rana of Oodipoor, about six years ago; and has ever since remained attached to his territories. The district contains eighty-four towns and villages; twenty-two of which are exclusively inhabited by Meenas;

who pay only personal service to the Sirkar. Each village has a *Kotwal*, or civil officer, of its own, who manages the affairs of the community according to their peculiar laws and customs. They intermarry with no other tribe, and among them the singular custom prevails of the second brother taking to himself the widow of the eldest: for this purpose, he purchases jewels and clothes, and produces her in the midst of his relations and friends assembled together, who sanction their union. This union, however, is not called marriage, though it has the same privileges and cannot be set aside; but is termed *Nata*. if the second brother should die, the third takes her; and so on, till she becomes too old to be taken by any one. They assured me that they could, upon any pressing occasion, assemble a body of twenty thousand men; of which number nearly a third were sprung from one family, the founders of their tribe: the rest are aliens, who have been incorporated at different times into the community. They profess to be thieves and robbers, and think it no more harm to maintain themselves by plunder than by entering into any military service. They are particularly fond of carrying off children from the villages or camps which they attack: the boys they breed up as Meenas, and the girls they sell as slaves in the neighbouring provinces. Their adoration is especially offered to Muha Deo; whom they invoke previous to engaging in any expedition, and pray him to give them two children for every man that may be slain. They complained loudly of the Muha Raj's treatment of them, who has only distributed five hundred rupees among them since they came to camp: and I make no doubt, but that in a few days, if he does not supply them better, they will quit his camp, and pay themselves as before, at his expense.

There is a general complaint throughout the army of a want of cash, and people of all ranks begin to feel the effects of it. A Mahratta chieftain, named Joota Bamania, left camp on the first instant with upwards of a thousand followers: but as he is still at a village only a few miles off, he probably meant this step but as a threat, and the usual stratagem to induce the Muha Raj to come to some settlement with him. Kumpta Gir, too, with his Gosaeens, finding that he could obtain no security for the payment of his troops, is gone off this morning. The Khans, and a Surdar named Raja Bawanee Purshad, have been sitting *D,hurna* upon the Muha Raj: the former have extorted from him many fair promises of a speedy settlement, and some trifling supply to answer their immediate necessities: but the latter was treated with the utmost contempt, and commanded instantly to quit the *Deooree*. He held lately a high situation in the service of the Nuwab Wuzeer, from which he fled upon some disagreement with his master, and came here in expectation of being employed by Seendhiya. The Muha Raj received him with the utmost attention, and promised to employ him: which promise enabling him to get what credit he pleased in the Bazar, the first use he made of it was to entertain the Muha Raj himself in a magnificent manner. Debts were soon incurred to the amount of half a lakh of rupees, and the merchants becoming importunate for payment, he applied for an advance, and was merely laughed at for his folly: he then tried the common Mahratta mode of enforcing demands, a *D,hurna*, but met only with scorn and contumely for his presumption. While Seendhiya is daily submitting to these and similar insults, he possesses a privy purse, stocked, as it is said, to the amount of fifty lakhs; which no distress either of himself or his troops is sufficiently powerful to induce him to violate, it being an established rule to put as much as possible into it, but never to take anything out.

The season for flying paper kites being now come in, the Muha Raj is to be seen every evening, attended by large bodies of cavalry employed to keep the ground, partaking of this princely diversion. It is a favourite amusement in every part of India. The kites have no tails, and bear some resemblance in shape to the ace of clubs.

Matches are fought with them, and frequently for large sums, which he whose string is cut loses, and his kite is reckoned lawful plunder for the crowd assembled to see the sport. A composition of pounded glass, called *Munjun*, is rubbed over the string to enable it to cut; and for this purpose all the empty bottles of the residency have been put in requisition by the Muha Raj; who also goes to the expense of having kites and strings brought for him from Delhi, which is celebrated for their manufacture. I can assure you that, ridiculous as it may appear to you, no small degree of skill and experience is requisite to manage one of these kites, and gain a victory.

Early on the morning of the 30th ult. there was an eclipse of the moon, when the whole camp resounded with shouts and the sound of drums and trumpets. The vulgar opinion of the Hindoos is, that a monster, called *Rahoo*, is attacking the planet, and they make these noises to drive him away. The Hindoos are enjoined to distribute charity during the eclipse, and one rupee bestowed at that time is deemed of more effect than a hundred given at any other. Long before three o'clock our camp was filled with beggars of all descriptions. Devotees keep a strict fast, which they do not break till they see the moon quite cleared of the shadow: unfortunately she now set eclipsed, so that these good people could eat nothing till they beheld her rise again in full splendour on the following evening. I send you enclosed the translation of a little Sunskreet poem, of the kind called *Eslok*, supposed to be addressed by a lover to his mistress looking at an eclipse of the moon from her terrace.

ESLOK

Enter quick, O fly the place !—
Veil, O veil, thy fairer face !—
See, yon Planet's fate delayed;
See, the Monster's grasp is stayed !
Thou, whose face no spot defiles,
Dread his force, and dread his wiles;
Soon a meaner prey he'll free,
And quit a Moon less pure, for thee.

LETTER XIII

Return of the messenger from Jypoor—Differences regarding Doonee adjusted—The treaty with Jypoor announced—Number of guns in camp—Establishment of the Jinsee—Part of the army marches—Clamours for pay—Balajee Juswunt confined—Curious message from Surjee Rao—Ambajee's death—His great wealth—Visit of condolence to Bala Rao—Miserable state of the cattle—Buniyas—Management of the Bazars—Imposts and taxes—Four girls exposed for sale by the Meenas.

CAMP, DOONEE, *May 13th.*

THE officer who was sent by the Buhora to Jypoor for fresh instructions, returned on the 4th and brought with him an answer favourable to the demands of this Durbar; or at least such an increase to the powers of the Ambassador as will enable him to conclude the negotiations to the satisfaction of both parties. The tents of the Muha Raj and his suite were, in consequence, removed into camp, and orders issued for breaking up the trenches and destroying the batteries. These orders, however, were immediately after suspended, till some difficulties, that occurred in treating for Doonee, should be adjusted. At length this knotty point was compromised, and it was agreed that the gun taken from the Mamma's battery should be restored, and then Doonee should be included in the general treaty. The gun was accordingly sent into camp on the evening of the 9th; and the troops were withdrawn from the trenches on the following morning. This important gun had not been fired at all during the latter days of the siege; and on examination a ball was found sticking in the chamber from the cartridge having been put in the wrong way—a mistake which the people of the garrison were unable to remedy.

On the 8th the treaty with Jypoor was announced to be concluded, and the principal bankers in camp were summoned to negotiate the payment of the contribution. The Raja agrees to pay seventeen lakhs in three instalments, only fifteen of which, however, go to the Sirkar, the other two being destined for the ministers and principal people of the Durbar, one lakh openly acknowledged, the other given secretly. Seendhiya, on his side, agrees to recall the whole of his troops from the Jypoor territory, and engages that no more shall enter it for the space of one year: and thus has ended this famous siege, on which everybody in camp seems to think with a sensation of shame and disappointment: a sensation not to be wondered at, when the relative strength of the parties is considered. The number of guns which Seendhiya has now with him amounts to sixty-six: twenty-seven with the park, of which ten are of large calibre, and the rest of various sizes and descriptions; seventeen attached to Jacob's brigade of regulars, and fourteen to Baptiste's; all of different sizes, but few so large as an English six-pounder. Besides these, he has eight curricle guns, each drawn by a pair of bullocks; they are very small, and are called the "Orderly guns," from their generally forming a part of the Muha Raj's *Suwaree*, or suite: the English word "orderly" being now in common use throughout Hindoostan.

The establishments allowed for the *Jinsee*, or park, are as follows: five hundred *Aleegols;* one hundred *Nagus* or *Uteets*, terms synonymous with that of *Gosaeen* and *Sunniasee;* *Naga* literally signifying naked, and *Uteet* abstracted: four thousand bullock-drivers, *Coolees* or porters, *Bildars* or pioneers, and *Khulasees*, which last are employed in the laboratory and yard. An officer called *Daroghu* of the Jinsee, has charge of the magazines, the arsenals, the bullocks and carriages; and commands the *Aleegols* and *Nagas:* another, who is termed *Daroghu* of the guns, commands the *Golundaz* or gunners, and Lascars or Matrosses : and a third is appointed to the general superintendence of the whole, who purchases the stores, issues pay to the men, &c., but whose charges are checked by a fixed allowance of every article that can be required.

The park and the *Baruh-B,haees* marched on the 10th ; and the rest of the army is to follow, as soon as the troops can be prevailed upon to move. Their clamours for pay have been so loud and so general, for a few days past, that the Muha Raj was obliged to call in a battalion of infantry, between whom and the Mahratta cavalry there always subsists the greatest jealousy, with four guns, for the protection of the *Deooree*. These last disturbances have arisen from the bills, which were given to them on the *Surrafs* or bankers, being protested, when presented for payment : but as the treaty with Jypoor offers a prospect of a speedy supply of cash, the present embarrassments will probably not be of long continuance. The minister has been trying, and successfully, one of his favourite schemes to raise supplies, by throwing Balajee Juswunt, a person of great respectability, and one of the richest men in camp, into confinement ; from which he was not released till he consented to advance two lakhs of rupees for the service of the state. A few days after Surjee Rao sent a watch to me, which had been presented to him by the Resident the day before, and broken through the neglect of a servant, with a request that I would endeavour to get it repaired ; and an assurance that, if I thought proper, he would order the fellow's nose and ears to be sent to me as a punishment for his carelessness.

Ambajee is at length dead. He died at the town of Bugera, not far from camp, on the morning of the 5th, and is said to have left immense wealth behind him : report states it at three *crores* of rupees ; or as many millions of pounds sterling. Report doubtless exaggerates in this as in all such cases ; but from his regular and long established habits of economy, and the many opportunities he had, during his protracted life, of amassing, there can be little doubt but that his wealth was very great. One of his sons, named Dajee, was with him at his death; and his brother, Bala Rao, set off from camp, attended only by five horsemen, upon learning his danger. He returned the next day, and on the following afternoon we went to pay him the customary visit of condolence. He was seated upon the ground, in a miserable tent, with no clothing, but a pair of common *gootinnas*, and a coarse cloth thrown over his head. On these occasions it is not usual for the visitors to take any notice of the mourner, either upon entering or departing, nor during the visit: a third person does the honours, communicating the speeches of condolence, and returning the answers which are made; and which always run in one common strain, upon the certainty of death, the virtue of resignation, and the futility of useless sorrow. Bala Rao, however, talked a little himself; and expressed himself with propriety and feeling on the loss he had sustained in his brother's death; who appears to have been very generally looked up to, and esteemed by his friends. In passing through the Bazars we were shocked at the miserable appearance of the cattle of all kinds: large heaps of carcases were lying about the camp, while the living bodies looked only like so many bags of bones. The general distress, however, affects not the Buniyas, who evince, in their sleek and well-fed persons, the advantage they reap from the necessities of all around them. These Buniyas, a general term for all descriptions of merchants, are generally either from the province of Marwar, or from Delhi; the former, however, are the most numerous. As a body, they are one of the principal supports of the Muha Raj's state; and consequently carry everything with a very high hand in his camp. The mode in which the Bazars are regulated may perhaps amuse you; and will at least serve to give you some idea of the consequence of these people, whose shops are their chief support and ornament. There are five principal Bazars, distinguished by the names of *Madoo-gunj*, *Duolut-gunj*, *Danuwullee*, the *Surrafa*, and the *Chuonree*. They are farmed out to such persons as are favourites, and are known to be rich enough to make good what they stipulate to pay; and they are calculated to produce each half a lakh of rupees annually to the Sirkar; at least it is known that *Madoo-gunj* yields this sum to the *Baee*, to whose use it is exclusively appropriated.

The farmers, who have the entire management of their own Bazars, reimburse themselves by the following imposts and taxes: viz., *Tuhbazaree*, a quarter of an anna levied daily upon each *dokan*, or shop; and eight annas every tenth day. This is either collected daily, or every tenth day, or sometimes two rupees are taken at once, at the end of the month.

B,heth; a present of one rupee from every *dokan*, in the month of *P,hagoon*, and another at the festival of the *Dusera*.

Choongee, a tax collected in kind from every corn-dealer, by a servant of the *Kotwal*, or superintendent, by dipping his right arm into the corn or meal, and scraping out as much as he can into a bag held close to receive it. This handful is called a *choongee*, and three and a half *choongees* are taken daily from every shop; two for the Sirkar (or the farmer, if the Bazar is rented), and the rest for the petty officers of the Bazar.

J,huree, and *Muhsool*; the former in kind, the latter in money, levied according to the following rules:

For every bullock load of grain belonging to a strange merchant, three and a half *seers* (each *seer* nearly two pounds), and two *annas*:[1] if belonging to a resident, one *seer* and one *anna*.

For every load of meal, three and a half *seers*, and three *annas*: or one *seer*, and one *anna* and a half.

For every load of rice, six or three *annas*, and the *seer* as above.

[1] An anna is the sixteenth part of a rupee. B.

For *Ghee*, or butter, and oil, twelve *annas* and six *annas ;* and the *seers* as above.

For drugs and spices, three rupees two *annas*, or one rupee nine *annas*, per load, but no *seers*.

Upon cloths, of whatever kind or description, two *annas*, and one *anna*, per piece.

Upon all other articles these duties are levied according to their value, and in the same proportions ; that is, double from all strangers.

Palputtee ; a tax levied for the professed purpose of providing a tent for the accommodation of the *Dundiya*, or constable, and other petty officers of the Bazar, but which is generally paid *en masse* to the Sirkar, or the farmer, by the *Kotwal*, who levies it upon all the shops of his Bazar, according to their ostensible means. It is estimated in four of the Bzaars at the following sums :

Duolut-gunj . .	3,000 Rupees.
Danuwulee . . .	3,000 ,,
Chuonree . .	2,000 ,,
Surrafa . .	6,000 ,,

In *Madoo-gunj* it is altogether dispensed with.

Ootagir ; three-fourths of such bags of cash or valuables as may be carried off by boys while the owner is looking another way. This curious tax is imposed upon the principle of punishing carelessness.

There are, besides the Bazars, fairs or revels held every day, except Friday, at a particular spot in the camp, which are called *Goodurees*, or *Nukas*. Cattle of all kinds, arms, and old clothes, are sold at them ; and the purchasers pay a duty of six and a quarter per cent. upon the price.

The *Goalas*, or milkmen, if Mahrattas, pay each one rupee per day ; if Hindoostanees, a rupee for every female buffalo ; and for every cow, their share of the *Palputtee*.

Chummars, or leather-workers, pay one rupee per month for their shops, and work for the Muha Raj gratis.

Nach girls are exempted from all taxes, though they pay

a kind of voluntary one monthly to a Fuqeer, who remains in their quarter of the camp, and who is called *Sooturisue*, their several proportions being adjusted according to the strength of the set, and the vogue in which its female members may chance to be at the time of payment.

The *Shodahs* I have already often mentioned; and have only now to add that two hundred and twenty-five out of their number are regularly employed, under Fazil Khan, by the Muha Raj, and receive each from five to ten rupees per month, according to their appearance, age, and talents. These are the accredited attendants at the licensed gaming houses. Two-thirds of their gains are accounted for to the Sirkar (out of which they themselves are paid), and the rest they are allowed to appropriate to their own use. There are at least as many more who acknowledge the authority of Fazil Khan, but live entirely by their wits, and it is these who are employed in carrying the Prince's baggage on a march.

Strangers who bring goods to the camp generally put up at the tent of some established merchant, who accommodates them, and disposes of their goods, upon the amount of the sales of which he receives a commission of six and a quarter per cent.

I mentioned to you in my last letter that the Meenas were in the habit of carrying off children and selling the girls. Two of our head servants intimated their wish of becoming the purchasers of four, to some of the Meenas now in camp, and desired that one or two of their party might accompany a man of their own to make the selection, but no agreement was entered into as to the price. A few days ago the party returned with the four girls, for whom three hundred rupees were demanded. The servants disapproved of them; and declared themselves both unwilling and unable to pay so large a sum, and the Meenas, who were very wroth at this conduct, and threatened loudly to complain of it, were with difficulty prevailed upon to take their charge to the Bazar; where they were publicly exposed for sale. The poor creatures are from eight to ten years of age, and appear to feel keenly the indignities to which they are exposed. One of my own servants, whom curiosity led to see them, told me that their eyes were swollen with weeping, and that they presented altogether a most distressing spectacle. Two of the four were soon disposed of, and bidders for the others crowd to the quarter where the Meenas remain throughout the day.

LETTER XIV

March to the Bunas—Mahratta women—Marwaree Buniyas—Must elephants—Slaughter of the Golundaz—March to Rioota Ghat—Plunder of the village—Adroitness of the Meenas—Body of a Surdar burned—March towards Sawur—Sagacity of elephants attached to the guns.

CAMP ON THE BUNAS, *May* 17.

WE quitted Doonee on the 8th, and after a short, though disagreeable, march of eight miles, encamped once more on the bank of this friendly river, near the spot from whence we moved on the 10th of March. A Mahratta line of march exhibits a collection of the most grotesque objects and groups that can possibly be imagined: and at no time is the difference in the treatment of women, between the Mahrattas and other natives of India, more strikingly displayed. Such as can afford it here, ride on horseback, without taking any pains to conceal their faces: they gallop about, and make their way through the throng with as much boldness and perseverance as the men. Among the better sort it is common to see the master of a family riding by the side of his wife and children, all well mounted, and attended by half a dozen horsemen, and two or three female servants, also on horseback: and I have often seen a woman seated astraddle, behind her husband, and keeping her seat with no small degree of grace and dexterity, while he was exercising his horse at a good round gallop. The Mahratta women are, generally speaking, very ugly; and have a bold look which is to be observed in no other women of Hindoostan. Their dress is unbecoming, and consists of a long piece of cloth, called *Saree*, one half of which is wound round the body and tucked up between the legs; while the other half is thrown loosely over the head and shoulders: those of the rich are made of a stout kind of gauze, with a border of gold, and are generally dyed either red, blue, or green: those of the lower classes are commonly of dark printed cotton. Beneath the *Saree* women of the better sort wear a *Choolee*, or short bodice, of silk, which just serves to confine their breasts; and when abroad, a *Chadur*, or large veil, and sometimes a shawl, which envelops the whole figure. The poorest women tie their infants in a bag, which they sling over their shoulders, and so trudge along a whole day's march without appearing to suffer the slightest inconvenience: and this is often done when the child has been actually born upon the road. They must, however, be very poor indeed who have neither a bullock nor a *tut,hoo* to carry their baggage. These *tut,hoos* are a breed of small ponies, and are the most useful and hardy little animals in India. It is surprising to see them getting on during a long march at a quick walk under loads which appear sufficient to break their backs, and which commonly consist of all the goods and chattels of the family, including the tent; with the mistress seated on the top, a child in her lap, and a pet kid, or a little dog, tied on before her. They are generally vicious, and will fight, after getting rid of their load, with as much vigour and spirit as if just loosed from their night's pickets. In the Company's provinces the *tut,hoos* are also used for draught, and are often to be seen dragging along at a canter a coarse kind of *cabriolet*, called a Hackery, in which three or four heavy fellows are seated, besides the driver. In this camp Hackeries and *Ruths*, as they are called when they have four wheels, are always drawn by bullocks, and are used, almost exclusively, by the *Baees*, the Nach girls, and the bankers. The Marwaree Buniyas are very conspicuous figures upon a march: they ride two and two on camels, which, like their masters, always present a picture of prosperity and good feeding. The Mahratta women seem to be particularly fond of a breed of little lap dogs, which are evidently of French origin, and were probably introduced among them during the reign of the French officers: not a bullock, a camel, or a *tut,hoo* passes along the road but has one or more of these little animals perched on the top of its load.

The day after this march an elephant, *must* as it is called, or pampered to make it wicked, got loose from his stand, and killed a man and his horse, close to our camp, before he could be again secured. Several of them are kept in this state by the Muha Raj purposely for fighting, and are serious nuisances to the camp.

Before we quitted that ground an event occurred which caused considerable sensation throughout the army, especially among the men of the artillery and regular brigades. A party of *Golundaz* had been for some days very clamorous for pay, and on the 12th proceeded so far as to seize and confine the *Daroghu* of the Jinsee. This act of violence was reported to Surjee Rao, who ordered that the demands of the mutineers should be immediately complied with, and themselves turned out of camp. The order was obeyed; but they had scarcely proceeded a quarter of a mile before a party of the *Baruh B,haees* was despatched after them, who overtook them, attacked and plundered them, killing six and wounding ten, of whom seven were afterwards brought into camp, and three left bleeding on the ground: others were bound, and brought in prisoners, and a very few only escaped. Among these unfortunate fellows were three veteran Jemadars, highly respected in the army, and several of inferior rank, who had served for years under Madoojee Seendhiya. Their wives and families were with them, and several of their comrades, who had accompanied them so far out of regard and attachment, suffered for their kindness, and were also plundered and wounded. This, which is the first act of notorious cruelty that has occurred since we have been in camp, is universally, and I believe justly, attributed to the minister.

The Muha Raj was so much vexed by it, that he put off his visit of ceremony to the Jypoor Ambassador, which had been settled to take place that evening, but was now postponed to the following one.

On the 14th we marched to Rioota Ghat, also on the Bunas, a straight distance of not more than nine miles; but from the circuitous road, which the line as usual followed, we marched at least fifteen: and as the *Beenee-wala* did not start till after day-break, the people suffered greatly from heat and a want of water. We passed on the march to the southward of a fortress called Rajmahl, built on the summit of the southern extremity of a range of hills, at the northern end of which is the town of Tod,ha. Immediately above Rajmahl there is an abrupt division of the range, through which the Bunas flows in a most romantic manner. Rioota is a miserable little village inhabited by Meenas and Goojurs, who, upon the approach of an enemy, take refuge in the hills, at the foot of which it is built. A party of infantry, destined for the attack of this village, led the line, and was followed by a multitude of horsemen, of all kinds and descriptions. The place was in flames in a minute, and everything it contained was greedily seized upon by these warriors, who came up in shoals, flogging their horses, and straining every nerve to get a share of the plunder, which, after all, could consist of nothing but a small quantity of grain, and the sticks and thatch which roofed the wretched houses. Mark the consistency and good faith of this Durbar: in the evening Seendhiya receives an entertainment from an Ambassador, upon the occasion of a peace being concluded, and the very next morning wantonly plunders a miserable little hamlet, for we are still in the Jypoor country, that chances to lie in his road: then, to complete the farce, writes letters to Meer Khan (whose troops are playing the same game in the vicinity of Oojyn, Seendhiya's own capital), remonstrating upon the unfriendliness and impropriety of his conduct. The park did not come up till yesterday, and Surjee Rao remained with it, report says, to quell some indications of mutiny which had appeared among the men. We had a specimen of the dexterity of the Meenas the other night: they contrived to enter the tent in which the Resident's own horses are picketed without being perceived; and cutting the head and heel ropes of one, which is commonly so restive as to require two men to lead him, actually conveyed him, under cover of an extremely dark night, beyond the sentries: he was fortunately then perceived, and the alarm given, at which the horse was so frightened that he broke from the thieves, and returned of his own accord to his stable. The villagers of Rioota soon after our arrival formed acquaintance with some of our Sipahees, and came without any alarm into the Bazar to purchase grain and liquor: one of them professed a violent attachment to a young lad, who wore a gold chain round his neck; and made an appointment to show him their retreat in the hills —an appointment which he was fortunately prevented from keeping by another Sipahee having been attacked by these new friends while going down to the river for water.

The body of a Mahratta Surdar was burned near our tents last evening, who died in consequence of a wound received on a foraging party. The funeral pile was raised on the bank of the river, and the body carried to it in great state, preceded by the elephants and horses of the deceased, gayly painted and caparisoned, and followed by a number of his friends on foot, weeping and lamenting aloud. Some pieces of money were scattered over the corpse, which with the clothes in which it was enveloped become the perquisites of the *B,hungees*, a set of men of the lowest *caste*, or rather of no *caste* at all, who perform the vilest offices for the living, and are remunerated by receiving, after death, that which no one else is permitted to touch, every thing that has been used about a corpse being deemed unclean by all classes of Hindoos. His most intimate friends and relations bore the couch on which the body was laid, and the nearest relation set fire to the pile.

This morning we marched ten miles, along the right bank of the river, and are encamped within sight of Sawur and Gutiaree—two forts in the province of Ajmeer belonging to Seendhiya. We saw not a solitary spot of cultivation, though we observed some large villages at no great distance, to the right and left of the road. About half way we overtook the Jinsee and the regular brigades, the only corps out of the whole army which move with any kind of regularity. Several elephants are attached to the former, and always march with it, occasionally lending their strength to push on the heaviest guns. In passing over swamps and other places of difficulty, they are taught to twine their trunks round the breeches of the guns, and to extricate them with the most admirable sagacity.

LETTER XV

March towards Jajgurh—Grove of date trees—Heera Sing,h joins the army—Bawanee Purshad—The Gosaeens—Projected march to Ajmeer—Remonstrance of the Buhora—Attacks of the Meenas—Consternation in camp—Melon Gardens—Tent of Kus—Seendhiya's extraordinary conduct at the Durbar—Filth of the camp—Disputes with Surjee Rao—Shuhamut Khan, and his wife—Seendhiya sits D,hurna—Ambajee's family arrives in camp—Ravages continued in Jypoor—Jypoorian faith—Discontent of the Buhora—Manners of the Rajpoots—Dokul Sing,h's Wukeels—Surjee Rao performs his ablutions; and feeds Brahmuns—Fuqeers—Hindoo songs.

CAMP NEAR JAJGURH, *June 2nd.*

WE marched nine miles on the 19th ult. to this place, over a continuation of the same almost boundless plain upon which we have been travelling ever since we crossed the Chumbul. To the front and rear, and to the right, our view was terminated only by the horizon; but on our left was a range of high hills, running nearly east and west, which form the northern boundary of Boondee and the district of Rajgurh, and about the centre of which lies the fort and town of the same name. We scarcely saw any appearance of cultivation, and no trees, except a few planted in the immediate neighbourhood of some villages, which we passed at a distance to our right. Upon coming to our ground, however, we found an agreeable shelter, while the tents were pitching under a large grove of date trees, the first we have seen in this part of India. They have ever since afforded a constant feast to the people of the camp, who cut them down for the soft pieces of pith which are found in the heart of the tree at its summit, and which, either raw or boiled, is esteemed a very great delicacy: it is called *Gaba*, and when dressed resembles in flavour the bottoms of artichokes. The tree also yields a pleasant liquor by tapping, but its fruit is very indifferent. Our camp is about four miles from Jajgurh, on the opposite side of the Bunas; the fort, which appears to be large, and is reckoned very strong, is built on the top of an oblong hill in front of, and detached from, the main range. It consists of two similar walls, flanked with round bastions, the outer being at a considerable distance from the inner one, and nearly half way down the hill, each wall having a ditch, said to be a good one, all round it. The town lies to the north-west, at the foot of the hill; and is large, well built, and fortified. On the day of our arrival here, a detachment of infantry, with some guns, was sent on to the place; although Zalim Sing,h, its possessor, is on the most friendly terms with the Muha Raj. They returned, however, the following day, it having been agreed that the Kota Wukeel, already in camp, should negotiate the terms upon which his master's country was to be exempted from plunder.

A corps of infantry, under the command of a soldier of fortune, named Heera Sing,h, joined the army on this march: it consists of four battalions of two hundred men each, and two guns; but the men have no uniform dress; and are armed with matchlocks only, to which bayonets have been affixed.

The Mahratta chief, who went off with his party from Doonee, has been induced to return, by a deputation, and the usual fair promises made upon such occasions. Bawanee Purshad has been trying the same plan, but with the most mortifying consequences: Seendhiya would not allow any one to be sent after him, and he was obliged to return uncalled and unwished for, except by his numerous creditors, who can entertain the faintest hopes of being paid their money only by his continuing in camp.

The Gosaeens have behaved with much more spirit; a very strong party was sent after them as far as Tod,ha, with orders to bring them back to camp, if possible, by fair means; if not, by force: they steadily, however, refused to listen to any offers which the Muhratta envoy made, and showed so determined a front, that he did not think it prudent to attempt compulsion. He accordingly returned alone, and the Gosaeens are fairly gone off.

Our march to this place has been a very sudden measure, for when we quitted Doonee it was intended to proceed directly to Ajmeer, under the pretext of mediating between the Rajas of Jypoor and Juodpoor. Against this plan, however, the Buhora firmly remonstrated; averring that those Princes were perfectly competent to settle their own differences, and would both regard such a movement with a jealous eye, independently of the injury which the whole country would sustain from the presence of the Mahratta army. Due attention has been paid to this representation, more likely in consequence of the first instalment of the Jypoor contribution not having been yet touched, than from the justice and reasonableness with which it is marked. The army has in consequence advanced to a point from whence either the Boondee or Marwar territories may be entered in one march, and which is also close to the province of Ajmeer.

We are in the very midst of the Meenas, who seem resolved to make the most of such an opportunity, and revenge themselves for the treatment which their friends—who by the bye have all gone off—met with, while they continued in camp. Not a day occurs without the most daring robberies being committed. The foraging parties are attacked wherever they appear, and it is absolutely unsafe for individuals to move a musket-shot from the camp. The main army is kept in a constant state of alarm, several attacks having been made on its skirts by bands of these daring mountaineers; and the stream of the river running under the bank opposite the army, the women and others, who are obliged to go for water, are perpetually stopped, and plundered of their clothes, brass pots, &c. Forage is scarcely to be procured, even in the smallest quantities, and all these united vexations have created such a general sentiment of discontent, that a number of the Surdars, taking their cattle of every kind with them, proceeded to the *Deooree* in a body, declaring that they would not stir from thence till the Muha Raj consented to march away from such an abominable place. Promises of complying with their wishes were made in abundance, and will probably be kept, for I do not see how it is possible that we should remain where we are. If it is determined to cross the Bunas, it will be necessary to do so soon, for we have already had some heavy falls of rain, and the river has begun to rise, and washed away the melon gardens which are cultivated in its bed. It is usual in this part of India to sow melons in the sandy beds of rivers, after the annual floods have subsided: the seeds are put in the ground in February, and the fruit is ripe about the beginning of May, and continues in season till the rains again set in.

I went yesterday with the Resident to the Durbar, which was held in a small tent made of *Kus*,[1] and being kept constantly wet, was exceedingly cool and pleasant. While Captain C—— was conversing with Surjee Rao, one of the Muha Raj's favourite companions came into the tent, and stood before him, and his Highness immediately began to amuse himself by making most indecent signs and gestures, and winking at him, whenever he thought himself unperceived. As the man was directly behind my back, I could not observe whether these extraordinary communications by signal were replied to by him, but rather suppose they were not, as it is contrary to the etiquette of this polite court to retaliate any of the Prince's jokes at the Durbar, especially in the presence of foreign Ambassadors. The stench arising from the numerous carcasses which lay strewed about the Bazar was almost intolerable; it is hardly credible that any people should

[1] The well-known *Khaskhas*, the roots of a plant *Andropogon muricatus* (Retz.), made into screens or mats which, when wetted, emit a fragrant odour. *See Bernier*, Vol. i., *C. O. M.*, p. 247.

prefer submitting to such a nuisance to the little trouble of removing it from their immediate neighbourhood.

Continual bickerings and disputes have lately taken place between the Muha Raj and his new minister; the former complaining that, with a revenue, as he states it, of a crore and a half of rupees, he does not receive the value of twenty lakhs: and the latter retorting that the bankers and merchants do not, and will not, place any reliance on him, while they perceive that he does not possess the entire confidence of his master. Surjee Rao has been making overtures to an old servant of the Muha Raj, named Deoba Kalia, who is supposed to possess more influence over him than any other individual about the Deoree; but his overtures hitherto have been met only with neglect. He has been equally unsuccessful in urging the Muha Raj to give a sufficient sum from his private purse to pay up the troops, and get rid at once of the multitude of inefficient men now attached to the army. Seendhiya, however, fears, and certainly with some reason, to trust so large a sum in such slippery hands as those of his politic father-in-law.

There are many plans at present under consideration; one of them is, to proceed with the whole army directly to Oojyn, and expel Holkar and Meer Khan, who have been ravaging the country, and levying contributions under the very walls of the city. They have been joined there by a Pithan chief, named Shuhamut Khan, who was, but a short time since, in the service of Seendhiya, but has now become his sworn enemy, in consequence of his wife having been forcibly detained by Baba Patunkur, the nephew of Surjee Rao. This lady, who has lately made a great deal of noise in camp, was sold in her earliest infancy by her parents, to the mistress of a set of dancing girls, by whom she was in due time placed under the protection of this Patunkur. From him she ran away, and attached herself to Shuhamut Khan, who married her, and has two children by her. By him she was left at Jypoor, about a year ago, when he himself proceeded to join Meer Khan's standard, and, disgusted at some ill treatment she had received from him, soon took again to her old profession, in every qualification for which she is said to excel in the highest degree. At the commencement of the late negotiations with Jypoor, a formal but secret demand for her being given up was made by this court, and she was accordingly sent to camp under the charge of Koosallee Ram; where she has once more been placed under the guardianship of her first lover, to the great scandal and indignation, however, of the Pithan, who has vowed unceasing vengeance against the whole set.

Seendhiya, who has been lately plagued by repeated *D,hurnas*, seems now resolved to partake also in the active part of the amusement: he had permitted this same Patunkur, as a signal mark of favour, to borrow fifty thousand rupees from the *Khasgee*, or private treasury, upon an assurance of its being repaid within a certain time: the time elapsed without the agreement having been fulfilled; and Seendhiya immediately despatched the treasurer to sit *D,hurna*, on his behalf, at Patunkur's tents. This act has greatly irritated Surjee Rao, who complains that it evinces a total want of confidence in himself. He was himself lately placed in very strict *D,hurna* for two or three days by the grandson of a Kundaharee chief, a lad of fifteen years of age, whose father was killed last year in the Surjee Rao's employ.

Ambajee's widow and son, with a large suite of followers, arrived in camp on the 24th, and were visited the same evening by Seendhiya, attended by the Mamma, Surjee Rao, and most of the principal Surdars in camp. He expects to receive a present of four or five lakhs of rupees, as a douceur to ensure his protection towards the family. The young girl, to whom Ambajee was betrothed, is now to be given in marriage to the favourite, Deoba Kalia; her father is a man of great wealth, and resides at Sawur, about five miles from our present encampment.

Bapoojee Seendhiya is still with his army in the Jypoor country, and has openly declared his resolution never to return to camp, while Surjee Rao continues in power there. The Buhora has warmly remonstrated against this delay in executing the terms of the treaty, and demanded to know whether Bapoojee, Jugoo Bapoo, and Baptiste, who with a third army has now invested the fort of Kiroulee, are under the control of this government, or not; that, if not, his master may immediately take means to rid his country of them by force. Seendhiya on his part probably expects, by keeping these detachments in the country, to force the Raja into a speedy payment of the contribution: for the mode in which the Jypoor Durbar is accustomed to execute such agreements is quite notorious. They pay one half, and agree to pay a quarter after a certain number of months, and the remainder after another lapse of time. The payment of the second instalment is generally delayed, upon various pretences, for about a year, and for the last they fight again, and if worsted enter into another treaty. The Buhora, in the mean time, begins to be heartily tired of his residence in camp, where he is not only tormented by perpetual demands for money from the Durbar, but his people have caught the infection of the camp, and become mutinous. A party of his Sipahees went off a few days ago, and were with difficulty induced to return; which they did amidst the jeers and taunts of the Mahrattas, who upbraided them for taking so disgraceful a step when they were only six months in arrears! His camp is close to ours, and his people have frequent communications with our men. They are in general fine-looking fellows, with intelligent countenances, and a bold soldier-like appearance. They are rigid observers of all old Hindoo customs, and look upon themselves as contaminated by their residence among the Mahrattas. When the waters of the Bunas rose, most of them abstained from bathing, lest they should be defiled by the numerous impurities washed down in its current: and such as did bathe made a second ablution in water taken from little wells dug in the sand. They not only abstain from eating all kinds of flesh, but take great care to prevent any life from being destroyed. The other day, when a Mahratta was about to shoot at some pigeons that were flying between our camps, a number of the Rajpoots rushed out in the greatest agitation to stay his murderous arm. Our people have learned to look upon all this as mere prejudice.

In company with Ambajee's family, two Wukeels have arrived in camp from Dokul Sing,h, a young pretender to the throne of Juodpoor, with the hope of prevailing upon Seendhiya to espouse his cause. The Muha Raj affects to lend a favourable ear to their representations, but probably with no other intent than to alarm the reigning Raja, with whom he is now negotiating a contribution, and whose Wukeels have expressed great indignation at these strangers being received in camp.

On the 24th ult. was the *Dusera*,[1] a Hindoo festival, from which is dated the commencement of the rainy season, and upon which it is usual for the rich to distribute charity, and give entertainments to the Brahmuns. Surjee Rao pitched upon this day for performing his first ablutions since his recovery from the wounds which he received at Doonee; on which occasion he bestowed five thousand rupees among the Brahmuns, entertained fifteen hundred beggars with a good dinner, and eight *annas* to each, and gave a piece of cloth to every Fuqeer who chose to take it. The number of Fuqeers in this camp is enormous, and they are of all descriptions, Moohumedans and Hindoos, men and women, boys and girls. They are an intolerable nuisance, wandering among the tents throughout the day, each attracting attention by some peculiar cry or sentence, and thronging around those who appear rich enough to bestow anything, asking, or rather demanding, alms with an importunity and perseverance that is equally insolent and provoking. The Moohumedans are the worst, many of them going about on horseback, and asking for rupees with as much assurance as others beg for pice; and the

[1] The Dasara takes place in September–October, and is known in Bengal as the Durgá Puja.

more impertinent they are, the greater is the idea entertained of their sanctity. When we first came to camp we were so much annoyed by crowds of these fellows, that we were obliged to give our sentries orders to prevent all but two or three from entering the lines. One of these lives almost entirely upon opium, who is said to have been once a leader of horse in this very army: he exists in a constant state of intoxication, and in his diurnal round through the camp breathes forth the most curious vows for our individual prosperity. A month or two ago one of our officers gave him a pair of pantaloons, an old military jacket, and a cocked hat and feather, and in this equipment he used to make the tour of the great camp to the no small astonishment and entertainment of the Mahrattas, till the things were all stolen from him during his state of insensibility. Another of our licensed Fuqeers sings his petitions, and dances, in a most ridiculous manner, to a pair of dry sticks, which he uses like castanets. Many go about in groups, and earn a livelihood by singing old Hindoo songs in a manner that is far from being disagreeable.

I have already sent you some specimens of these compositions, and now enclose two more, in a different style, which I have picked up from these itinerant bards. The first is of the kind called *Doha*, and is meant to ridicule the proverbial thrift of the *Buniyas:* one of whom made a vow to give a handful of meal to every beggar who came to his shop; but, that his charity might cost him as little as possible, warily dealt it out by the small hand of his lovely daughter. The second is a *Kubit*, and is merely a little *jeu d'esprit*, not, however, without a moral point.

DOHA

The frugal father's sage commands,
Dealt by his daughter's smaller hands,
  His daily pittance to the poor.
Bad thrift;—her beauty to behold,
In beggar's guise, both young and old
  Came thronging round the crowded door.

KUBIT

Your beast perverse ; your man a rogue ;
  Your heart to amorous courses given ;
Your friend a fool ; your master mean ;—
  Can greater plagues be sent by Heaven ?

Dinner to seek abroad ; a house
  Built in some little dirty town ;
Long journeys on cold rainy days ;
  Are miseries all mortals own.

Yourself with wantons sporting oft,
  While wife at home to love is given ;
An itch to cheat, oppress, or rob ;
  A child, whom from your love you've driven.

Folly, old age, a sickly frame ;
  A lack of means ; a memory gone ;
These, these are hell, a present hell ;
  Talk not of others still to come.

LETTER XVI

March towards Shahpoora—Dokul Sing,h—Jypoor treaty still unexecuted—Alarming discontents in camp—The Khans sit D,hurna—Are driven from camp—Disturbances in the battalions—Mahratta chiefs offended—Balajee Juswunt tortured—Method of raising supplies—The Khasgee—Seendhiya intimates his intention to befriend Dokul Sing,h—Wukeels from Krishngurh—Physicians of Ajmeer—Number of snakes and scorpions—Deoba Kalia's wedding—Marriage creemonies among the Mahrattas—Marriage of Madoojee Seendhiya—Dancing girls.

CAMP ON THE TINEL, *June 16th.*

WE quitted the ground, where the army experienced so many inconveniences, yesterday, and after a march of nearly fifteen miles encamped near two ruined villages, about six miles to the eastward of Shahpoora, a large town, containing many fine buildings, and surrounded by a strong wall of stone and a ditch. The country through which we marched belongs to the Raja, who is nominally a tributary of the Rana of Oodipoor, but has for many years been sufficiently powerful to maintain himself in a perfect state of independence. We passed by many villages, some of them very large, and all in ruins, and plundered of everything that could possibly be turned to use by the people of the camp. This morning we marched about ten miles over the same uninteresting plain, but found the villages to the westward of Shahpoora presenting a less desolate picture than those which we passed the day before; some of them remain still to be plundered, and many are surrounded by small clumps of trees, which are yet to afford forage for the Mahratta elephants and camels.

These marches have been made with the double view of

frightening the Shahpoora Takoor into better terms (who has as yet offered to give the Muha Raj only twenty-five thousand rupees), and at the same time intimidating the Raja of Juodpoor: the expediency of supporting the cause of his nephew Dokul Sing,h having been seriously considered for some days past. This young prince, still a mere boy, is, or is supposed to be, the posthumous son of the late Raja, the brother of the reigning one, of Juodpoor. He was rescued from the power of his uncle by some Takoors, attached to his father's family, and placed under the protection of the Raja of Putialee, where he continued, till the Raja of Jypoor, about two years ago, proclaimed his resolution to restore the young orphan to the throne of his ancestors: and marched for this purpose to Juodpoor, with a more powerful army than had appeared in India for many years. Raja Man Sing,h, however, the Juodpoor prince, found means to sow dissension among the chiefs of the Jypoor army, and so ably defended his capital, that they were obliged to retire without effecting anything of importance, and covered with disgrace. Since that time the friends of Dokul Sing,h have been soliciting various powers in favour of their young charge, and their Wukeels are now said to have been listened to with attention at this Durbar. His cause I believe to be a just one; but hastily adopted, without due consideration, or any plan being digested for ensuring its final success, what can be foretold of it but certain failure? It is the distinguishing characteristic of Surjee Rao to enter eagerly into any measure which offers the dazzling prospect of immediate profit, without considering for a moment his power to carry it through: and it will be fortunate for Seendhiya if his headstrong rashness, unsupported by any sure resources, does not plunge his affairs very speedily into total ruin. The treaty with Jypoor has not yet been carried into execution in any one point; Bapoo Seendhiya still continues to ravage the country, and not one rupee has been paid of the contribution: the old Buhora is even accused of having paid too much attention to Seendhiya's interest, at the intriguing and suspicious court of his master Jugut Sing,h.

Before we marched from Jajgurh, the discontents which prevailed throughout the army had broken out into some alarming disturbances. The resolute conduct, however, of the minister has probably quelled this spirit of mutiny, at least for a certain time. The two Khans, whom I have mentioned to you in former letters, commenced a strict *D,hurna* upon the Muha Raj, with drawn swords, and every appearance of a resolute struggle for their rights. A commotion in the camp was apprehended, and in the evening two thousand rupees were sent to them, and the most positive promises made to bring their affairs to a speedy settlement. This induced them to return to their own tents, which they had scarcely reached when they were surrounded by a couple of battalions and eight guns. Seendhiya sent them a peremptory order next day to move out of camp, and prepare to march upon the following morning, but promised at the same time to settle their debts in the Bazars, which amount to nearly three lakhs, and also to send them twenty thousand rupees for their immediate expenses. They accordingly did move out of the main army, and pitched their tents in front of our lines. Here they continued three days, during which they suffered the severest hardships: credit, of course, they had none: and indeed Seendhiya was obliged to place two companies of Sipahees over them, to protect their persons from the rage of their creditors. They sold every spare article of dress or arms for such trifling sums as they could procure to answer their present demands, and many individuals of the corps, who had previously parted with everything, were driven to the miserable shift of killing field rats, which swarmed upon that ground, to appease the cravings of nature. All this time negotiations were going on with Surjee Rao, who protested that his master was drunk when he ordered them to quit the camp: and assured them that he would interpose to make up the dispute. As this *Risalu* was not only the strongest, but in every way the most respectable of all the Hindoostanee ones in camp, it was supposed that an accommodation would have taken place: it failed, however, and on the fourth morning the party marched away. The disturbance, it seems, originated with the private men of the corps, who suffering the keenest distress from want of pay, entered the tent of the Khans with drawn swords, and forced them to go to the *Deooree* in the manner I have described. It is hardly necessary to add that Seendhiya forgot to send the twenty thousand rupees he promised: and as for settling their debts in the Bazars, it is a thing quite out of the question. The regular battalions have also been riotous, and confined their *Mootusudee*, the officer who keeps their accounts, and transacts the public business of the corps on the part of the commandant. Seendhiya sent them word to be quiet, and he would settle with them in eight days. They released the *Mootusudee*, and replied to the Muha Raj's message that they had now obeyed him; but if he did not keep his word, *they would certainly mutiny*. such a trifle as seizing the person of a public officer not being regarded by them in that light. This lenity, always shown to the *Kampoos*, as the regular brigades are called, though the men are beyond all comparison the most mutinous and disorderly in the army, has greatly offended the Mahratta chiefs, many of whom have made it a pretext to demand their arrears and dismissal from his service. The scarcity of cash is felt more severely than ever, and the minister, who becomes daily more unpopular, is driven to the most desperate means of raising supplies. He has compelled Balajee Juswunt, whom I before mentioned to you as having been forced to contribute towards the exigencies of the state, by torture, to restore *Burats*, or bills, for eight lakhs of rupees: six of which he has given to Nimalkur, the richest and most powerful of all the chiefs who support his administration; and who, in return, gives up two lakhs, which he claims as due to him by the Sirkar, and pays down four lakhs in ready money, but at a discount of about thirty per cent. The usual mode of raising money here is by making out *Pats*, or statements of the sums required for the public expenditure, which are negotiated with the bankers of the camp, and fetch a price regulated by the value set by these bankers upon the security offered by the government for repayment. These securities are generally either assignments of the revenues of a province actually under the authority of the Muha Raj, or about to be attacked; or else bills upon the different states, from whom a claim of tribute is set up. The *Pats* are always sold at a considerable discount, and when the bargain is concluded, the purchasers accept bills drawn upon them, generally at a long date, which are called *Burats*, and which are issued to the troops as pay. They who receive them are commonly so much in want of ready cash, that they are obliged to sell the drafts, often at a discount of twenty or thirty per cent. to procure a present supply of necessaries: and the bankers on whom they are drawn (and not infrequently the agents of the Muha Raj himself), eagerly purchase them again at this rate. You will be no longer at a loss to conceive the distresses of a government supported by such a system of finance as this; or that the bankers, by whose means it is entirely conducted, should be the richest and most powerful set of people attached to it. But you will probably be a little at a loss to understand how such a government exists at all. And this is a problem which, I confess, I am totally unable to give any satisfactory solution of; unless, indeed, we pitch upon force and habit: the former exerted in the lawless and violent contributions levied by this government upon all the neighbouring states without exception; the other exemplified in a starving army, still clinging round the shadow of a lately powerful state, under whose standard they were formerly led to frequent victory and to constant plunder. Two such rotten props as these, however, must fail sooner or later;

and indeed their insufficiency begins already to be pretty evident. Seendhiya is almost deserted by his Hindoostanee troops, whose reports throughout their own provinces must, in time, operate so as to prevent any but the most needy and desperate adventurers from seeking such a service; and, probably, even his Duk,hunee troops will soon find it more to their advantage to remain quietly upon their own estates, or enter the services of the more fixed governments of the Peshwa and the Bhonsla.

Surjee Rao, in spite of the opposition he meets with, has been endeavouring to strengthen his party by heaping favours on the few powerful individuals who are attached to it. He has taken the districts of Shahduora and Aruon from Jacob, an Armenian who commands one of the regular brigades, and given them to Bala Rao, the brother of Ambajee. He has also repeated his solicitations to Seendhiya, to allow of a large sum being taken from the *Khasgee* at once, to enable him to put the army on a respectable and efficient footing. This term was formerly applied only to the treasury of his hereditary states, which was supposed to be particularly at the Muha Raj's own disposal, in opposition to the collections made in the name of the Peshwa, under whose authority he still professes to act. It is now, however, used in a more extended signification, and means generally the treasury: any cash that once goes into it is considered as sacred, and never allowed to come out again; except now and then in small sums to particular favourites, who repay them at the stated times, and with exorbitant interest.

There seems to be now some hope entertained of raising money, from one of the parties at least, by supporting, or affecting to support, the cause of Dokul Sing,h. Seendhiya sent for the Juodpoor Wukeels, and told them that his, Dokul Sing,h's, agents were very pressing for him to declare himself, and had offered very favourable terms if he would do so in their favour; that he had no particular predilection towards the cause; but that if their master did not come to a very speedy settlement with him, he should be obliged, in his own defence, to adopt it. He recommended that Goolab Sing,h, a Takoor of high rank, who had been nominated Plenipotentiary to his Durbar, should hasten his arrival in camp, and complained loudly that Moohumed Shah Khan was still retained in the Raja's service. This personage is the commander of a very strong brigade of regulars, nominally in the service of Meer Khan, but at present paid by the Raja of Juodpoor.

I received a visit, some few days ago, from the Wukeels of the Raja of Khrishngurh, a small but independent principality in the neighbourhood of Ajmeer. They were both Rajpoots, of a most respectable appearance, and very pleasing manners: and the little history they gave of their master and his court will, I think, interest you. His territories were once much more extensive than they are at present, several districts having at different times been seized upon by the more powerful princes of Jypoor and Juodpoor, and incorporated with their own. The revenue of Khrishngurh does not now exceed four lakhs, or about fifty thousand pounds sterling. The Raja's relations, and the descendants of his family, are all fed and clothed at his expense. They amount to nearly five thousand in number, and each receives a daily order for his bread, according to his actual consumption: the bread being baked on the Raja's premises, where the single men eat it, and those who are married receive it for their families. They all serve him as soldiers, and if one is wounded, he has a small *Jagheer*, or estate, assigned to him as a reward. Their marriages are likewise conducted at the Raja's expense, whose government, in its simple and economical regulations, is quite patriarchal. As one of the errands of the Wukeels to our camp was to procure medicine for their master, the conversation turned upon doctors and physic, and they described with much spirit the modes of practice of two very celebrated physicians residing at Ajmeer; one a Hindoo, the other a Moosulman. One of the Wukeels had a fever, and the former of these learned men was sent for, who shut up his room quite close, wrapped him in blankets, and gave him strong bitters to drink: till, as he expressed it, his body was hissing hot, and he was driven almost mad. The rival doctor was then summoned to his assistance, who threw open all the doors, poured cold water upon him, and gave him sherbet and other cooling liquors to drink. The Wukeel declared that he was instantly relieved, and in a few days got perfectly well.

We are not here quite so much troubled with thieves as at our last halting-place; but instead of them we are pestered with snakes, scorpions, and a large species of yellow spider, whose body is nearly an inch in length, though the animal is quite innoxious. It is not uncommon to see men who will take up the most venomous snakes, and allow them to creep about their persons. with impunity: they pretend to do this by a certain *muntur*, or charm; and if we refuse them their claim to supernatural powers, we must at least acknowledge some art by which they render so dangerous a creature quite harmless. I have known a Sipahee dig out one of these snakes, and keep him for several days in a cloth tied about his loins, feeding him daily with the utmost care and assiduity. Scorpions are easily rendered innocent by pinching their tails just below the sting; which deprives the animal of the power of darting it forward. It is, to be sure, rather a nice operation, but all that is requisite is to keep the hand behind and below the creature, who can only inflict a wound forwards and over its back.

I mentioned to you that the intended bride of Raja Ambajee was to be given to Deoba Kalia, an old servant and great favourite of the Muha Raj. The wedding took place on the 7th, on which day Surjee Rao himself, with many of the principal Surdars in camp, accompanied the bridegroom's procession to Sawur, where the lady's family reside. The customs which prevail among the Mahrattas in carrying on marriage contracts differ but little from those of the Hindoos in general. With the former, the bride's father receives, instead of giving, a portion with his daughter; and that often when there exists some flaw in the descent of the bridegroom which he wishes to repair by marriage. With the Mahrattas, too, the marriage is generally concluded within a few days after the *mungnee*, or betrothing; and the female relations of the bridegroom accompany his *burat*, or procession, to the house of the bride. When the friends of both parties are assembled there, the father takes a little water in the palm of his hand, and proclaiming his daughter's name, descent, &c., pours it into the hand of the bridegroom, declaring that he thereby freely gives her to him. The scarf of the bridegroom and the veil of the bride are next tied together in a knot; and they walk hand in hand seven times round a fire, into which oblations of clarified butter, milk, &c., are poured, to the various *deotas*, or deities, who are invoked on the occasion. The bridegroom then makes a public profession of fidelity and kindness towards his bride; who, in her turn, declares her resolution for ever to honour and obey him, to study his interest, be guided in all her actions by his advice, to follow his mode of worshipping the gods, and never to quit his protection upon any pretence whatever. She then places herself on his left hand, and a loud flourish of drums and trumpets, mixed with the acclamations of the whole party, announce them to be man and wife. A day or two previous to this final ceremony, another of a ridiculous nature takes place. The bride's mother goes with much ceremony to visit the bridegroom's, and invite her to her house. The latter is prevailed upon, after a deal of importunity, to accept the invitation, and sets out in great state, accompanied by all her friends and relations, some of whom hold a canopy over her head, while others let off fireworks before her. After she has thus proceeded, at the pace of a tortoise, for a short distance, she pretends to be fatigued, sits down, and declares herself unable to go a step further. The other lady has then again recourse to entreaties; presses little presents of ornaments, &c., upon her acceptance, and washes her feet with warm water, prepared for the occasion. The delicate matron, thus coaxed, exerts herself to the utmost, and advances a few yards further on the way, when the same farce is acted over again, and is repeated at intervals, regulated by the distance which may chance to be between the habitations of the parties, great care being taken that the procession should not move at a rate above a mile in an hour. When arrived at the house of the bride, she is, for the first time, presented to her intended mother-in-law, who takes her in her lap and caresses her, and then gives her the present of jewels, articles of dress, &c., according to her means, which she has brought along with her. An excellent dinner is prepared for the ladies of both families, and little presents are distributed among the attendants of the visitor.

A striking instance of the rapidity with which matches are concluded among the Mahrattas is that of the late Muha Raj. Madoojee Seendhiya upon his return to the Duk,hun, after an absence of many years in Hindoostan, went to offer up his vows in a celebrated temple at Tooljapoor, remarkable for Mahrattas only officiating at the sacrifices instead of Brahmuns. He there observed a very interesting girl, apparently about twelve years of age, ministering at the altar of the goddess. The Muha Raj inquired who she was, and was informed that she was a poor orphan, who supported herself and two uncles, her only surviving relations, by selling flowers for the offerings, and performing other little services in the temple. He next asked respecting her family, and learned that they were *Bohpas*, a tribe held in great respect among the Mahrattas. The Muha Raj, whose own family is from a low origin, and who was, moreover, himself a natural son, immediately sent a deputation of his favourite servants to the uncles of the little girl, with an offer to make her his wife, and to settle a *Jagheer* of ten thousand rupees upon themselves. The offer was joyfully accepted, and the Muha Raj went on the following morning, magnificently dressed and attended by his whole court, to the humble cottage of his bride, where the ceremony was performed, and in the afternoon of the same day she accompanied him as his wife to camp. Madoojee Seendhiya did not survive this marriage above two years, and the fate of his interesting young widow is affecting; she died some years after at Dutteah, of poison, administered by herself, to conceal the too apparent effects of a subsequent and illicit attachment. I had this story from a very respectable *Pundit*, who was himself in attendance upon the Muha Raj at the celebration of his marriage.

On the 4th we wished to celebrate the birthday of our revered monarch, but our means of rejoicing, outwardly at least, are so circumscribed, that we were obliged to content ourselves by seeing a *Nach*—a mode of rejoicing of all others the least joyous that can be imagined. It is almost everywhere uninteresting, but pre-eminently so in this camp, where dancing girls of any celebrity very seldom make their appearance. You Europeans are apt to picture to yourselves a *Nach* as a most attractive spectacle, but once witnessing it generally dissolves the illusion. Nothing can be more deficient in grace than the whole figure of a dancing girl: the dress consists of a pair of loose satin trowsers, and a gown, called *Peswaj*, made with a very short waist, long straight sleeves, and skirts that reach only to the calves of the legs, but so full that it would triply envelop the largest bell-hoop that ever was worn at any court in Europe. The gown, which is made of thin muslin or gauze, is commonly dyed either red, blue, or orange, and trimmed with a quantity of tinsel lace. She covers her head with a shawl or *sela*, which hangs down over the shoulders, and is then wrapt about the body: the whole figure thus presenting the appearance rather of an Egyptian mummy than of a living female tricked out to captivate and allure. The principal dancer stands in the middle, and is generally accompanied by an inferior female singer or two to assist her. The in-

FIG. 7.—A GIRL DANCING THE KUHARWA.

strumental performers range themselves behind, consisting commonly of a couple of fiddlers, a man who plays upon two drums, called *tubla*, fixed in his girdle, and a boy, who clashes a couple of little brazen cymbals, called *munjeera*. Some of the Hindoostanee airs are very pretty, but the mode of execution, which is to scream as loudly as possible, and introduce the most ridiculous *apogiaturas*, destroys the tune, and renders the words quite unintelligible. In dancing, they never spring off the ground, but slide along in a kind of measured pace, marking the time very exactly by striking the foot against the ground, and so ringing a parcel of little brass bells fastened round the ancle. When a girl is to dance the *Kuharwa*, she ties a sash round her loins, through which she pulls up her gown, puts another across her shoulders, and a man's turban upon her head, and in this dress, unless she is naturally very pretty, she looks worse than before : though to a fine animated countenance it gives a certain spirited and roguish air, which seldom fails to attract a due degree of admiration. In this favourite dance the most indecent gestures are used, meant to raise admiration and desire, but which, in uninitiated English bosoms, seldom excite anything but disgust. Such attractions has it, nevertheless, that it is always called for ; and young and old, great and small, Europeans as well as natives, look forward to the *Kuharwa* with anxiety, and sit for hours to witness its performance. It is no uncommon thing for one woman to continue dancing and singing throughout the whole night, and to desist some time after the day has broken without evincing any symptoms of fatigue after so great and continued an exertion.

LETTER XVII

Surjee Rao goes to Shahpoora—March to Irwur—Province of Ajmeer —Protection afforded to the villages—The perambulator—Loan with Gokul Paruk—Universal distress in camp—Contributions not realized in the neighbourhood—Visit to the Durbar—System of espionage.

CAMP NEAR IRWUR, *June 30th.*

WE were to have marched from our last ground on the 17th instant, but the order for that purpose having been given during the absence of Surjee Rao from camp, he considered it as an infringement of his office, and insisted upon its being countermanded, which was accordingly done on that very morning, after a part of our tents and baggage had been packed and sent off. The minister had been to Shahpoora, where he was splendidly entertained by the Raja, and settled his contribution at forty thousand rupees: which sum Seendhiya promised that he should appropriate towards the payment of his own troops.

We did not come here till the 19th, and there is a report that we are to make a long halt upon this ground. Our tents are pitched on the bank of a small river called the *Mansee*, where there is a plentiful supply of water, though it is at present a little brackish. We have an extensive plain round the camp for many miles, and the country abounds in game of all kinds. On the opposite bank of the river commences the province of Ajmeer, or *Chuoaleesa*, so called from its containing forty-six *Purgunus*, or small districts. It was rented by Ambajee, and since his death has been continued to his brother Bala Rao. This province is reckoned one of the finest in this part of India, and is certainly one of the most important, from its situation in the centre of the Rajpoot states of Jypoor, Juodpoor, and Oodipoor. Had the magnificent and enlightened plans which the Marquis Wellesley meditated for the welfare of India been carried into effect, this commanding station would probably have been occupied by a British force, which would have secured to the fine countries around the blessings of peace and tranquillity, instead of leaving them for ever exposed to the attacks and ruinous extortions of the different Mahratta chieftains in turn. All the villages that are in sight from our tents appear to be large and flourishing; and are so scrupulously protected from the ravages of the camp followers, that not a stick or a blade of grass is to be procured without the express sanction of the Muha Raj: a sufficient proof that, where they have an interest in the case, the Mahratta generals are quite able to control the individuals of their armies, and restrain their usual licence and depredations.

Upon a march our perambulator still attracts the wonder of the Mahrattas, who are unable to comprehend how it should point out the distance passed over. They call it *Jadoo-ka-chukkur*, the magic wheel; and being, from the highest to the lowest, implicit believers in witchcraft, they find a kind of satisfaction in attributing to its influence everything wherein they feel our superiority over themselves.

The Muha Raj has concluded a loan for ten lakhs of rupees with a rich banker named Gokul Paruk, and, it is said, on rather hard terms. This sum is to go towards a general settlement with the army, and indeed it is high time that some step of the kind should be taken, for the distress in camp is fast approaching to a climax, and is felt by all ranks and descriptions of people. A detachment has been formed for some time to proceed to the southward, but the troops composing it have positively refused to march without pay. The Hindoostanee Surdars have, one and all, demanded their discharge, and the *Hydrabad*

Risalu, a corps of horse so named from the birthplace of their leader, and upwards of four hundred strong, moved out of camp a day or two ago, threatening to go off, if some plan for satisfying their demands was not speedily adopted. Raja Bawanee Purshad and his nephew, whom the Muha Raj has been amusing with a promise of a *Jagheer*, upon their finding a sufficient security, have been driven to the necessity of selling or pawning their goods for support. A *Tumoolee*, or seller of *Pan*, went yesterday to demand payment of his bill from them, and not getting it, seized and forcibly carried off a copper vessel, in which the water for their immediate use was kept. Another of the same class, who went upon a similar errand to the Poona Wukeel, with still less success, cut his throat, and fell dead at the door of the envoy's tent. The people about attempted to remove the body, but the man's relations and friends collecting around it, declared that it should not be touched; that the Wukeel had caused his death; and that the blood lay upon his head. The Wukeel, who was greatly shocked at the event, sent to Seendhiya, who caused the body to be removed, and appeased the people by promising himself to settle their demand. A Mahratta Surdar, who had been repeatedly put off with fair promises, and as often disappointed, in a fit of vexation put to death fourteen of his horses, which with himself were actually starving. You must not, however, suppose that any feeling for the sufferings of the poor animals dictated this act, which was the effect solely of impotent revenge, and the miserable satisfaction of knowing that it would heap obloquy upon him who drove him to such extremity. Another Surdar of rank went with his horses, camels, and elephants to sit *D,hurna*, at the Deooree, and contrived so to work upon the Muha Raj s apprehensions, that he procured an order on the *Khasgee* for one hundred and fifty rupees a day, and the promise of a bill for one lakh, at the next general settlement of accounts. Surjee Rao continues to urge the conclusion of this settlement, and as six lakhs of the Jypoor tribute are said to have been paid into the hands of Seendhiya's agent at that Durbar, it is probable that the distresses of the army may at last force the Muha Raj to do them justice. The fact, however, of any money having been actually paid may fairly be doubted, as Bapoo Seendhiya still continues to ravage and raise contributions in the Jypoor territories. Some people, who lately brought supplies to us from Agra, described that part of the country through which they passed as being quite ruined by his troops. Kumpta Gir with his Gosaeens is at Jypoor, where he has been well received, and invited to take service: he has, however, written to the Muha Raj, offering to return to his camp if he will give any security for the payment of his followers.

Seendhiya has not been very fortunate in realizing his contributions hereabouts. The Shahpoora Takoor has not paid a rupee of what he agreed for with Surjee Rao; and it has, in consequence, been intimated to him that the army will continue in his country till the money shall be forthcoming: neither has anything been collected in the districts which Seendhiya holds in Mewar. Bala Rao took an opportunity of recommending that some person of character and consequence should be sent into that quarter with the rank of Soobu, and the Muha Raj replied that if he would pay two lakhs into the *Khasgee*, he himself should go. From Kiruolee, however, Baptiste writes word that he has received fifty thousand rupees, and from a small fort, in the neighbourhood of the camp, called Dabra, they have got seven thousand rupees; after battering it, however, for ten days. Dabra is at present in the possession of Zalim Sing,h, but belongs of right to the Raja of Shahpoora; and was to have been delivered over to him for a handsome consideration, if it had been taken. An affair of such trifling consequence does not at all interrupt the good understanding that subsists between Seendhiya and Zalim Sing,h.

We have paid a visit to the Durbar since I last wrote,

the purport of which was to demand restitution of the contributions levied by Bapoo Seendhiya on our friends the Rao Raja and the Nuwab of Kutpootlee. The principle on which the demand was made was immediately acknowledged by the minister, and the demand itself acceded to; more probably from its affording him a fair pretext for quarrelling with Bapoo Seendhiya than from a conviction of its justice and propriety.

He has now established a system of *espionage* throughout the camp, which pervades even the retirement of private families, and has excited universal terror and disgust. Such a state of things is so unusual in this army, and so irksome to the individuals which compose it, that in all probability some violent explosion will soon be the consequence.

LETTER XVIII

March to Roopahelee—Body of a murdered girl—Surjee Rao's influence declining—Fresh quarrels with the Muha Raj—The Minister remains behind—He prepares to quit camp—Detachment formed for Malwa—Violent dispute with the Mamma—Part of the Jypoor contribution paid—The Rana of Oodipoor—Disturbances in his country—Villagers of Boorkera—Temple of Nathdooara—Boldness of the thieves—Huts erecting in camp—Influence of his companions over the mind of the Muha Raj—The Bala Baee.

CAMP AT BOORKERA, *July* 18.

OUR expectations of a long halt were soon disappointed by an order for marching on the morning of the 4th, when we encamped in the neighbourhood of two villages belonging to the Rana of Oodipoor, called Roopahelee and Bojras, and about ten miles to the westward from our old ground. The country was still one continued flat, with fewer villages than before, and consequently fewer trees, for none seem to grow spontaneously in these districts; nor do the inhabitants appear to think of planting them, except in the immediate vicinity of their villages, or round a well. Soon after commencing our march on that morning we saw, within a very short distance of our tents, the body of a young girl, apparently murdered but a few hours before, lying upon the ground. She was deeply wounded about the throat and neck, and both her feet, and part of one hand, were cut off; the former probably to secure the rings or other ornaments that were upon them. Her clothes, however, which were good, and seemed to have been wrapped carefully around the body, remained untouched. She bore the appearance of a *Butkee* belonging to some woman of rank, and in all likelihood had fallen a victim to the jealousy of her husband or a lover. Every one that passed by turned to look at this shocking spectacle, but the only idea it seemed to excite was a transient sorrow, no one appearing to wonder, and still less to think it of sufficient consequence to make any inquiry after the murderer.

Before we left the camp at Irwur a large body of the *Silahdars* waited upon Surjee Rao to remonstrate against an order which he had issued for the *Hazree-nuvees*, or muster-master, to keep his accounts in the Persian as well as the Hindee characters—an innovation which they did not comprehend the drift of, and therefore greatly disapproved. The Minister, incensed at their folly and insolence, drove them away with a severe reprimand. He will not, however, I am inclined to think, have it much longer in his power to reprimand any one; his influence is evidently on the decline, and it is even rumoured that consultations have been held upon the expediency of bringing back Ana Siknuvees to camp, and placing him again in power.

The Muha Raj and his father-in-law have had some serious disputes, which commenced upon the bullocks of the Baee's carriages being carried off, while grazing, by the Meenas; a party was sent in quest of them, but returned unsuccessful. Seendhiya was exceedingly angry, and upbraided Surjee Rao that under his management camels, and horses, and bullocks, and everything else, were taken away. The other replied that if the management of affairs was really entrusted to him, without the interference of favourites, not the value of a straw would be lost. High words ensued, and they parted with mutual disgust. Seendhiya makes no scruple of uttering his complaints in open Durbar, and among other things, upbraided the Minister for having given so large a sum as forty thousand rupees to his favourite Juwahir, which, if properly distributed among the troops, would have pacified their murmurs, and kept many with the army who have since deserted from it. That the complaint is just cannot be denied: but it must also be acknowledged to come rather oddly from Seendhiya.

On the next march, which was to the ground we now occupy, Surjee Rao remained behind, and declared his resolution of going away altogether. The Muha Raj seemed very indifferent about it, and for a long time refused to allow any Surdar to be sent to entice him back. He also gave a positive order that Juwahir, who had come on to camp, should not be suffered to return to him. This was a deprivation, however, which the old Minister could not support; he sent a number of his people to conduct his beloved mistress to his tent, and at the same time wrote to the Muha Raj, that "life was not life without this Juwahir, who, at least, was guiltless of any injury to him or his state!" This dispute was at length made up by the interference of Bala Rao, who was himself deputed to escort the Minister back to camp. The breach, however, between them is too wide to be cured by temporizing measures, and a very short time must decide whether he is to continue in power or not. If Mahratta politics were to be judged by the same rules which regulate those of other states, it would be at once decided that he must fall; for he has not only lost the confidence of his master, but possesses not the support of a single man of rank or influence in the whole army; with the exception alone of Nimalkur, his colleague the Mamma being a mere cypher. Three days ago he gave an entertainment to the Muha Raj, at which they got drunk together, and passed the night in every species of riot and debauchery, and the next day they had so violent a quarrel that Surjee Rao quitted the Durbar highly incensed, and gave orders for preparations to be made for his immediate departure. Juwahir, with part of his equipage, under an escort of two hundred men, actually marched yesterday; and he himself was about to follow them this morning, when Seendhiya, who hardly expected so much resolution, sent a summons for him to attend the Durbar. The event I do not know, but the most probable one is, that they will again be reconciled, to commence fresh quarrels, and so go on, till the other party shall be fully prepared to take some decisive steps. Small sums of money have been distributed among the troops destined for the province of Malwa, and they have consented to proceed, but are still delayed by some merchants of the Bazar sitting a strict *D,hurna* upon Jugoo Bapoo, who was appointed to lead them. The command was then offered to Gopal Rao, and subsequently to the Mamma, but was declined by both: the latter, however, has since been prevailed upon to accept the situation, on condition of the troops being paid the whole of their arrears, and sent off perfectly satisfied. Upon these terms it is not probable that he will soon march: and in the meantime he has been involved in a serious dispute with a man named Gunga Dur Raste, the agent of a rich and powerful Mahratta, to whom the Mamma is deeply indebted, and in whose hands he has placed his little island of Colaba as a pledge. The period fixed upon for the liquidation of the debt expired a few days ago, without any portion of it having been paid: the agent accordingly proceeded to the Mamma's tents, and commenced a strict *D,hurna;* so greatly to his annoyance, that he applied to the Muha Raj for relief. Seendhiya sent a battalion to protect his person, who drove away the people employed in sitting the *D,hurna*, seized upon the cattle and other effects of Gunga Dur, and carried him prisoner to the Deooree. The Muha Raj has since exerted himself strenuously to reconcile the parties, but hitherto in vain; Gunga Dur refusing to listen to any terms, except the actual payment of the sum due: and boldly declaring that by resorting to force the Mamma has forfeited his word, and Colaba also: that his principal, Kundoo Rao, was sufficiently powerful to resist any attempt to dispossess him, and that he himself would no longer be answerable for any consequences that might ensue. The Mamma's wife and family were at this time about to march for Oojyn, and when it was known that they had proceeded far enough to be out of danger from any attack by Gunga Dur's people, his effeets were restored to him, and he himself was set at liberty.

On the 9th Surjee Rao reported one half of the first instalment of the Jypoor contribution to be paid, and that he was assured the remaining half was prepared, and would be paid, together with the second *Kist*, or instalment, upon the Buhora receiving leave to depart from camp. This the Muha Raj refused to grant till the whole contribution should be paid; in opposition to the advice of the Minister, who observed, that he was still on the borders of the Jypoor country, and as the *Kureef*, or second crop, was now nearly ripe, he could at any time enter it, and recommence his devastations, should any unnecessary delay take place in fulfilling the treaty. A small detachment has been sent out to make collections in the neighbouring villages; and has been generally successful: having taken hostages at those places where the inhabitants were obliged, from poverty, to postpone the payment of their contribution till after the approaching harvest.

The unfortunate Prince of this country, the Rana of Oodipoor, once the most powerful and still the most exalted of all the Hindoo Princes of India, has written to Seendhiya, entreating him, now he has entered his country, to advance and take upon himself the task of settling his affairs, which, he truly states, are going rapidly to ruin: that his revenues are dilapidated and his principal Takoors disaffected, many of them having thrown off all subjection to his authority, and proclaimed themselves independent. Seendhiya, as the surest mode of relieving his distress, proposes to send a *Soobudar*, with powers to redress all grievances, and put the affairs of the state to rights. The Takoor of Deogurh, the name of a strong fortress and the district attached to it, about fifty miles from camp, who bears the ancient Hindoo title of *Rawut*, and Surda Sing,h, an *Oomrao*, or nobleman of the first rank, and related to the

Rana, are now rivals for power in this distracted state, and are both courting the favour of the Muha Raj.

The village of Boorkera, which is close to our tents, belongs to the district of Bednohr, the capital of which is about twenty miles off in a north-westerly direction. The Takoor to whom it belongs is of the Juodpoor family; he has come to camp, and thrown himself upon the protection of the Muha Raj: in consequence of which, his village and the crops around it have been preserved from plunder. About six miles beyond Bednohr is the district of Mugruolee, celebrated for its hilly fastnesses and impenetrable jungles; it forms the boundary between the countries of Marwar, or Juodpoor, and Mewar, or Oodipoor; but the daring race of robbers who inhabit it acknowledge the authority of neither. They subsist by levying contributions on the inhabitants of the plains around, when they are not checked by the presence of a still greater evil than themselves, a large army of Mahrattas.

The little chief of Boorkera, with some of his villagers, came to my tent a few days ago: it was the first time they had ever seen a European, and everything astonished them: while I, in my turn, was as much interested by a kind of primitive simplicity, which characterized all they said and did. They are a tall, decent-looking race of men, equally distant in their manners and demeanour from insolence and servility. The general state of the peasants appears to be always comfortable, but never luxurious; there are no great landholders among them, but each head of a family rents a moderate farm immediately from the Takoor, which is sufficient to supply his family with all the necessary comforts of life. At the time of harvest, the Takoor sends round an officer, who collects his dues without any trouble or violence: they consist of two-fifths of all kinds of grain, collected in kind; and two rupees for every *beegha* of land sown with cotton.[1] They manufacture

[1] A Beegha is about the third of an acre. B. [It varies greatly in different districts.]

themselves what little cloth they require for their own expenditure, but none for exportation, and as they carry on little or no commerce with other parts of India, they are strangers to the commonest luxuries of other countries. I presented the *Zumeendar*, or head man of the village, with a small cotton carpet, with which he appeared to be as much pleased as if it had been made of the most costly materials, and promised that it should be preserved in his family as long as it could hold together. These villagers are on the best terms with our Sipahees, whom they freely admit into their houses, and readily supply with milk, butter, &c., favourably contrasting their conduct towards themselves with that of the Mahrattas. They all joined in feelingly deploring the ruined state of Mewar, which, at least the completion of it, they with one voice attributed to Ambajee and Bala Rao, who with large armies had been marching about the country during the last two years.

The capital of Oodipoor is a hundred and twenty miles from hence, situated in the midst of vast ranges of mountains, and about twenty miles on this side of it is the celebrated temple of *Nat,hdooara*, or "the Dwelling of God." It is held in such veneration, that the town in which it stands has always been respected by the Mahratta and other armies that have chanced to pass near it. The revenues of many villages are appropriated to its use, as well by the Rajas of Juodpoor and Jypoor as by the Rana himself. The former Prince keeps five hundred men constantly ready for the service of the temple, and has a *dak*, or post, laid from his own capital, a distance of two hundred miles, for the sole purpose of conveying fresh flowers, which are offered every morning at sunrise upon the shrine of the idol. The Mahrattas seem everywhere to be regarded with dislike and contempt: the people here tell a ridiculous story of Seendhiya, when he was at *Nat,hdooara* about four years ago, having uttered some sarcasms against the image, which he called *Parusputtur*, "the Philosopher's Stone." A piece of wit so offensive, that it quitted the temple, and did not return till the Muha Raj had himself departed without performing his devotions.

The simple manners of the peasantry are strikingly contrasted by the boldness and dexterity of the thieves in this part of the country: a most determined attack was made a few nights ago on the shop of a merchant, in the centre of the Bazar, which was known to contain a large sum of cash, many valuable jewels, and a quantity of gold and silver ornaments. The robbers came, with flambeaux, went directly to the tent, and having dug up the treasure they came in search of, retired without any loss on their part: but one or two persons belonging to the Bazar, who were attracted to the spot by the noise, were cut down. No troops came forward to give assistance to the merchant; and a servant, who ran towards Surjee Rao's tents calling aloud for aid, was, by his orders, well flogged for making a noise that might have attracted the thieves to that quarter of the camp. On the following night a tent was robbed in our camp, in which fourteen *Hirkarus* were sleeping: two of them had drawn swords by their sides, which the thieves made use of to cut their way into the tent. While we were at *Irwur*, one of the Muha Raj's finest horses was carried off by a fellow who observed the rider dismount and give the bridle into the hands of an attendant: he darted forward, cut the reins with his sword, and springing upon the animal's back, was out of sight in a moment. Some horsemen were sent in pursuit of him, as soon as the robbery was made known, but returned to camp without success.

The rainy season has now completely set in, and the whole plain around us is covered with the finest verdure. The principal Surdars here have a curious custom at this season of the year, when grass is in plenty, of appropriating to their own use large spots of ground near the camp, over which they place servants, with orders to allow no other people to cut the grass. We have, in consequence, often found it more difficult to procure a supply of this necessary article when it abounds, than at other times when it is found with difficulty. Many of the people in the great camp have begun to build huts, with the idea of remaining on this ground for a long time. Sticks and bushes are collected for this purpose in all directions, and firewood has already become scarce. When this latter article is difficult to be procured, small flat cakes of cow-dung, mixed up with a little chopped straw and water, and dried in the sun, are used for fuel; they are called *Kundhas*, and answer all the purposes of common cookery perfectly well.

The Hydrabad *Risalu*, which went off at Jajgurh, returned to camp on the 9th, upon the persuasions of Nimalkur, who was deputed to them for that purpose. On the 12th, however, they again decamped, concluding, from the general state of affairs, that it would be folly to expect any security being given for the regular disbursement of their pay. These events vex the Muha Raj for an hour; he quarrels with his ministers in consequence, and then drowns all his cares in the society of his gay and debauched associates. The influence they hold over his mind is evinced in every transaction: a few days ago a horseman, in a fit of passion, put to death his own father-in-law; the relations of the deceased went to Surjee Rao for redress, who stated the circumstance to Seendhiya. The murderer, however, belonged to the troop of Appa Kandra, the chief of the infamous crew who perpetually surround the Muha Raj; he had already told his story, and the Minister was informed that the unfortunate man must doubtless have committed some heinous offence to have drawn down upon his head so signal a punishment; and that, at any rate, it was no business of his: no further notice of course was taken of the matter. The more respectable people of the camp feel and resent this influence highly: all parties, however, seem now to have united against Surjee Rao, to thwart and displace whom former animosities are, for a time at least, to be laid aside.

The Wukeels of Dokul Sing,h are very urgent for the

army to march to Ajmeer, where their master would join the Muha Raj: and Surjee Rao now openly supports his pretensions. For this very reason, probably, Seendhiya is evidently not hearty in the cause, though he seems to acquiesce, with the hope of bringing the Raja of Juodpoor to a more speedy and favourable settlement. Bala Baee, the daughter of Madoojee Seendhiya, a lady who possesses great influence in camp, has avowed herself the supporter of those who oppose the present Minister. She sent for the Muha Raj lately, and read him a long lecture upon the state of his affairs, adding abundance of good advice, and many exhortations to reform before it was too late: to all of which he listened very attentively, promised to give it his serious consideration, and quitted her, to mix again in the orgies of a set of wretches, who have already brought him to the brink of ruin, and who will assuredly not quit him till they have completed their noble work: for what but ruin must be the consequence of a system of measures as much distinguished by weakness and rapacity as they are deficient in justice, honour, and good faith!

LETTER XIX

March to Nimara—Increased disputes between Seendhiya and Surjee Rao—Intrigues respecting Gwaliur—The Buhora urgent to quit camp—Plans proposed for Mewar—The Ukhara—Gymnastics—Puhlwans.

CAMP AT NIMARA, *July 21st.*

THE ground about Boorkera was found to be so low and swampy that it was deemed impracticable to continue there during the remainder of the rainy season, and we accordingly marched here this morning—a distance of about eleven miles, in a direction south-west. The face of the country is still an unvarying flat, but the ranges of hills seen at a distance are more numerous than before, and among others which are in sight are those in which the fort of Deogurh and Bednohr are situated. This village belongs to the latter: it is tolerably large, and has an old stone fort in the centre. The villagers have not quitted it, and their property is protected.

Surjee Rao has not left camp, though his visit to the Durbar, which I mentioned in my last letter, was far from producing a reconciliation with the Muha Raj. On the contrary, their disputes have been since carried on with more bitterness, and the breach between them is wider than ever. He complained, and certainly with justice, that the Muha Raj took every opportunity of showing that he no longer possessed his confidence or support; in consequence of which all descriptions of people thwarted and insulted him: that the *Silahdars*, or privates of the cavalry, when distressed for pay, sat *d,hurna* upon the *Risaludars*, or commandants, who in their turn came to him, and that the merchants and bankers behaved towards him still worse, refusing to lend him any assistance, or to advance a single rupee. Seendhiya then took up the discourse, and, among other things, upbraided him with his private expenses; upon which the old man, taking off the little dirty cap which he always wears, displayed it, and protested that his own expenses were in strict conformity with that simple article of personal decoration. After some further bickering, Surjee Rao retired to his tents, angry and uneasy, and immediately ordered a camel, a blanket, and three *tolas*, or rupees weight, of silver to be distributed among the *Fuqeers*, as a propitiatory offering. After he had quitted the Durbar, Bala Rao generously endeavoured to interest the Muha Raj in his favour; but Gokul Paruk, the rich banker coming in at the moment, openly declared that so long as Surjee Rao continued at the head of affairs they never would prosper, but that upon any change being made the effect would be instantaneous and evident. The Muha Raj continued so angry throughout the day, that even the greatest favourites stood aloof, nor ventured to intrude upon him. Since that day Surjee Rao has only been once to the Durbar. One of the principal subjects of dispute at present is the Soobuship of Gwaliur, which is now held by Deoba Kalia, and which the Minister's party have been straining every nerve to appropriate to themselves. They have apparently succeeded so far as to get Dajee, the son of Ambajee, nominated Soobudar; and he has even been presented with the customary *Khilut* upon the occasion. He has agreed to pay a *peshgee*, or advance, of eleven lakhs for the appointment, which is three more than Deoba Kalia gave for it: but the security for this sum is only conditional, and provides for Dajee's being put in actual possession of his government. Deoba Kalia has signed a *chook-chit,hee*, or order for evacuating the garrison: but notwithstanding all this apparent success, it is pretty certain that Dajee will in the end be disappointed in his expectations. His rival possesses a greater share of the

FIG. 8.—AN UKHARA, WITH A VIEW OF THE BRITISH RESIDENT'S CAMP.

Muha Raj's regard than any other individual; and when he represented to his master that he had in vain bestowed this favour upon him, if after the heavy expenses of reducing the neighbouring fortress of Bind, and other refractory *Zumeendarees*, he should take the Soobuship from him, Seendhiya desired him to keep himself quiet, and rest assured that he would never forsake him.

Nothing has yet been settled respecting the *Buhora's* departure, who is very urgent for permission to return to *Jypoor*, where his enemies have taken advantage of his absence to injure him in the opinion of his master. He has proffered the most solemn assurances that he would, upon reaching the capital, despatch a person to camp, vested with full powers to settle everything to the Muha Raj's satisfaction; and in answer, has been desired to give accepted bills upon some banker for four lakhs and a half, payable as soon as he himself should reach Jypoor. This he refused to do, and the discussions recommenced, with as little prospect of being brought to a conclusion as ever. The same indecision exists respecting Mewar. Bala Rao wants the Minister to give him a *Sunud*, or warrant, for the general superintendence of the whole province, as well the personal estates of the Rana, as those of the different Takoors: for which appointment he offers to pay an annual sum of three lakhs and a half, and to allow the Rana five hundred rupees per day for his private expenses, whose complaints, however, both parties agree must be strictly kept from reaching the Muha Raj's ears.

A great deal of rain has fallen; and our Sipahees have commenced the exercises which are customary at this season of the year. The natives all over India are exceedingly fond of these diversions; which are regulated by certain ceremonials, observed with the most scrupulous etiquette.

A sufficient space is marked out, generally in the smoothest ground, and, if possible, under the shade of trees, which is carefully dug up, and cleared of all the stones, hard

lumps, &c. This is called the *Uk,hara*, and is held sacred; no one entering it with his shoes on, nor any impure thing being suffered to be brought within its limits. At one end a small heap of earth is raised, to which each individual, as he enters, makes an obeisance, and adds a handful of earth. The most skilful among them is appointed *Khuleefu*, or superintendent, for the season; who regulates the exercises, and instructs the young *Put'has*, or scholars. Every one strips to his *dhotee*, which is drawn as tight as possible about the loins, and rubs a particular kind of white earth over his body. The first exercise is generally the *Dhun*, or, rather, *Dund*, which is thus performed. The exerciser having balanced himself upon his hands and toes, each about two feet apart, throws his body forward, till the chest comes within three or four inches of the ground; loosening his elbows and tightening his knees, but without moving his hands or feet from their original position: in which motion almost every muscle of the body is exerted. He then straightens his elbows, and erects his head and chest; and having remained in this position a few seconds draws back to his first posture, and repeats his *Dhuns* as long as his strength will allow him to continue. At first it is difficult to exceed ten or twelve, but by practice a man may bring himself to make so many as two or even three hundred. The next exercise is the *Kooshtee*, or wrestling, at which the natives of India exhibit great skill and activity. They salute by striking smartly, with the right hand, upon the left arm doubled on the breast, and upon the hollow of the right thigh; and they do not consider it a fall, unless one of the wrestlers is laid flat and helpless upon his back. In these contests strength is much less exerted than skill; yet a broken or dislocated arm is by no means an uncommon event. The other principal exercises are with the *Moogdurs* and the *Lezum*: the former, thick clubs of hard wood about two feet or upwards in length, and from fourteen to twenty pounds in weight, which are wielded about somewhat in the manner of our dumb-bells; the latter is a stiff

bow of bamboo, bent by a strong iron chain, to which a number of small round plates of the same metal are affixed, for the purpose of increasing the weight and making a jingling noise. The bow is used by alternately stretching out the right and left arms to the utmost extent, the other arm pulling firmly in the opposite direction. All these modes of exercising tend to open the chest, set up the body, and strengthen the muscles, and the effect produced by them upon a young lad at the end of the season is astonishing. When the business of the day is over, the players gather round some individual of the party, who repeats a *Kubit*, or little poem, upon the occasion; they then perform the salute, first to the *Khuleefu*, and afterwards to each other, and conclude by a few *Dhuns*, performed by the whole party drawn up in a line, with the *Khuleefu* at their head. A large dish of sweetmeats or of steeped grain is generally produced, of which they all partake, and the party breaks up. A man who wishes for distinction as a wrestler prepares himself by a fixed régime; which consists chiefly in drinking a certain quantity of milk and clarified butter, and, if he ever eats meat, in devouring an increased allowance of it every day. When his body has by these means imbibed an additional portion of vigour, and he has acquired a certain degree of skill, he is dignified by the appellation of *Puhlwan*. The Muha Raj, who is a great patron of these people, retains a celebrated wrestler in his service, to whom he makes a daily allowance of a sheep and twenty pounds of milk. A *Puhlwan* came lately from Muttra, for the express purpose of trying his skill with this Mahratta champion, and was conquered—an event at which Seendhiya was so highly pleased, that he presented his favourite with a golden bracelet worth five hundred rupees. Great men in India take a pride in having the best wrestlers in their service, who are permitted to make use of their horses, elephants, &c., whenever they please. Nay, to such a pitch is this passion for gymnastic exhibition carried, that the art is sometimes practised by women, who study to make their

bodies hardy and their flesh firm by following the prescribed regimens, and go about challenging the wrestlers in the different villages though which they pass to try a fall. These Amazons sometimes attain to such a degree of proficiency, that it is rare for the most experienced of their male opponents to overthrow them. It must be added, however, that the best wrestlers often decline engaging in these contests from the fear of incurring the disgrace of being worsted by a woman.

LETTER XX

Death of Surjee Rao—His character—Distress of the Baee—Friends of the late Minister confined—Juwahir and Khueratun—Seendhiya and Deoba Kalia make Kurum-Durum—Begars.

CAMP AT NIMARA, *July 27th.*

THE career of Surjee Rao is at length fatally closed, and in a manner the most violent and tragical: he was murdered yesterday evening in the open Bazar. The particulars of this event are, as well as I have been able to collect them, as follows:—The Minister had gone to the Durbar, and was earnestly pressing Seendhiya to accede to some of his proposals, to which the Muha Raj, as usual, returned evasive and unsatisfactory replies, and ordered his equipage to be got ready to go to an elephant fight. As he was about to depart, Surjee Rao repeated his remonstrances, and at length had the temerity to seize the skirt of his gown, and endeavoured to detain him forcibly in his seat. Some of the *Hoozooriyas* present, incensed at such an insult, thrust him back, and Seendhiya escaped from the tent, giving an order, however, to secure his person. The Minister snatched his sword from the hand of an attendant, and resisted those who attempted to execute the order of Muha Raj. A violent scuffle ensued, in which some individuals of both parties were killed, and several wounded, and Surjee Rao at length effected his retreat to his tents, after having killed two men with his own hand. He was followed thither by the enraged party from the *Deoree*, headed by Anund Rao and a son of Mannajee Fankra, two distant relations of the Muha Raj's family. In one minute the ropes of the tent, in which the unfortunate Minister had taken refuge, were cut, and he himself dragged from beneath it, and in the next he fell dead in the public street, pierced with a dozen wounds inflicted by his pitiless enemies, Anund Rao himself having set the example. The commotion excited by this event was much less than could have been expected. At first all was uproar and confusion; of which the *Shohdas*, and other rabble of the army, took due advantage, and plundered everything that came in their way. The troops, however, were almost immediately under arms, and the whole camp was speedily surrounded by parties of horse, who received orders not to allow any individual whatever to enter or to quit it. This morning all was again as quiet as if nothing of any consequence had happened. So universally was the very name of Surjee Rao detested, that none were found even to feel a moment's pity for his sudden fate, much less to think of revenging it. Thus has fallen the most unprincipled, sanguinary and daring public man that has for many years figured in Hindoostan. He was bold and hasty in conception, but so little scrupulous in the means by which he endeavoured to attain his end, that instead of conciliating those whose concurrence was necessary to ensure success, he only inspired them with doubt and apprehension. Hence his enterprises were always characterized by rapacity and ambition, and were very rarely conducted to a fortunate issue: witness the siege of Doonee, and the treaty with Jypoor. Wanton cruelty was another principal feature in his character, and he is supposed to have caused more innocent and respectable blood to be shed than any Minister who ever conducted the affairs of a Mahratta state. Justice, however, obliges us to acknowledge, that during his last short career he was not guilty of any very atrocious acts, and that he did not meet from the Muha Raj with that confidence and support which could alone have enabled him to exert the military talents he is generally allowed to have possessed. Seendhiya is said to have given orders, when he heard the scuffle, to spare his father's life, and from the known lenity of his disposition it seems probable that he did so. His pursuers, however, either wilfully or ignorantly mistook these orders, and in all probability rejoiced at an opportunity of getting rid of a man who was an object of hatred to themselves, of dislike to their master, of terror to the whole army, and apprehension to every court in India.

The Baee is in the deepest affliction at the sudden and shocking fate of her father. Seendhiya sat up with her the whole of last night, endeavouring to console and comfort her, and with his own hands wiping away the tears which she shed in abundance. Her situation indeed demands his utmost tenderness, being nearly six months gone with child.

The principal members of Surjee Rao's party, with the exception of Dajee, who made his escape with five attendants upon the first alarm, together with all their followers, are placed in confinement, and Seendhiya, to save appearances, has ordered Anund Rao and his accomplice to quit the army, furnishing them, however, with a liberal supply of money for their immediate expenses.

Juwahir, the mistress of the late Minister, and her friend Khueratun, the wife of the Pithan chief, have both been put in close confinement, and their effects seized upon by the Muha Raj's orders.

Among the people of rank who fell in the affray, were the Raja of Moongee, and Bugwunt Rao Punwar, a member of one of the first families in the Mahratta empire; their bodies, together with those of the Minister and such of his friends as fell in his cause, were carried out of the camp and burned, during the night, on the bank of the little river which runs past our tents.

It is difficult to conjecture who will immediately succeed Surjee Rao in the directions of affair, but whoever it may be will probably have Deoba Kalia as the principal coadjutor. He and Seendhiya made *Kurum-Durum* together a few days ago, a ceremony at which the parties swear eternal friendship, and solemnly bind themselves to study, and be faithful to, each other's interests.

Reports of marching have been prevalent for the last two or three days, in consequence of the *begars* being seized for the service of the *Deooree.* This is a term applied to poor people employed to carry burdens without hire: there are many thousands of such in camp, who subsist by selling grass and wood during a halt, and carrying loads upon a march for those who will employ them, and are not powerful enough to get them for nothing: a certain number being always seized, on the evening before a marching day, to assist in carrying the baggage of the Muha Raj and his courtiers. A quantity of bread is distributed daily among these poor people at Seendhiya's expense, which, though not sufficient for their support, is, neverthcless, a considerable aid towards the maintenance of their families. In all parts of India bread is made into cakes about the size of pancakes; and either baked on the convex side of an iron plate, or fried in meltcd butter in the concave side of the same vessel: a few sticks, or some *Kund,has,* serve for firing, and everybody is early taught to dress his own dinner.

LETTER XXI

The Mourning of the Baee—Punishment of Juwahir—Khueratun—Disposal of Surjee Rao's property—Treatment of Bala Rao—Intrigues for office—Bapoo Seendhiya—Justice of the Durbar—Remonstrances with the Juodpoor Wukeels—Distresses of the army—Soobudarees—Bawanee Purshad—Kulamuts—Restoration of the old officers of government.

CAMP AT NIMARA, *August* 5.

SEENDHIYA and the Baee ate on the evening of the 28th ultimo, for the first time since the death of Surjee Rao: abstaining from food being deemed, throughout India, the most unequivocal proof of grief that can possibly be evinced. She has directed the bones of her father to be collected, and they are to be carried in a white cotton bag, by a number of Brahmuns, to the banks of the Ganges, and deposited in its sacred stream. Her days of mourning are commenced, during the continuance of which she is considered impure, no one being permitted to eat with, or even to touch her, till after ten days are expired: when she will effect her purification by bathing, and feeding a number of Brahmuns. Her tribulation, however, has not taught her humility or compassion. The unfortunate Juwahir, doubtless a natural object of her dislike, was sent for to the *Deooree* on the 29th, and, in the presence of the Baee, severely beaten with a cane, and afterwards, as a greater mark of indignity, received several blows from a slipper; report adds, though I trust unjustly, inflicted by the hands of the indignant Princess herself. The Muha Raj, on his part, threatened her with the loss of her ears and nose, but contented himself with plundering her of a considerable sum in jewels and money, which she had contrived to collect during her short hour of sunshine and prosperity; and then, satisfied with this manly vengeance, generously ordered her to be set at liberty. Khueratun, who shared her confinement, has also shared her punishment, and has been plundered of property to the amount of nearly a lakh of rupees. She exclaimed vehemently against the injustice of taking from her what she termed "the honest gains of her profession, amassed during twelve long years of constant practice;" offering, at the same time, to give up freely whatever she had received from Patunkur since she was last restored to his protection. Finding, however, that all remonstrances availed nothing, she sent a spirited message to the Muha Raj, declaring she would wring the whole from him again, whenever she gained access to his presence, by a single song. She is said to possess clothes and jewels to a much greater amount than that of which she has been robbed, secured in the hands of different merchants and bankers. Surjee Rao's property has been seized upon by the Muha Raj, the jewels and other valuables have been confiscated; and his camp equipage, horses, elephants, &c., sent off to his family in the Duk,hun. Most of the chiefs of his party have been released, except Bala Rao; and he is kept under some restraint, in the charge of the Mamma, who, together with Nimalkur, has become security for his person. An order for the evacuation of the garrison of Ajmeer has been, with some difficulty, obtained from him; and a Surdar deputed to take possession of the fort. Bala Rao at first objected to sign this order, upon the plausible pretence that the garrison, knowing him to be under restraint, would certainly refuse to obey it. It is now reported that the army will move towards that quarter as soon as the rain, which has fallen heavily, will admit of continued marches.

No administration has yet been formed; and the parties contending for power are so many, and so nearly balanced in strength, that its completion must be a work both of time and difficulty. The Mamma wishes himself to be appointed Minister; and the other Surdars now in camp, puffed up with the idea, that without their support nothing can be done, seem loth to declare for any one: the friends of old Ana look upon him as the only person fit to be placed at the helm; and Deoba Kalia, proud of his wealth, and the acknowledged favour of the Muha Raj, but still more of the recent downfall of his rival, openly vaunts that his interest alone will decide the matter. Seendhiya has very wisely left the determination to the principal Surdars, declaring that he will sanction their choice, whoever it may fall upon; but, when once made, will admit of no more disputes and cavils, and will expect them all to join heartily in supporting their own administration. In the meanwhile Deoba Kalia and the banker Gokul Paruk conduct all the public business; and it is very probable that it will be finally continued in their hands; especially if the Mamma can be prevailed upon to join them, and give that *éclat* to the junta which the want of rank in the other two would prevent its possessing.

Bapoo Seendhiya has at length arrived within a few marches of the army; and will, in all likelihood, start as another and most formidable candidate for power. He has been desired to come to camp with only his immediate followers, and to leave the bulk of his troops at some distance. The motive for this request is, that if they should join the main army, they would also join it in looking to the Muha Raj for pay, as well of the arrears due during their expedition as what they may henceforth become entitled to; whereas if they continue a separate corps, they will have no claim upon any one but Bapoo Seendhiya himself, it being an invariable rule at Mahratta courts that every leader of a detachment shall find the means of supporting it while under his command. It has also been intimated to him, through his brother, that a handsome sum, in the present conjuncture of affairs, would materially tend to advance his interest at the Durbar; which he cannot be at any loss to procure, as he has for so long a time been laying the whole Jypoor country under contribution, without any demand being made upon him, or any control exercised over his actions. The wily chief has returned no answer to these advances, and seems reserving himself till he shall arrive in camp, and be better able to judge how matters actually stand.

A message has also been sent to the Buhora, desiring him to be under no apprehensions respecting the treaty, which the Muha Raj considers himself as much bound to abide by as if the Minister who made it were still alive. Meer Mukdoom, the leader of the Hydrabad Risalu, has been treated with much less attention and honesty. He himself continued in camp after the departure of his corps, with the hope of being paid the long arrears due to them; but has been dismissed without a single rupee, upon the shameful pretext of his being considered exclusively in the service of Surjee Rao. It was at the same time intimated to him, however, that he might, if he pleased, be entertained in the service of the Muha Raj, on a fresh score : an offer which he listened to with all the contempt and indignation which it merited.

Warm remonstrances have been made to the Juodpoor Wukeels, upon their master persisting to retain in his service the strong and efficient brigade of Moohumed Shah Khan, to which they candidly replied that the Raja retained it only from the alarm and mistrust which he could not avoid feeling of his Durbar, and that he neither could nor would discharge that corps till he had come to some settlement with the Muha Raj, and received satisfactory security against further molestation, at least for a certain time.

Seendhiya will, after all, be obliged to accede to the Raja's offer, for the threat of espousing Dokul Sing,h's cause, especially since the death of Surjee Rao, appears to have lost all its terror; and it is even said that his Wukeels have been directed to quit a court which appeared to listen to them only for its own purposes, and with the paltry view of extorting from them as much money as possible.

The distress for cash continues to be severely felt throughout the army, and in order to answer the demands of the troops it is proposed to raise thirty lakhs, in the following proportions: *viz.*, ten from Deoba Kalia, and from Bapoo Seendhiya, Gokul Paruk, and Zalim Sing,h, five each. The latter is to have the Soobuship of Mewar given to him as an equivalent, but what good things are to fall to the lot of the others is not yet determined upon: it is, however, much more easy to talk of such a sum than to raise it. I do not well know how to explain to you precisely what is now understood by a Soobuship: the office somewhat resembles that of the Proconsuls of ancient Rome, who were sent into distant provinces to superintend the interests and possessions of the republic. Holkar, as well as Seendhiya, has at present large possessions in Oodipoor, or Mewar, and each has a Soobudar in the province. Their original claims were for no more than a tribute of eight lakhs of rupees, imposed by Muhadajee Seendhiya for the restitution of *Chuetohrgurh*, which he had conquered from the Rana, one half of which was made over by the present Muha Raj to Holkar as a testimony of his friendship, when they united their forces to act against the English in 1806. In the provinces which belong entirely to Seendhiya the Soobudar is simply the governor, as in Malwa, Ajmeer, Gwaliur, &c.

Raja Bawanee Purshad continues to be one of the greatest sufferers amidst the general distress of the army; horses, jewels, and even his tents have been sold to procure the necessaries of life. An elephant, which had been long the pride of his family, and was offered for sale in the morning at a quarter of his value, died before night, literally starved.

A merchant to whom he was indebted for the clothes, &c., which he presented to Seendhiya, upon his arrival in camp, had the boldness to seize the person of his nephew, and carry him off to his tent, where he confined him for a day and a night. Bawanee Purshad complained to the Muha Raj of this outrage, who ordered the youth to be set at liberty, and promised to pay the debt, whenever he himself should settle with the Raja. In the midst of this universal distress, proceeding solely from a want of ready money, three or four *Kulamuts*, or musicians, the favourites of the Muha Raj, are abundantly supplied from his own purse, and parade about the camp with the retinue and magnificence of Nuwabs ; to the great scandal and indignation of the more respectable members of the army, who are unable to give their horses a feed of corn, or even to afford their servants a hearty dinner.

Many of the inferior servants of the government, who were displaced to make way for Surjee Rao's friends, have been reinstated in their offices, and among the rest Atmaran has returned to his post in our camp, greatly to the satisfaction of all parties.

LETTER XXII

Seendhiya's designs upon the Wukeels of Dokul Sing,h—The Takoor of Kuliawas—The Muha Raj discontented with his new advisers—Superstition of the Mahrattas—Siege of Soopoor—Kafilus to Ajmeer and Pokur.

CAMP AT KULIAWAS, *August* 14.

SEENDHIYA has discovered, within these few days, that Dokul Sing,h's Wukeels have brought with them *Hoondees*, or bills, for two lakhs of rupees, and jewels to half that amount, intended as a present for him, whenever they should be convinced that he had in earnest adopted the cause of their young Prince ; one lakh to be paid upon the army's arrival at Ajmeer, the rest upon its reaching Meerta. Upon this discovery, the Juodpoor Wukeels were sent for, and desired to give a conclusive answer as to what sum the Raja would agree to pay : to which they tauntingly replied that as the Muha Raj had at length resolved upon taking possession of the whole country, they must wait and see what should be left for their master before they could venture to specify what was so very uncertain. They boldly warned him, however, to be prepared for a resolute struggle, and averred that the moment he should enter the Juodpoor territories, the Raja of Jypoor would lay aside his private disputes with their master, and march immediately to his assistance. Seendhiya, finding that the Wukeels were not to be intimidated, has since changed his tone : he now professes to feel a sincere friendship for the Raja of Juodpoor, and a hearty wish to remain on good terms with him ; nor has he blushed to reveal to them his intention of acceding, in appearance, to the wishes of Dokul Sing,h's friends, with the honourable view of getting possession of the money which the Wukeels are furnished with to reward his sincere co-operation. In pursuance of this plan we made a march yesterday of about six miles in the direction of Ajmeer. The ground, however, over which we passed was so swampy, that the artillery could only proceed half way, and we have accordingly halted to-day for it to come up. Kuliawas is a large village belonging to the Rana of Oodipoor; it has a good stone fort, or castle, attached to it, and appears to be full of inhabitants. The head man of this, as in every village in the Rajpoot states, is dignified with the appellation of Takoor; we had a visit from him this morning, for the purpose of consulting the surgeon of the Residency for a disorder which he labours under, and which is very prevalent among the Rajpoots—dyspepsia—caused, probably, by the great quantity of opium which they eat; this fascinating but destructive drug being produced among them upon all occasions, and presented to visitors as *pan* is in other parts of India. His manners, like those of the generality of his countrymen, especially the better sort, were pleasing and unassuming. He conversed freely, and was very inquisitive respecting our manners and customs, especially as to the mode in which we treated the *Rueyuts*, or peasantry. He palliated the immoderate use of opium upon the score of its exhilarating and making those who partook of it happy; and for the same purpose, he said, his countrymen were accustomed to drink liquor and smoke tobacco. He did not attempt to disguise his hatred and contempt of the Mahrattas, and declared that he had paid two hundred rupees the preceding day for the protection of his village.

The Muha Raj has already begun to find fault with Deoba Kalia, and complains that he has effected nothing since the death of Surjee Rao; whose ghost, by the bye, is asserted by the whole army to haunt the Deooree. The superstition which prevails among these people, and even influences the acts of the Muha Raj himself and his Durbar, is of the most ridiculous nature, and operates in every event that occurs. A very general sensation was lately excited throughout the camp by our having substituted a white ensign, with the union in one quarter, for the old union-jack, which was worn out. It was immediately asserted that the English were about to assume the general sovereignty of Hindoostan, of which the white flag was the emblem; while the coloured canton represented the contracted space which the Mahrattas were still permitted to occupy. This curious idea received additional force from one of the gentlemen attached to the Residency having unwittingly pitched a new baggage tent, made of coarse red cloth—the colour which designates the imperial tents of the King of Delhi. So universally was this opinion received, that wherever our servants or sipahees appeared they were questioned upon the subject; and at length a Surdar of rank was deputed, under the pretence of transacting some trifling business with the Resident, to find out the truth of the matter—which was, that a white flag being more readily distinguished from a distance than a coloured one, the people with the baggage would be more certainly directed on the march to their own camp than they were before.

The odes of Hafiz are constantly consulted by this Durbar upon any important event, in the same manner that the poems of Virgil were in former days. This belief in omens, however, often lays the Muha Raj open to the extortions of the wily and interested Brahmuns, who maintain a powerful influence over his superstitious mind. I remember once the whole Durbar being thrown into confusion by a crow flying through the tent: it was said to predict some fatal event; and to avert it, the Muha Raj was enjoined to construct a crow of gold, with a chain of pearls round its neck, and present it to the Brahmuns—an injunction with which he literally complied. The whole army was alarmed a few nights ago by the *Sohaba*—a number of phosphoric lights which sometimes appear and disappear suddenly during the night, especially in low damp places

N 2

where dead bodies have been laid. The natives suppose them to be the spirits of the slain, and the lights are often seen in such numbers, that they have the appearance of an army moving with torches. The Sohaba is regarded as an ill omen ; but Seendhiya jokingly observed to some persons, who pretended to be greatly alarmed, that it could not be meant for him, whose fortunes were already sunk to so low an ebb that it was quite impossible to sink them deeper. He has attended himself to business, since the death of his father-in-law, much more than he was ever accustomed to do: and was highly gratified yesterday by receiving advices from Baptiste, who has been for some time besieging Soopoor, intimating that he had taken the town with a heavy loss on the part of the enemy, and hoped in a few days to become master of the fort also. The Juodpoor Wukeels have been instructed to intercede for the Raja of Soopoor, and Koosallee Ram has offered to negotiate for him ; but Seendhiya replied to both, that the Raja having failed in performing the treaty he had entered into, it was necessary to take the place, not only as a punishment for his present want of faith, but as a security against a repetition of such conduct in future.

Several *Kafilus* of pilgrims, both Moosulmans and Hindoos, have lately gone from camp ; the former to pay their vows at the tomb of Kwaja Moouen-oo-deen Chishtee,[1] a celebrated Moohumedan Saint, at Ajmeer ; the latter to worship at and bathe in the sacred lakes of Pokur[2]—a town

[1] Khwaja Mu'in-uddin Chishti was born in Persia in 1142 A.D., came to India and was residing at Ajmír when Pithaura, the rájá of that place, was taken prisoner and put to death by Shahab-uddín Ghorí, in 1192. This saint died in 1236, and his shrine is venerated by Muhammedans and Hindoos alike.

[2] Pokhar, or more correctly Pushkar ; where is situated the only temple in all India dedicated to Brahma, the creator, who here performed a peculiar Brahmanical sacrifice, whereby the lake became so holy, that the greatest sinner, by bathing in it, earns the delights of paradise. A great fair, combined with a celebrated horse and cattle market, is held here in October–November, when many pilgrims come from all parts to bathe in the sacred tank.

but a few miles distant from Ajmeer, and esteemed one of the holiest, as it is the most ancient, *teeruts*, or places of religious resort, in India. We have now become strenuous advocates for the cause of Dokul Sing,h, with the selfish hope that its being adopted may afford us an opportunity of seeing these two celebrated places.

LETTER XXIII

March from Kuliawas—Naked Fuqeer—Battle of the Bunjaras—The Juree Putkee—Bapoo Seendhiya—Disputes with the Buhora—Alliance between Jypoor and Juodpoor—Discontent among the troops—Tent erected for the Junum-ushtoomee—The Rakia—Preparations for the Baee's confinement—Succession to the Raj—The Takoor of Roopahelee—Seendhiya transacts public business—Buffalo fights.

CAMP AT ROOPAHELEE, *August* 30.

WE marched from Kuliawas on the 15th, and are again encamped on the banks of the *Mansee*, within a mile or two of the ground we occupied in June last. Upon the march we observed a number of Fuqeers mounted on capital horses, or riding upon elephants, the property of the Muha Raj and the principal Surdars of the camp, who think it meritorious so to accommodate this lazy and generally insolent race. One man in particular attracted our notice; a fair good-looking fellow of about five-and-thirty years of age, perfectly naked, and close shaven; and so fat and sleek, that at first we supposed him to be some rich *Buniya* who had taken the opportunity of bathing in a piece of water close by. Upon inquiry, however, we were informed that he was a very celebrated *Purhumhuns*—a term applied to those Hindoo ascetics who, by a life spent in a series of the severest austerities, have arrived at the fourth order of religious poverty, and have established a high reputation for holiness and sanctity. The man in question, however, had much more the appearance of having passed his time amidst the good things of this world, than in meditation upon the next.

A violent dispute took place, on this march, between two Bunjaras, the leaders of their respective parties, about precedence; which grew to such a height, that it was at length agreed to proceed to the open plain and settle it at the point of the sword. The partisans of each champion began immediately to prepare for combat, girding on their swords and shields, and loading their matchlocks. The parties drew up in regular array, and it was then determined that the Muha Raj himself should be a witness of their prowess. Everything was prepared for engaging; to the no small astonishment and interest of the army, who were assembled in crowds to behold this extraordinary conflict. It being very late, however, before Seendhiya came up, the Bunjaras retired to their respective camps, and sent a deputation to inform him of their intention to fight next day, and entreat him to honour them with his presence: to which he very properly replied that they were a parcel of fools, and desired them to remain quiet in their tents. Such a termination of the business, however, did not appear to them at all reconcilable with their honour, which was pledged for the strife, and accordingly one party proceeded about dusk to attack the camp of the other. A few shots were fired on both sides, when they rushed on with their swords and spears, and a desperate conflict, hand to hand, ensued, which lasted till eight o'clock; the assailants were then beaten back, with the loss of twelve killed, and nearly thirty wounded, the other party having suffered somewhat less. The dead of the vanquished party were abandoned on the field of battle, and on the following morning a mission from a third corps, more powerful than the other two, proceeded to their camp, accompanied by two bullocks bearing white flags of truce, to invite them to return and bear away the bodies of their friends, assuring them at the same time of safety and honourable treatment. They urged them, however, in vain, the worsted Bunjaras refusing to quit their camp, where they remained brooding over their defeat and meditating future vengeance.

Upon marching days the Muha Raj generally sends on the *Juree-putkee*, or golden standard, the ensign of the Mahratta empire, with great state, when arrived within a few miles of the new encampment, and remains out, with his attendants, till the afternoon, amusing himself with hunting and shooting, at both of which he is reckoned a skilful sportsman. On these occasions he wears a suit of deer-skin, dressed rough, and always fires from a match-lock, with common Hindoostanee powder, though he prefers that of our manufacturing for priming. When he goes in pursuit of deer he often makes use of a bullock trained for the purpose, behind which he is enabled to approach the herd and take his aim with precision.

We went to Durbar on the 21st, where we met Bapoo Seendhiya, who had arrived in camp two days before. He is a large, fat, vulgar-looking man, talks and laughs a great deal, and has the reputation of being the least scrupulous of all the chiefs of this unprincipled Durbar. Seendhiya went some miles out of camp to meet him, who, when he approached, threw himself at the Muha Raj's feet, and was honoured with a most gracious reception, ensured by a report of the great wealth he is said to have collected during his command. He has left his army at some distance from camp, but has been promised to be continued in the command of it. It consists nominally of twelve thousand men, but the troops are very discontented, and are deserting daily in great numbers. Since his arrival in camp he has been solely employed in intriguing with the different parties that are struggling for influence in its councils; but a detail of his manœuvres, even if it were possible to obtain it correctly, would only present a tissue of bribes, threats, lies, and boastings, which would disgust, without affording you any information. His chief arts have been called forth to induce the Buhora not to press the final execution of the treaty until he himself shall have effected a settlement of his own accounts. The veteran Minister, however, has been proof against his attacks, and has required that Bapoo Seendhiya's accounts should be adjusted without loss of time, in order to facilitate a speedy conclusion of those of his own court. He has informed the Muha Raj that he has received bills for three lakhs and a half of rupees, to be paid on the following conditions: first, that the agreement for twelve lakhs, entered into three years ago, when Bapoo Seendhiya was detached to the assistance of the Jypoor Raja, and which was the foundation of the late treaty, should be cancelled; secondly, that the collections made by Bapoo Seendhiya and Baptiste should all be accounted for; and thirdly, that he himself should immediately be permitted to depart from camp. These conditions have excited the Muha Raj's highest indignation; he calls them, and with some justice, gross violations of the treaty just concluded: he has severely upbraided the Buhora with a breach of faith, and averred, upon the assurances of Bapoo Seendhiya, that the collections made in Jypoor since the conclusion of the treaty at Doonee amount to the petty sum of only fifteen or sixteen thousand rupees. He has become, however, a little more humble with regard to Soopoor, having, upon the Buhora's renewed offer to treat for it, declared himself willing to accept of double the original contribution, and to desist from all further proceeding against the place. Baptiste's late reports have not been quite so favourable as were expected: the fort still holds out, and there are some apprehensions of reinforcements coming both from Kota and Jypoor. He has, however, dug mines, and prepared boats to cross the ditch, and still holds out hopes to the Muha Raj of final and complete success.

Bala Rao has been set at liberty, and has received a *Khilut* upon the fort of Ajmeer being delivered up to Seendhiya's officers, the Mamma, however, still continuing security for his person. A present of a handsome pair of shawls has been also sent to the nephew of Bawanee Purshad. Both the uncle and nephew have claims upon the Muha Raj, having been now kept nearly a twelvemonth in expectation of something being done for them. These shawls have been given as a slight token of remembrance, and may just serve to keep hope alive for another year.

A report has been circulated, which has afforded no small degree of alarm to the politicians here, of a projected alliance between the Rajas of Juodpoor and Jypoor, to effect which a Takoor of high rank was about to be despatched from the latter court. The Juodpoor Wukeels have been informed that such an alliance would immediately produce a breach between their master and this Sirkar, an information quite unnecessary, as such a union, if entered into with sincerity, and supported with wisdom and firmness, would, in all probability, be the immediate forerunner of the ruin of both this Sirkar and that of Holkar, by completely excluding them from a field in which they had been, for so many years, employed in reaping a rich and abundant harvest. A confederation of the Rajpoot states, under the powerful control of the British government, appears to be a measure of all others the best calculated to ensure the permanent security of the whole continent of India, by at once connecting the eastern and western limits of our empire, presenting a formidable barrier, quite across the head of the peninsula, to any invader from the north, and circumscribing the Mahrattas within their natural limits, the only people now in India whose habits and principles lead them to increase their own power by a constant demand upon the resources of their neighbours.

Some symptoms of the usual discontent which prevails among the troops breaking out into open violence having appeared, Deoba Kalia assembled the Silahdars of the whole army, and promised them an immediate supply of fifteen rupees per man if they would remain quiet, at least till something should be decided upon in the Durbar. They agreed to consult together upon his offer, but have not yet made known their determination. A report of the same spirit having manifested itself among his troops has been made by Ram Chund Buo, the temporary Soobudar of Mewar; and a reinforcement of two battalions and some cavalry from Bapoo Seendhiya's army has, in consequence, been sent to him.

Great preparations are making for the approaching Hindoo festival of the *Junum-ushtoomee*, the anniversary of the birth of Krishna. Sets of dancing boys, called *Rahus-d,harees*, are arrived from Muttra for the occasion, and all the principal people in camp have received invitations to be present at their performance. A large temporary tent is always prepared for this entertainment by the Muha Raj, the materials of which he purchases from the merchants of the Bazar, and, when the festival is over, proffers them again as payment for their own goods—an offer to which they gladly accede, rather than submit to a certain and total loss. A more economical mode of giving a splendid *fête* has not, I believe, yet been discovered by any of the ingenious votaries of fashion in your colder hemisphere of the globe.

On the 25th, which was also the last day of the Hindoo month *Sawun*, was another festival called *Rakia*, on which Brahmuns go about fastening little bracelets of floss silk, called *Rakees*, upon the wrists, swords, spears, &c., of those whom they wish to compliment, and receive, in return, a small present of money.

Besides the great tent preparing for the *Junum-ushtoomee*, another is also being erected for the accommodation of the Baee, whose confinement is expected to take place in a short time. The hopes of an heir have been raised to the highest pitch in the bosoms of the Muha Raj and his family, by the confident predictions of all the astrologers in camp.

The presumptive heir to the *Raj*, Raja Desmookh, is now lying dangerously ill, and should he die, there is no one whose relationship is sufficiently near to give him a fair claim of succeeding to the honours of the family, females being excluded among the Mahrattas from the succession. He is the only surviving child of Bala Baee, the daughter of Madojee Seendhiya, by the late Raja Desmookh; *Desmookh* being the title of an inferior officer of the state, under the *Putel* (or Zumeendar), by which latter title Madoojee himself was frequently designated.

Roopahelee is a considerable village,[1] and, like most others in this part of the country, is surrounded by a wall of mud excavated from a ditch, which runs entirely round the place; it is also defended by a small square fort, but of no strength, in the centre of the place. The Takoor rents twelve other villages besides Roopahelee, but resides entirely at the latter: he is a relation of the Takoor of Bednohr, but holds his estate immediately from the Rana himself by an annual payment of forty thousand rupees and the military service of a certain number of horsemen. This sum is collected among the different villages, which also furnish their quotas of horse according to their means. The proportion fixed for Roopahelee is eight thousand rupees and twenty horsemen, but in the present distracted state of Mewar the former is seldom paid, except when levied by force, and the latter as seldom attend at Oodipoor, except upon a special demand from the Rana. These little feudatory bands were formerly summoned to appear at the court of the Rana once in three or four years, whence they were commonly sent back, after a week's attendance, unless any urgent occasion should call for more protracted services.

The little river, upon which we are encamped, must be of essential service in the cultivation of the fields about Roopahelee. Like all other streams, however, in this part of the country, it is seldom full, except after the heaviest rain, when it rises in a few hours to the top of its banks, and falls again as suddenly. This has already happened twice since we have been here.

Nothing like the arrangement of a ministry has taken place, the Muha Raj continuing himself, with very unusual assiduity, to superintend the transaction of public business during the morning, and to amuse himself in the afternoons with buffalo fights. These animals are sometimes opposed to tigers, and a strong buffalo will toss a moderate-sized tiger to a considerable height into the air.

[1] Close by is now a station—Rupaheli—on the Malwa section of the Bombay, Baroda, and Central India Railway.

LETTER XXIV

The Junum-ushtoomee—Conduct adopted towards Bala Rao—Coolness between the favourites—Baptiste's battalions join the army without orders—Jooruor Sing,h—Seendhiya proposes to take a muster—Proceedings at Soopoor—Fresh preparations for the Baee's confinement.

ROOPAHELEE, *September* 8.

THE *Junum-ushtoomee* took place at twelve o'clock on the night of the 2nd, when the image of the infant Krishna was placed in the *Phool Dhol*, a kind of swinging cradle, and the important event announced by the sounding of drums and concas, and the firing of cannon. There often happens a schism among the Pundits as to the proper time for keeping this festival, one party asserting that it should be determined by the recurrence of the *Ushtoomee*, or eighth day, of the month *B,hadon*, the other, averring it to depend upon the ascendency of the star *Rohunee*; both these data having occurred at the birth of Krishna. The *Bueshnoos*, or followers of Bishn, are guided by the star, which always appears in a certain position on the eighth, or on the preceding or succeeding day, while their opponents regard only the day of the month. On the third the great tent was consecrated by a *Pooja*, or worshipping, at which the Muha Raj was present. In the evening the customary dances commenced, and all the Surdars were summoned to attend. A thousand rupees were also distributed among the Brahmuns. On the following evening we paid our usual visit on this occasion. The tent in which we were received was about one hundred and fifty feet long, divided lengthwise into three compartments, by a double row of posts ornamented with coloured paper, and to each of which was

FIG. 9.—THE JUNUM-USHTOOMEE.

affixed a sconce of candles. At the further end was a stage, raised about two feet from the ground, and made to represent a kind of gothic hall, with pillars and arches highly painted and gilded. This is called the *Sungasun*, or throne, and in the centre of it was placed the *Phool Dhol*, covered with a profusion of pearls and jewels, and wreaths of flowers fancifully disposed, in which lay the image of *Bal Govind*, the name by which Krishna was distinguished in his early infancy, and which literally signifies "the happy infant." A number of Pundits and attendant Brahmuns sat about it, and were employed in rocking the cradle and fanning the little idol within. The centre space of the tent was left open for the dancers, and those on either side filled up to the level of the stage, and appropriated to the accommodation of the Muha Raj and the numerous spectators assembled on the occasion. Among these, when the candles were lighted, we perceived, to our utter astonishment, the fat *Purhumhuns* whom I mentioned in my last letter, in the same state of disgusting nudity in which he appeared upon the line of march. He sat immediately opposite to the Muha Raj, of whom, however, or of any one else, he took not the slightest notice. The attendants, who sat about Seendhiya, did not seem much to like the distinguished post which this man of mortified passions had taken up, and Atmaram made a kind of apology for his appearance, by saying, that as it was a religious spectacle, it would not be proper to exclude a *devotee* from being present at it. He strenuously denied, however, the man's pretensions to the title of *Purhumhuns*, asserting, that if he were really so refined a being, he would neither be so fat, nor have exhibited himself in such a place. After one or two sets of common Nach girls had performed, the *Rahus-d,harees*, who were seated at the upper end of the tent on a kind of raised sofa surrounded by *Chobdars*, *Chuonree-burdars*, and a crowd of other attendants, came forward. They are boys, always Brahmuns, who are educated at Muttra for this purpose, where a large tract of land is appropriated for their support. Parties of them travel about at this season, to perform at the different Hindoo courts of India ; that now in camp consists of four, besides the musicians, and are all eminently handsome. The eldest represented the young Kunya, the name by which Krishna was distinguished in his boyish days ; the youngest, his beloved Rhada, and the other two her youthful companions. The performance was a kind of *Ballet*, descriptive of the sports of this amorous and inconstant, but interesting deity, with the *Gopees*, or virgins of Gokul, during which they sung stanzas in the *B,hak,ha*, or language of *Brij*, the name by which the country, for a certain distance around Muttra, was formerly designated, and which was the scene of the early exploits of Krishna. This language, which is very little known among Europeans in general, is forcible and comprehensive, though, from abounding in monosyllables, it sounds harsh to ears unaccustomed to hear it pronounced. It contains beautiful specimens of the ancient Hindoo poets, which, I am persuaded, would amply compensate the trouble of any one who should apply himself to their study.

I have procured copies of some of the songs performed on this occasion, and, as you expressed yourself gratified by the former specimens of Hindoo poetry which I sent you, have added translations of two of them, which particularly pleased me. The first is supposed to be a dialogue between Kunya and one of the *Gopees*, who returned to him, after a former visit, sooner than he expected. The second contains a description of the effect caused in the bosoms of the Muttra maids, by the sound of the pipe of their darling shepherd, and a dialogue between them and Jasooda, in consequence of their interview with him in the groves of Mudbun,[1] a village in the neighbourhood of Muttra. The only figure, peculiarly oriental, which requires explanation, is, in the first poem, an allusion to the gathering clouds,

[1] The present Madhu-ban is near the village of Maholi, about five miles from Muttra, and the banks of the Jumna.

which the Hindoos suppose to be peculiarly incitive of the tender passion; and the only personages introduced, with whom you are not already well acquainted, are Nund,h and Jasooda, in the second poem: the former the principal *Go,ala*, or cowherd, of Gokul, with whom Krishna passed his boyish years; the latter, his wife. Both poems are of the kind called *Kubits*.

KUNYA

Again, my fair one!—hast thou purchased me?—

THE GOPEE

Think'st thou uncalled I boldly come?—Ah, see!—
The gathering clouds, dear youth, invite to love.

KUNYA

How could a frame so soft, such dangers prove?
While e'en thy pretty self was lost in night,
How see thy way?

THE GOPEE

The lightning gleam'd so bright!

KUNYA

O'er broken roads, through mire, and tangling thorn,
Thy tender limbs must ache, thy feet be torn?

THE GOPEE

Steps light and firm will weariest way o'ercome.

KUNYA

Yet dark's the night; and thou wert all alone.

THE GOPEE

No, my soul's lord!—for love was with me still;
Pointed my path, and warded every ill!

KUBIT

The pipe is heard of *Nund,h's* sweet boy;
The *Goalins'* hearts beat high with joy:
To the cool woods in crowds they speed;
Nor danger fear, nor toil they heed.
And if by chance the youth they spy,
Away go prudence, modesty:
They gaze, by his bright beauties burned,
And soon,—their pails are overturned!

Jasooda!—listen to our prayer;
Thy son's audacious frolics hear!
To Bindrabun we bent our way;—
He seized our arms, and bade us stay.
Lady! our cheeks with shame were red;
Like modest girls away we fled:
In vain we've milked, in vain we've churned
For he—our pails has overturned.

Go, bold and forward *Goalins*, go!—
No one your wily ways can know.
Often in laughing groups you're seen,
Bending your steps to coverts green;
There in the cool retreats you rove,
And pass the hours in mirth and love;
Then tell me, from your pranks returned,
Forsooth—your pails are overturned!

Both the dancing and singing of the *Rahus-d,harees* was far superior to that of common performers; their attitudes were exceedingly graceful, and their voices were never raised beyond the natural pitch. The dresses were appropriate and elegant, especially that of Kunya, who wore a brilliant sun upon his head, and a quantity of superb jewels about his neck and breast; all of which, as well as the dresses of the other boys, were furnished from the wardrobe of the Muha Raj. After the dances were over, they exhibited in groups representations of the most celebrated statues of Krishna and his relatives, with an accuracy and steadiness quite surprising in such children. The instrumental performers who accompany the *Rahus-d,harees* are, as well as the boys themselves, all Brahmuns; and it was pleasing to see them, after the performance, instead of making the usual obeisance, lifting up their little hands, as invoking a blessing upon the Muha Raj, who rose, and bowed to each as he retired. We quitted the tent soon after, highly gratified by the entertainment of the evening.

The festival of the *Junum-ushtoomee* lasts six days, and is, upon the whole, the most classical and pleasing of the Hindoo calendar. Various rites and ceremonies take place at stated periods of the infant's growth, allusive to events which occurred at those times, till the sixth day, when the *Takoor* (that word, as with us, being equally applied to a spiritual as a temporal lord) is removed from the cradle in which it had lain. An earthen pot, filled with sour curds tinged with turmeric, is then hoisted upon a long pole, from whence it is dropped at a signal made by the Pundits; and the by-standers besmear each other with the mud, and throw about a quantity of the mixture, which each had brought with him for the purpose, in the same manner as at the *Hohlee*: a part of the ceremony which was announced by salutes of cannon in the Muha Raj's camp. The whole concludes with a dinner given by the Pundits; the only occasion, I believe, on which these holy men ever incur such an expense.

A *Phool-dhol* was constructed in our lines, before which some of the younger Sipahees danced and sung, in imitation of the *Rahus-d,harees*, every night during the festival; though to dance in public, upon any other occasion, would be reckoned a disgrace to which no decent man could possibly submit.

The hopes, which were for some time held out to Bala Rao, of being reinvested with the Soobuship of Ajmeer, diminish every day. The private advisers of the Muha Raj are endeavouring to persuade him to march there; and, if he likes the place, to retain it in his own hands, or, more properly speaking, in theirs; and they urge him, consequently, to stipulate for such security from Bala Rao, as they well know he cannot possibly comply with. The Mamma takes this conduct in dudgeon, as it was upon an implied promise of the reinvestiture that he prevailed upon Bala Rao to evacuate the fort. He has in consequence refused to appear at the Durbar for some days past, and talks of quitting camp.

A coolness has taken place between the rival favourites, Gokul Paruk and Deoba Kalia, and the latter is said to have written privately to Ana Siknuvees, urging his return to the army; he has also openly espoused the cause of Bapoo Seendhiya, against whom several complaints have lately been made, by the petty Takoors in the neighbourhood, of the lawless and disorderly conduct of his troops, which are dispersed about in detached parties, and employ themselves in plundering everything that comes in their way. I met a party of them lately who had come to camp with the hope of bullying their general out of some money, but were forcibly driven away and abused for their insolence. They vented their anger in loud invectives against Bapoo Seendhiya and the Mahrattas in a body; and called out to ask me if I would take them into the Company's service, which, they had candour enough to acknowledge, was the only one in India that was worth going into. Three battalions of Baptiste's brigade, which were detached towards *Boondee*, returned a few days ago to the army of their own accord, and have pitched on the opposite bank of the river, a little below our camp. They were so much harassed by the *Meenas* during their march, as to be in the most imminent danger of losing their guns, and were at length obliged to apply to Zalim Sing,h, who exerted his influence with their tormentors to procure them a safe passage through the country. They are dreadfully ashamed of this brilliant exploit, for which they have been laughed at and upbraided by all classes of the army.

It was in one of these battalions that an interesting young girl was discovered, about a twelvemonth ago, who had served with it for two or three years as a Sipahee; in which capacity she had acquired the favour of her superiors, and the regard of all her comrades, by her quiet and inoffensive behaviour and regular attention to the duties of her station. It was observed that she always dressed her own dinner, and ate it, and performed her ablutions by herself; but not the slightest suspicion of her sex was entertained till about the time I mentioned, when it was discovered by the curiosity of a young Sipahee who followed her when she went to bathe. After this she continued to serve for some months, resolutely declining the patronage of the Baee, who proposed to receive her into her own family, as well as the offers of the Muha Raj to promote her in the corps she belonged to. The affair soon became the general subject of conversation in camp; and I having expressed a strong wish to see Jooruor Sing,h, the name by which this Indian D'Eon went, one of our Sipahees, who was acquainted with her, brought her to my tent. She appeared to be about twenty-two years of age, was very fair, and, though not handsome, possessed a most interesting countenance. She spoke freely of her profession and her immediate situation, but betrayed neither the affected bashfulness nor forward boldness which such a situation was likely to have produced; and let it be recorded to the honour of every party concerned, that, from the moment when her sex was discovered, she met only with increased respect and attention from her comrades, not an individual presuming to utter a word that might insult her, or breathing a doubt that could affect her reputation.

At length her motive for enlisting and remaining in the service was discovered; an only brother was confined for debt at Bopal, and this interesting young creature had the courage to enrol herself as a common soldier, and afterwards persisted in exposing her person to the dangers and difficulties of a military life, with the generous idea of raising money sufficient to liberate this loved relation from confinement. When Seendhiya was informed of this anecdote, he liberally ordered her discharge to be made out, gave her a handsome present in money, and sent her with a letter to the Nuwab of Bopal, warmly recommending both the brother and sister to his favourable notice and protection.

Seendhiya has offered to take a muster of the troops, as a preliminary step to settling their accounts; but with one accord they have declined the offer, stating, and with reason, that a great many of their horses have died since the commencement of the rains, which would necessarily be excluded from a new muster, but which they have been obliged to support for a long while. They insist, therefore, that their accounts should be adjusted by the last muster, which was taken nearly three years ago.

The Jypoor Wukeel has been strongly urged by his court to conclude a treaty for Soopoor, a proposition now but coldly received by this Durbar, although one or two conferences have actually taken place upon the subject. Baptiste writes word that he has met with more obstacles than he expected, although he still continues sanguine as to the final result of the siege. Among his other disappointments, the Raja of Kota refused to send him a considerable supply of powder and ball, which he had promised, when he learned that it was to be employed against Soopoor.

A temporary wooden house has been substituted for the tent prepared for the Baee's confinement, which is expected to take place in less than a month; and a lucky moment has been fixed upon by the *Nujoomees*, or astrologers, for its erection. Should she be confined about the time expected; we shall halt here till she is perfectly recovered: if not, we shall probably make a march or two in the direction of Ajmeer previous to the important event taking place.

LETTER XXV

Increasing perplexities of the Muha Raj—Kundoojee—Violent conduct of the Sipahees of the regular battalions—First instalment of the Jypoor contribution paid—The young Pretender Man Sing,h—Usurped power in different states of Hindoostan—Raja of Jypoor—Pindara delegates—Attempts upon Holkar and his family—Bawanee Purshad demanded by the Nuwab—The Shub-i-burat—The Puttur Chuot,h—The Pitr-puch.

CAMP AT ROOPAHELEE, *Sept.* 26.

WE now look upon ourselves as stationary for some time: the wooden house has been erected, and all the tents which are usually pitched around the *Deooree* have been removed, to make room for those of the Bala Baee, who wishes to be near her cousin in her confinement. Seendhiya seems to find, in the certainty with which he looks for an heir, some relief from the vexations which are multiplied upon him from all quarters, and it is now pretty generally believed that he means to recall old Ana to camp. The Rana of Oodipoor has written to him, stating that during the life of Surjee Rao he was regularly paid a daily sum of five hundred rupees, and complaining that since that *unfortunate* event this remittance has been suspended, and he has in consequence run deeply into debt. The *Mamma* complains loudly on the same score, averring that his salary, which was settled when he came into office at twenty thousand rupees per month, has been allowed to fall greatly in arrears. He also seizes every opportunity of urging the claims of Bala Rao to some compensation for the loss of Ajmeer; claims which the Muha Raj and his favourites do not seem at all inclined to admit, or at least to attend to.

They have nevertheless written to his elder brother Kundoojee (who for many years superintended the affairs of *Nurwur* on the part of Ambajee, and now holds that Soobuship on his own account), setting forth, that by the death of his brother he has acquired an immense accession to his wealth, which, on account of his advanced age, it would be unreasonable to think of employing for himself alone; that he has long been in the enjoyment of a very lucrative command, without contributing a rupee to the support of that state by whose favour he held it; and finally, that it would be highly becoming in him to aid the present necessities of the Sirkar by a seasonable donation of ten or fifteen lakhs of rupees, on the receipt of which his Soobuship should be guaranteed to him for life, and an engagement entered into that no further demands should ever be made upon him. Kundoojee will probably return a civil answer to this very civil demand, but will assuredly send no money, for he has evinced his ability to resist the just claims of the Sirkar too long to yield to them upon the bare receipt of a few fair promises. Baptiste continues to send assurances of final success from Soopoor, but no tidings of having made any real progress towards obtaining it. His agent, with the four battalions which lately arrived here, complains daily of the insults to which he is subjected by them; and among others, of having been immersed up to his chin in a pit filled with mud and cowdung, in which he was kept for a whole day and night. The officers of the same corps have represented to the Muha Raj, that the men are daily deserting; and that if something be not speedily done for them, there will in a short time be nothing left of the battalions but the guns and themselves. The Baee too, taking advantage of the Muha Raj's distresses and her own situation, sent a message to him the other day, purporting that as he had taken her *Jagheer*, or rather her father's, into his own hands, he must also find money to pay her establishment, for she had none herself.

The first instalment of the Jypoor contribution has at length been honestly paid; and the Buhora has formally demanded permission to quit the camp, which has as positively been refused by Seendhiya until the second payment shall also have been completed. From this payment it has now been agreed that two lakhs and a half shall be deducted on account of Bapoo Seendhiya's collections; and this is probably a pretty fair adjustment of the dispute. That chief, however, is by no means satisfied with it; as he well knows that the loss will be made up to the Muha Raj, some time or other, at his expense. He has accordingly warmly espoused the cause of *Man Sing,h*, a lineal descendant of a former Raja of Jypoor, who was deposed and murdered by his cousin, the father of the present Raja; and has recommended that the youth should be proclaimed Raja, and supported in his just claims to the *Musnud* by a powerful force, if the reigning Prince does not immediately perform the whole of the engagement which he entered into. It is a very curious fact that among the principal states of Hindoostan the greater part should be now governed by Princes whose right to the dignity they enjoy is at least disputable. I have already mentioned the young pretenders to the Rajpoot states of Juodpoor and Jypoor, and the usurpation of Zalim Sing,h in the province of Kota. The government of the little principality of Bopal has been wrested in the same manner from its legitimate ruler by the Minister, Wazeer Moohumed, and the Nuwab himself excluded from all participation in it. The assumption of supreme power in the Mahratta confederacy by the *Peshwa* has continued so long, that it is now scarcely considered as such. Holkar is a natural son, and having gotten the reins of government into his own hands, has secured them by the murder of his brother and his nephew; both of which events took place very lately, and are universally attributed to him. The right of Seendhiya himself to his rank and station is denied by many, who assert that Raja Desmookh, the grandson of Madoojee

Seendhiya, ought to have succeeded before his grand-nephew.

That the *Muha Raj* should take up the cause of the young Prince of Jypoor is most improbable; but were he to do so, and the event prove successful, it would be impossible not to rejoice at the fall of the present Raja, who is a disgrace to the rank he holds and the distinguished family from which he is descended. Although a very young man, he is already reduced to a state of perfect debility, both of body and mind, by unlimited indulgence in every species of excess and debauchery. His caprices are without end, and absolutely intolerable; and in the indulgence of them he neither regards whom they may affect, nor what may be their consequences, pursuing his aim with the most boundless extravagance and open contempt of all honour and decency. He has lately bestowed his affections, if his brutal passions may be ennobled by such a name, upon a common prostitute named *Rus Kufoor*—literally "essence of camphor"!—and has given such proofs of his passion as would, in any European state, entitle him to a private apartment in a mad-house. He began by bestowing on her a *jagheer* which had been appropriated to maintain the dignity of his legitimate wife and family. He has since presented her with a palace furnished in the most costly and magnificent manner, and assigned her a splendid establishment of servants of all descriptions, elephants, camels, &c. &c., to be paid regularly from the public treasury. He has not even blushed to escort her in person to this luxurious abode, through the streets of his capital, seated behind her on an elephant, and fanning her with a *Chuonree* which he held in his hand, to the astonishment and indignation of the Rajpoots, who flocked from all quarters to witness the degradation of their Prince. He had summoned the noblest Takoors of his court to attend him in this extraordinary procession; but their blood revolted at the indignity, and, with very few exceptions, they sent him a spirited and positive refusal.

Two delegates from the *Pindaras* have been for some time in camp, endeavouring to persuade Seendhiya to assemble their main body once more under his standard, and to place the two chiefs, Kureem Khan and Cheetoo (whom he retains in close confinement) at their head.[1]

Upon this measure the opinions of the Durbar are as various as on most other topics: some openly condemning the encouragement of Pindaras under any circumstances; while others as warmly support them, upon the true Mahratta principle of their bringing a body of fifteen thousand horse to the service of the state without putting it to any expense whatever. I believe the Muha Raj himself is rather inclined to the latter opinion: at any rate, he has required the delegates to state expressly how large a sum they are able and willing to pay if the measure they propose should be adopted. Kureem Khan joined this army three years ago, with nearly four thousand followers: visits of ceremony took place between him and the Muha Raj, and a treaty was almost concluded by which the latter agreed to increase the *jagheer* which the Pindara chief already held from him for military services. Seendhiya's avarice, however, was in the meantime inflamed by accounts of the great wealth which the Pindara camp contained. He accordingly invited the Khan to a friendly conference, at which everything was to be settled between

[1] "The name of Pindara is coeval with the earliest invasion of Hindoostan by the Mahrattas. . . . The designation was applied to a sort of sorry cavalry that accompanied the Pêshwa's armies in their expeditions, rendering them much the same service as the Cossacks perform for the armies of Russia. . . . The several leaders went over with their bands from one chief to another, as best suited their private interests or those of their followers."—Prinsep, "History of Political and Military Transactions, 1813-1823." Cheetoo—rendered famous in the poem of "The Old Pindaree"—was devoured by a tiger in the jungles adjoining the fortress of Asirgarh in January, 1818. Kureem Khan afterwards surrendered himself to Sir John Malcolm. For many notices of the Pindarees and their leaders, *see* James Grant Duff's "History of the Mahrattas."

them, and immediately upon his reaching the Deooree, seized upon his person and gave the signal for a general attack and plunder of his camp. Most of the *Pindaras* escaped, but their leader has ever since been rigorously confined in the fort of Gwaliur. Seendhiya soon after obtained possession of the person of Cheetoo, the leader of another band of Pindaras, by a similar act of treachery, but not executed in his own camp.

The dispute between the Muha Raj and his troops as to the terms of the proposed muster is still carried on, without any symptoms of yielding upon either side; and, indeed, all public business seems to be entirely superseded by the various intrigues and animosities that agitate the Durbar. The Muha Raj himself has been alarmed by accounts of a recent attempt to poison the wife and child of Holkar, by administering ratsbane to them folded up in a *pan*: the former, perceiving something extraordinary, took the *pan* out of her mouth, and the drug was discovered. The servant who presented it was flogged, but no further notice was taken of the affair. About two months ago a more serious attempt was made to assassinate Holkar himself, and the man, who was prevented from perpetrating the act, gave up a Surdar of high rank as his employer, who was immediately blown from a gun.

Bawanee Purshad, of whom I have so often made mention, has been demanded by the Nuwab of Oude, upon the score of his being considerably indebted to him upon public accounts. Seendhiya declined interfering in the matter, asserting that so many people of a similar description took refuge in his camp as to render it impossible for him to be answerable for them. The real motive of his refusing the Nuwab's request, however, was the style of superiority assumed by the latter in his quality of Wuzeer of the empire, deigning only to address the Muha Raj by the simple designation *Rao Sahib*.

I have more than once noticed to you the observance which is paid by the Mahrattas to Moohumedan customs and festivals. Last night was the *Shub-i-burat*, or "night of portions," on which God is supposed to allot to each of the faithful his share of good and evil for the ensuing year It ought to be passed in prayer and meditation, but the modern Moslems have converted it into a watching of mirth and gladness, making entertainments for their friends, letting off fireworks, &c. It is notorious, indeed, that the Moohumedans of India have deviated so widely from the institutions of their forefathers, and have adopted so many of the customs and prejudices of the Hindoos, that they form almost a distinct class from their brethren in other parts of the world. When a battalion of volunteers from the Bengal army went to Egypt, under the gallant General Baird, the Moohumedans of that country refused to eat or associate with the Moosulmans attached to it, calling them *Kafirs*, or infidels, and *Hindoo Moslems*. On the celebration of the *Shub-i-burat* Seendhiya directed five thousand rupees to be distributed among the *Paegas*, or corps of Mahratta horse, and a like sum among the Hindoostanee Risalus. Of the latter there are so very few remaining in camp that it must have been, in these times of distress, a most acceptable donation to them. On the night of the 12th, a curious Hindoo festival, called *Puttur-chuoth*, occurred, on which it is customary, when the evening has closed in, for such as love mischief to throw stones about in all directions, sorely to the annoyance of the more sober part of the community, and sometimes to their serious injury; some laughed and some cried, and the grossest *Galee*, or abuse, resounded throughout the camp. Any one who should be discovered, however, in the act of throwing would pay severely for his fun. During this night the influence of the moon is reckoned so baneful that the Hindoos sedulously avoid looking at her for the short time she remains above the horizon. Atmaram, who is a *Pundit*, very gravely assured me that so strongly was this influence felt by all nature, that the wild hogs hid their heads in bushes to avoid its powerful effect!

Another Hindoo festival began on the 23rd, called *Pitr-puch*, it commences with the full and ends with the new moon of the month *Koowar*, during which time every Hindoo whose father is dead goes down at break of day to the river, and standing in the stream, with his face turned towards the east, repeats the prayers called *Turp,hun*, and, first invoking the *Deotas*, then the hills and mountains, the streams and rivers, the forests and green trees, pours out a libation to each from the palms of both hands. He then turns to the south, and calling over his ancestors for many generations, again pours out water to each as he repeats his name. He next faces the north, and makes a like oblation to *Sunkaduk*, the first offspring of *Brimha*, and lastly, turning again to the east, he concludes with a libation to the sun. During the whole of this fortnight a Hindoo who performs the *Turp,hun* is enjoined to abstain rigidly from everything impure; he must restrain his passions, bestow charity, let his hair and beard grow, and even refrain from indulging in connubial pleasures.

The weather, which, till within these few days, has been pleasanter than I ever experienced it at this season in any other part of India, has become very hot during the day, and as remarkably cold at night; and to this great variety of temperature we attribute the fevers which have been lately very prevalent in camp. That part of the rainy season is now approaching when every shower that falls is esteemed so precious by the farmers, that the Hindoos, with the usual luxuriance of Asiatic fancy, suppose pearls to be formed by every drop that is imbibed by an oyster.

LETTER XXVI

Confinement of the Baee—Doubts respecting the sex of the child—Influence of evil eyes—Women pour out water at the Deooree—Great disturbance among the troops—Capitulation of Soopoor—The Mamma's allowance—Bawanee Purshad's flight from camp—Anecdote of Raja Takoor Purshad—The Dusera—Husbandry of the Oodipoor provinces.

CAMP AT ROOPAHELEE, *October* 20.

THE anxiously expected confinement of the Baee has taken place, and all the Muha Raj's high raised hopes have been at once dashed to the ground by the unwelcome intelligence of the birth of another daughter. His vexation at this unexpected event has been equalled only by the shame and confusion of the *Pundits* and *Nujoomees*, who so confidently predicted that he would have a son. Some of them have fled from camp, to avoid the effects of his anger; an unnecesssary precaution, as the utmost punishment that he could inflict upon a *Brahmun* would be some token of disgrace, or dismissal from his service. The consternation and disappointment which the birth of this little stranger produced has however been relieved, or at least suspended, by a report, which was quickly spread abroad, and which has not even yet been authoritatively contradicted, that the child's sex has been purposely concealed from the Muha Raj, and that the Baee had actually been delivered of a son. In great families this species of deceit is not uncommon, especially where the birth of a son is known to be anxiously wished for. People of all ranks throughout India have the utmost dread of the *Nuzur*, or *evil eye*, of the envious, and it is presumed that the malice of all such will be disarmed and warded off by the lamentations of the father over the sex of his child. Madoojee Seendhiya lost several boys in early infancy, whose deaths were all attributed to this malignant influence; and it is by no means improbable, however ridiculous it may appear to us, that in the present case the Baee has had recourse to a stratagem of this kind to avert so fatal an evil, and perhaps to increase her own influence in proportion as her husband's joy would be greater from so agreeable a surprise. In many parts of Hindoostan the natives have so great a dread of the *Nuzur*, that it is deemed an affront to tell them they look in good health, are getting fat, handsome, or the like; and this superstition is carried to such a length, that they often dress their children in mean clothes, lest they should attract the glances of an evil eye. It is even disagreeable to them to call a horse, a bullock, or any other animal belonging to them fat. These doubts, respecting the sex of the Muha Raj's child, have gathered strength from the circumstance of several women, called in to the assistance of the *Accoucheuse*, not having yet been suffered to quit the Baee's apartments. The sceptics of the army, however, account for the delay in disclosing the truth, by the infant's having been born under the influence of a certain star, and its not being usual for children so born to be presented to their fathers, or seen by any strangers, during twenty-seven days. This will, I fear, prove after all to be the real state of the case, and that the Muha Raj's hopes have been re-excited only to be again overthrown with heavier disappointment. Ever since the confinement of the Baee, the women of the camp, and even of the neighbouring villages, have gone daily in large parties to the *Deooree*, carrying pitchers of water upon their heads, which they empty at the walls of the enclosure. The origin or motive of this curious ceremony I have not been able to learn, but it will be the means of ascertaining the real sex of the child, the number of days on which it is repeated being regulated by that. As each woman pours out her water from the pitcher she offers up a prayer to *Bawanee*, a favourite goddess with the

Hindoos, that the Baee's temperament may now, for a certain time, remain cool and comfortable.

The disturbances among all descriptions of the troops have, since my last letter, been greater than ever. The Silahdars to a man have refused to stand a muster, upon the terms which the Muha Raj proposes ; he has, however, been tampering with some of those who have most influence in the army, and will probably induce them, by bribes, finally to acquiesce in his plans. The regulars of Baptiste's battalions have been more violent than any others ; they have thrown all their officers, together with the *Mootusudees*, into confinement, and sent a message to Seendhiya, by one of his confidential servants deputed to soothe them by promises of speedy payment, that if the money did not come very soon, they should be under the necessity of presenting themselves at the *Deooree*, to make known their grievances to the Muha Raj himself. The leaders of the different detachments in *Mewar* have written word that they are unable to pursue any operations, in consequence of the troops having refused to march till they were paid. Baptiste, however, has been more successful at Soopoor. He made a grand attack upon the fort, which failed with considerable loss, in consequence, as he states, of his ladders breaking down ; this, however, added to the annoyance of a large battery constructed upon a cavalier which commands the interior of the fort, produced such an effect upon the inhabitants, as induced the Raja to capitulate : he has resigned his fort, and the whole of his territory, with the reservation only of a *Jaedad*, or estate, for himself of ten thousand rupees per annum ; and it was agreed that half a lakh of rupees should be distributed by the captors among the garrison and the principal public servants of the Raja, as an indemnification for the losses they had sustained during the siege. Baptiste has accompanied his report with a pressing demand for a supply of money, without which he declares himself unable to keep his battalions any longer together.

The Mamma, as usual, has borne his share, both passively and actively, in the disturbances of the camp. The merchants, to whom he is largely indebted, have been sitting *D,hurna* upon him; and he, in turn, has warmly remonstrated with the Muha Raj upon the conduct which has been observed towards him respecting his salary. It was first fixed at twelve, then at six lakhs per annum; and, at the formation of Surjee Rao's ministry, was reduced to thirty thousand rupees per month, not *one anna* of which, he declares, has ever come into his hands. Seendhiya, to get rid of his importunities, and perhaps somewhat ashamed of allowing so near a relation to starve in his camp, has fixed his allowance at a thousand rupees per day, and has given an order on the treasury for that sum, accompanying it with an intimation that he expected to be no more troubled upon this subject. Out of the thousand rupces, however, the Mamma has discovered that he will realize no more than seven hundred, the remainder being swallowed up in *Butta*, or the difference between nominal and real money, and the innumerable fees of office, which form the salaries of most of the public functionaries in the camp. Deoba Kalia still continues to transact the public business, under the superintendence of the Muha Raj; and has consented to receive a paper from the Buhora, in which he agrees to become personally responsible for the whole remaining amount of the contribution if, on the second instalment becoming due, five lakhs of rupees should not be paid down by his government; and on the strength of this paper he has demanded his leave, which has been promised to him. Raja Bawanee Purshad, wearied out with the fair speeches and empty promises of the Muha Raj, has fled from camp; but it is not yet known where he has taken refuge. Upon hearing of his flight, Seendhiya ordered all his tents and cattle, miserable as they were, to be seized and brought to the *Deoorec*. I mentioned in a former letter that his person had been demanded by the Nuwab of Oude, and have since learned a curious story respecting his father, who was one of the wealthiest officers under the government of Shuja-ul-duolu. He had formed a strong attachment for a common dancing girl named *Boolhun*, the daughter of a Moohumedan butcher, and, though himself a Brahmun, resolved to marry her. Accordingly he proclaimed his intention, and invited upwards of two hundred Brahmuns to be present at the wedding feast, concealing, however, the name and rank of his bride. The party assembled, and had begun to eat the dinner prepared for them, when you may imagine the horror with which these pure and immaculate persons were struck, upon the bride and bridegroom appearing, with their garments as usual tied together, and preparing to give to each guest a portion of rice from their own hands! Loud murmurs were heard among them, and a resolution was instantly adopted to refuse the customary handful, by partaking of which the bride's claim would be established to participate in the *caste* of her husband. Raja Takoor Purshad, the name of the bridegroom, was prepared for this resistance, but, well knowing with whom he had to deal, gave a signal, upon which the whole party were instantly surrounded by a band of fierce-looking fellows with drawn sabres; at the same time he himself came forward, and exhibiting a couple of gold mohurs for each guest, operated so powerfully at once upon their fears and their avarice, that they consented to eat, and were, with their whole families, for ever deprived of *caste* from that moment. Their number, however, was so great, that they immediately determined upon taking a decisive step and boldly supporting each other in maintaining their claims to all the privileges of Brahmuns, a rank which they still retain, with the distinguishing affix, however, of *Boolhun Sues*. They intermarry only amongst each other, no other Brahmuns deigning to have any communication with them, and are held in contempt by all the Hindoos of that part of the country. Raja Bawanee Purshad and his two brothers retained their original *caste*, by separating themselves from their father's family upon learning this

P 2

scandalous transaction, and ever after refusing to communicate with him.

The grand festival of the *Dusera* took place on the 18th, which is always observed among the Mahrattas with particular magnificence. It is the commemoration of the victory gained by *Ram Chundur* over the giant *Rawun* in the island of Ceylon, and is properly called *Beeja dusumee:* the true *Dusera* occurring in the month of *Jeet,h*, and being reckoned the commencement, as the *Beeja dusumee* is the conclusion, of the rainy season. At this period the Indian armies are accustomed to take the field; and accordingly warriors of all castes and descriptions are to be seen busily employed throughout the preceding day in bathing their horses, polishing their arms, and preparing new trappings for the exhibition of the following morning, when every one prides himself in displaying as much magnificence as he can. The battalions and the park were under arms soon after daybreak, and formed upon a plain adjoining the camp; the first brigade (or the *Bura Campoo*, as it is called) on the right, a battery of twelve guns in the centre; then the battalions of Baptiste's brigade, and on their left the corps of *Aleegols*, blazing with the tricoloured banners of France, which I noticed in a former letter.[1] The *amende honorable* was offered, however, to our British feelings on the present occasion most satisfactorily, by each company of the regular battalions displaying a standard on which an imitation of the English union was most carefully portrayed. There is not, I am convinced, an individual in camp aware of the folly or impropriety of displaying either of these flags. The regulars' corps have drums and fifes, both made in camp, on which they play French and English tunes in very good style. But the *Aleegols*, who despise any approach to discipline or regularity, were attended by a band of Indian drums and trumpets, on which they performed their own execrable

[1] *See* page 50.

music, occasionally interrupted by loud shouts to God and the Prophet, uttered in grand chorus by the whole corps.

Although the line was formed at so early an hour, the Muha Raj did not make his appearance till past three o'clock in the afternoon. He was preceded by the *Juree Putkee* and his own standard, both borne on elephants, kettle-drums, bands of Indian music, and a countless host of spearmen and flag-bearers, and was attended by all the Surdars in camp, and the whole of the cavalry now present with the army. The latter made a street as he advanced along the line by galloping up, and forming, in single ranks, in front of the infantry; while the men of his own *Paegas*, or body-guards, kept prancing about, and manœuvring their horses in every direction over the plain. The whole exhibited a most splendid and striking spectacle. Some paces in front of the centre a branch of a tree was planted, to which the procession advanced; and when the Muha Raj alighted from his palankeen, the *Pundits* in attendance commenced the Pooja, or sacrifice, by pouring milk and curds upon the branches, and smearing over the leaves with wetted rice. The Muha Raj himself then struck off a branch with his sword, which was the signal for several jays, kept in readiness for the occasion, being let loose, *Ram Chundur*, when he set out upon his expedition to *Lunka*, having observed one of these birds on his right hand and hailed it as a propitious omen. To behold a jay flying at the festival of the *Dusera* is still reckoned fortunate by the Hindoos. The youths of all classes range the fields in groups for this purpose; and if they chance to see a jay upon a bush, throw stones at it, to make it fly, taking care, however, not to strike or otherwise to injure the bird. The common people firmly believe that all the jays in the country purposely conceal themselves on this important day. When the flight of the jays was discovered, the music struck up, the cannon were discharged, the horsemen fired off their matchlocks, and the crowd rushed towards a field of grain, preserved for the purpose, which they quickly demolished, every individual returning home triumphant with a handful of the spoil. This concluding part of the ceremony is peculiar to the *Mahrattas*; and is designed, aptly enough, to remind them at once of their origin and their profession. After the salute was fired, Seendhiya mounted an elephant, superbly caparisoned with massive silver chains about his legs, neck, and tusks, and returned down the line, which then wheeled into divisions and marched off to their respective camps. Baptiste's brigade was on this occasion commanded by his son, a lad about fourteen years of age, very short and thick, and so fat that he seemed to move with difficulty, and who, being dignified with the title of Major, appeared in an old-fashioned English uniform, a cocked hat with the flaps down, jockey boots, and a pig-tail. Under him was an European who had been formerly a sergeant in the Company's army, and who gave the word of command. The whole of the road from the parade to the Muha Raj's tents was lined, on either side, with stages covered with fireworks, which, it being nearly dusk when the procession returned, were let off as the Prince advanced; they exhibited, however, nothing either very brilliant or novel. Appakandra, whom I have before mentioned as one of the Muha Raj's prime favourites, was placed behind him in the seat called *Kuwash*, and fanned his master with a *chuonree*, a kind of fan made of cow's tails.[1] To be so distinguished is esteemed in India a mark of the highest trust and honour.

It is usual at the *Dusera* for the Muha Raj to send *Khiluts* to the principal Surdars in camp, and he, in return, receives *Nuzurs*, or offerings, from all those employed about the *Deooree* and in the public offices. When a great man touches a *Nuzur*, but declines taking it, it is sometimes usual for the person who presents it to enclose it, if money, in his fist, and, waving his hand three times round

[1] These fly-flappers are made of the bushy tails of the Tibetan yak. Chowries were usually called "cow-tails" by Anglo-Indians in the last century.

the head of him to whom it was offered, to give it to the servants in attendance; this is called *Warna* by the Moohumedans, and *Nichuor* by the Hindoos.

The nights and mornings are become cool and pleasant, and the labours of the field have commenced, though the days are still very hot. The thermometer yesterday at sunrise was at 55, at noon 84, at sunset 78, and at bedtime 67. The villagers, assured of not being disturbed in their labours, have been for a fortnight past busily employed upon their farms, and it has afforded us no small degree of pleasure to watch their agricultural economy. Three weeks have not elapsed since the *Kureef*[1] crop, which consists of *Bajru*, *Jooar*,[2] several smaller kinds of grain, and cotton, was cleared from off the fields, and the same ground is already ploughed, up to the very ropes of our tents, and sown for the great *Rubbee* crop of wheat, barley, and chunu.[3] They use a drill plough, which, like all their other implements, and operations in husbandry, is exceedingly simple. The drill part consists of a piece of bamboo, about two feet long, split and widened at one end, where it is covered with leather, so as to resemble a funnel, and which is fixed behind the main stick of the plough. In this wide part the driver keeps his left hand, filled with grain, with which he at the same time steadies the plough; while in the right hand he holds the reins of rope and a long stick, with which he guides the bullocks that draw it. One man only is required for each plough, and one pair of bullocks; the man will work throughout the day, but the bullocks must be relieved at noon. In this simple manner the ridges are turned very regularly, and the grain sown

[1] The *kharif* crops are those sown at the commencement of the rains in June, and ripening in autumn. For the spring harvest or *rabi*, the seed is sown in September or October, at the close of the periodical rains.

[2] The well-known joár, great millet, or Guinea corn, *sorghum vulgare*, Pers.

[3] Familiar to all Anglo-Indians as gram, the food of horses all over India; botanically, *Cicer arietinum*, L.

pretty equally. When the field is thus ploughed and sown, it is gone over by a rude kind of harrow, called *muee*, consisting only of a large, heavy log, upon which two men sit, and which is commonly dragged by four bullocks, serving both to break the large clods and to cover up the grain. When the farmer has completed this part of his work, he goes over his fields once more, collecting the large lumps of earth in ridges with rakes, exactly similar to those used in England, for the purpose of irrigation. This last operation takes place when the corn has been about a month above the ground; and the water is drawn from wells or reservoirs dug at the sides of rivers, by chain-pumps, whose machinery is equally rude, simple and efficacious. When the crop is ripe, it is cut with hooks, and carried to the village, where it is piled in large stacks. A space is then cleared for a threshing floor, on which the grain is trodden out by bullocks muzzled, and afterwards winnowed by the simple operation of pouring it out before the wind. The farmers of these provinces appear to be far less slovenly than in most other parts of India, but their toils are not rewarded by so rich a crop, owing probably to the quantity of saltpetre with which the soil is everywhere strongly impregnated.

LETTER XXVII

Violent disturbances in the battalions—European officers turned out of camp—Character of the Sipahees—Difference of the two brigades—Seendhiya visits Nimalkur—Naming of the Muha Raj's child—Ceremonies upon the occasion—The Buhora moves out of camp—Muster of the cavalry taken—Offers of aid to the Muha Raj—Shikarees—Productions of Mewar—The Ramzan—Eras observed by the Mahrattas—Khueratun.

CAMP AT ROOPAHELEE, *November* 2.

THERE have been serious disturbances in the battalions of Baptiste's brigade since I last wrote to you. On the evening of the 23rd ultimo they proceeded, with their guns, in a tumultuous manner to the great camp, and drew up opposite to the *Deooree*, declaring that they were come only to demand their due; and that they would not depart without obtaining it. The Durbar was thrown into the greatest confusion, and an order sent for some Mahratta troops to get under arms immediately. Before these could arrive, however, Seendhiya himself had come out, and, by dint of promises and many soothing expressions, prevailed upon the mutineers, after they had stated their grievances, to return to their own camp. They complained in general terms of the shameful detention of their arrears; of the tyrannical treatment they experienced from Baptiste, under whose command they declared they would no longer serve; of the preference shown in every instance to Jacob's brigade, of the Muha Raj not having gone down their line, or even received their salute at the *Dusera*; and concluded by requesting that he would pay up their arrears, take back their guns and accoutrements, and discharge them at once from his service. To all these remonstrances the Muha Raj replied by the promise of an immediate distribution of a lakh of rupees, and the removal of Baptiste from the command of the brigade; by which temporising policy he got rid of their importunities for the moment, though, as the money is not yet paid, the spirit of mutiny still exists in the corps. Baptiste has besides been offended, and has warmly remonstrated against any diminution of his power, and Seendhiya in reply has assured him that the measure is merely one of a temporary nature, dictated by necessity, as the only means of keeping the men in any kind of order; and that, as soon as their minds are tranquillised, he should be reinstated in his command. The outrages of the Sipahees were carried to the utmost pitch; they seized and confined the whole of their officers, flogged a great number of them, including some unfortunate Europeans, put gun-locks on the ears of others, and the next day fairly turned out of camp all the Europeans (*Topee-Walas* or *men-with-hats*, as they are called) who were attached to the battalions. More than forty of these poor fellows, Europeans, native Portuguese, Armenians, and half-castes, of all ranks and descriptions, are now wandering about the army in a state of the utmost wretchedness and want. In vain they applied for redress to the Muha Raj, who not only positively refused to listen to them, or afford them the slightest assistance, but ordered them to quit camp within three days; rejoicing in so easily getting quit of their claims for large arrears of pay that are due to them. One of these unfortunate men, an Englishman of the name of Fosset, wrote to me the day after this happened, representing his case, and entreating me to send him some trifle, however small, to enable him to return to the Company's provinces, declaring that he had not a rupee in his pocket, and that even his tent, his horse, and all his property had been plundered by the scoundrels who drove him from their head quarters with ignominy and insult.

Returning from a ride a few evenings ago, I passed along in front of the camp of the mutineers, but on the opposite side of the river; in a moment a number of them ran down to the bank, calling out to me to move off, and accompanying this injunction with all the gross and horrible abuse that the Hindoostanee language is so fertile in, and which they continued to pour upon me till I was fairly out of hearing. These men are certainly the very worst of their kind; they have become callous by bad habits, and hardy by indulgence. Perhaps their peculiar situation may be some palliation of their insolence and mutinous spirit; but they are nevertheless the same sort of men who compose our armies, they come from the very same towns and villages, and they belong to that class of "*poor innocent oppressed natives*" for whom your European philanthropists have taken such pains to excite the indignation of honest John Bull against some of the greatest and wisest statesmen that ever administered the affairs of England.

In justice, however, to the Hindoo character, I must repeat, that where they are well treated, no people on the face of the earth are more obedient, or are more easily governed. This is even here exemplified in the difference of behaviour between the Sipahees of the two regular brigades, those of Jacob being rarely guilty of any disturbances or excess, whilst those of Baptiste are as seldom out of a state of absolute mutiny; a difference attributable chiefly to the different modes in which they are paid—Jacob holding certain lands in *Jaedad* for the payment of his corps, while Baptiste is entirely dependent on the Sirkar, and obliged to have frequent recourse to *D,hurna*, mutiny, and other Mahratta expedients to extort the smallest portion of the dues of himself and his troops.

It is always at a time when these kinds of vexations occur that the Surdars prefer suits calculated to embarrass the Muha Raj. Nimulkur has accordingly demanded payment of a part, at least, of the large debt due to him from the Sirkar, amounting to upwards of ten lakhs of rupees.

Seendhiya, as usual, had recourse to coaxing and promises of a speedy settlement, and among other things intimated his intention of honouring him by a visit. The visit accordingly took place, at which he was presented with a string of pearls, and a *sirpech*, or ornament of jewelry for the head, sent by the Muha Raj himself, the price of which is to be deducted from the general account.

The sex of the Muha Raj's child is at length placed beyond dispute, and he has still to hope for the birth of an heir. On the evening of the 29th ultimo a salute was fired upon the naming of the infant, who is called Kistna Baee Saoon Baee. Her mother received the compliments of the wives of all the principal Surdars in camp upon the occasion. A grand *Pooja*, or sacrifice, was made, and alms and a good dinner distributed among the Brahmuns; after which the ladies were entertained with a *Nach*. The Mamma, and other chiefs of the highest rank, sent *Khiluts* to the Muha Raj, and presents of fine *Sarees* and *Choolees* to each of the Baees; the inferior Surdars presented only *Nuzurs* to the Muha Raj. The mode in which this part of the transaction was managed is highly characteristic of the delicacy and good management of this court: each individual went to the keeper of the *Tosha-Khanu*, or wardrobe, and desiring him to write down so many rupees, according to his means and rank, received, from the Muha Raj's own stores, the necessary pieces of cloth, &c., which were then presented, in his name, to the Prince himself.

The *Buhora* has at length received his audience of leave, and has moved his tents a short way out of the camp, though I believe he has not actually marched away, it being contrary to etiquette to remain within the precincts of the camp after having taken leave. The terms on which his departure has been permitted are, security having been given for the payment of five lakhs within a month after the Wukeel himself shall have reached Jypoor, the remaining two and a half lakhs having, as I before stated, been allowed for the ravages committed by the army, and the contributions levied by Bapoo Seendhiya. Previous to his taking leave, the Buhora had the modesty to make an application, a fruitless one—of course—for the restitution of Soopoor to his master.

The Muha Raj has since been employed in taking a muster of his troops, the terms having with much difficulty been agreed upon between them. For this purpose a set of tents are pitched at some distance from the camp, whither each *Risalu* is summoned in its turn, and immediately surrounded by the Prince's guards, to prevent any strange horses from being introduced and palmed upon the muster-master. Seendhiya superintends in person, and sees the marks, &c. of the different horses entered in a book, to guard as much as possible against imposition. He had a long contest with the *Risaludars* respecting the particular kind of muster to be taken, but at length the distressing want of money, together with a promise from the Muha Raj to be as lenient and fair in his proceedings as possible, induced them to yield the matter and agree to the muster proposed, which is nevertheless not conducted without many impositions on one side, and as glaring injustice on the other.

Raja Bawanee Purshad has, we have learned, taken refuge in the camp of Moohumed Shah Khan, the commander of a strong brigade of disciplined Sipahees now in the service of the Raja of Juodpoor. The Khans, who, as you may remember, were turned out of camp at Jajgurh, are at the same place, but have written to the Muha Raj, stating that their quarrel was with Surjee Rao only, and that, as they always considered themselves attached to his service, they were ready, on the promise of honourable treatment, to return to his camp whenever he chose to summon them. The Soobudar of Mewar has also written that he has four thousand fighting men and thirty guns with him, and has entered into a negotiation with Heera Sing,h, the commandant of another brigade at Juodpoor, whom he expects to bring over to Seendhiya's service.

Even Meer Khan has tendered a portion of his troops to be employed by Seendhiya, upon a *Jaedad* being appropriated for their subsistence. All this is calculated to operate on the fears of the Raja of Juodpoor, with whose Wukeels conferences are still carried on, and whom they yet hope to induce to pay a handsome sum, without coming to extremities.

Among the number of poor people in this camp, there is one class who earn a livelihood by catching and selling game, for which purpose they make use of match-locks, nets, and snares; the last are made to fold up like screens, with a noose of horse-hair in each fold, and are used to catch partridges, quails, hares, and rock-pigeons. Deer and bustards are driven into nets, or shot with balls; the huntsmen, who are called *Shikarees*, using frames covered with grass[1] or boughs, and sometimes bullocks well trained to the sport, behind which they creep along till they are near enough to make sure of their aim. These men have had constant employment since the army has been in this part of the country, which is as productive of almost every kind of game as it is of the mineral and most valuable vegetable productions of nature. Of the crops I have already sent you an account, and have only now to add that in several parts of *Mewar* there are rich mines of copper, tin, and lead, and some quarries of tolerably fine marble. The soil is everywhere strongly impregnated with saltpetre, so much so, that out of ten or twelve wells which have been dug within our lines the water in many is very salt, while that in others, not ten yards distant, is perfectly sweet. The water of the river has also become brackish since the rains have ceased.

It is now the month of *Ramzan*, during which the Moosulmans observe a strict fast throughout the day, abstaining even from smoking their *hooqqus*, and drinking cold water: after sunset, however, they are allowed to eat

[1] *See* the illustration, from an Indian painting, of "The Emperor Akbar Deer-stalking," 183, Vol. III. *Constable's Oriental Miscellany.*

what they please. Devotees pass the greater part of the night in meditation and prayer. Some are even to be found who have learned by heart the whole of the *Qoran*, and, during the *Ramzan*, repeat it every night from beginning to end, between the hours of sunset and sunrise. Such persons are distinguished by the appellation of *Hafiz* , and I have been assured that it is not uncommon to see them, at the completion of their task, sink to the ground exhausted by so great an exertion. Every Moosulman is exhorted to keep this fast, but it is allowable to break it, or even to put it off to another month, in case of sickness or any great and emergent difficulty. Should any one, however, break his fast unnecessarily, the prescribed expiation, for a single day, is to observe a strict fast for two months, and give a good and full meal to sixty poor people, or to emancipate a slave. Fasting and prayer are the two indispensable duties of a good Moslem ; if a man breaks the fast he is accounted a sinner, but if he never keeps it, he is reckoned a *Kafir* or infidel : at the risk even of such an implication, however, there are many among the lower order of Moosulmans in India who do not keep the fast of Ramzan. Among the numerous Moohumedan customs which have attained prevalence with the Mahrattas, one of the most extraordinary is the era they make use of in their public records :[1] it is an Arabic one, and is styled *Alf-o-meeatuen-o-ashr*, or 1210. The names of the months are the same as those of the Hijru, or common Moohumedan era, and the year, as in that, commences with the month of Moohurum, but in reckoning they always retain the twelve hundred, and return again to *one* after the completion of every decade. I have endeavoured to obtain some further information respecting this era from different Pundits, and other ranks of Mahrattas, but my inquiries have produced nothing more than that it was probably adopted from some of the Moohumedan sovereignties

[1] For an account of the Shahúr or *Soor* era of Maháráshtra, see pp. 171–172 Prinsep's *Useful Tables*, edited by Thomas, Lond. 1858.

which formerly flourished in the Duk,hun: the generality of those to whom I applied appearing quite ignorant even of the meaning of the words by which the era is designated. They are equally ignorant of a number of Arabic words, to which they have given Mahratta terminations, and which they constantly use in the introductory compliments of their letters. On common occasions, however, the Mahrattas use the Hindoo eras of *Virkurmajeet*[1] and *Shuhaliwan*,[2] the former prevailing to the northward, and the latter to the southward of the Nuhrbudda; while among the tribes in the neighbourhood of *Arungabad*, the Moohumedan era called *Fuesulee*[3] is generally adopted.

We celebrated the glorious 21st of October,[4] as usual, with a *Nach*, when I had, at length, the pleasure of seeing the celebrated Khuerutun. I was, however, somewhat disappointed at beholding a woman of at least forty years of age, and without any pretensions to beauty, though possessed of a good countenance and fine expressive eyes. She is only now recovering from a fever, and was in consequence able to sing but two songs. These, however, she executed with a degree of taste and feeling far beyond what is generally met with in Indian singers: her voice is rather soft than powerful, but she has a perfect command over it, and seldom raises it beyond its compass. She was dressed very richly and was attended by a number of people, whom she says she is obliged to keep constantly about her to protect her from the violent attempts of her husband; he having declared his resolution to put her

[1] This era is said to have been established by Vikramâditya, a king of Ujain, to commemorate his victory over the Sakas. It is reckoned from the vernal equinox of the year 57 B.C.—*Cunningham*.

[2] The year 1 of the era Sâka Sâlivâhana begins with the vernal equinox of Kâli Yuga 3180, or A.D. 79.—*Cunningham*.

[3] There are various Faslí, or harvest, eras derived from the Hejira of the Moslems. The one here referred to is that which was established by Sháh Jahán for the Deccan in 1636 A.D.

[4] The anniversary of the battle of Trafalgar, fought in 1805.

little daughter to death, if he can effect it, to save her from the infamy of being hereafter prostituted. The child, who is about eight years old, accompanied her mother, who assured me it was by no means her wish to bring her up to her own *profession*.

LETTER XXVIII

The Muha Raj's birth-day—The Buhora marches from camp—The Teeka—The Baee completes her purification—Anajee writes to Seendhiya—Disturbances near Oojyn—Troops go over to Holkar—Defeat of the expedition against Rutlam—Baptiste's intrigues at the Durbar—Grand D,hurna—Mode of torturing among the Mahrattas—The Mamma's distress—Ajmeer given to Bapoo Seendhiya's brother—The Diwalee.

CAMP AT ROOPAHELEE, *November* 15.

THE 5th instant was the anniversary of the Muha Raj's birth, on which he completed his thirty-second year. Upon this occasion, he gave a grand entertainment to the Brahmuns, and distributed a quantity of clothes and money among them. He also presented the head *Nujoomee*, or astrologer, with a fine pair of shawls and a turban, and, when these religious duties were performed, he and his friends retired to the *Deooree*, to partake of the more congenial festivities of a Nach. The same day had been pitched upon, as a lucky one for the departure of the Buhora, who accordingly marched a few miles, leaving two persons of his suite in the camp, to receive the *Teeka* from the Muha Raj, and convey it to the tents of the Ambassador. This is the term for a *Khilut*, presented by friendly powers to any Prince upon his accession to the *Musnud*, and is regarded as an acknowledgment of his rights. It has hitherto been withheld, upon various frivolous pretences, by Seendhiya, who promised, however, that he would, upon the Buhora's taking leave, send it to the Raja under his care. The demand of these two Wukeels was again evaded, and an offer made of half the customary presents, which was of course rejected on their part. This fresh discussion has stayed the march of Koosallee Ram towards Jypoor, and will very probably retard it for some weeks, though his master is so anxious for his return to the capital, that he has stationed relays of *Ruths*, or carriages drawn by camels to expedite his progress. The old Minister, however, has declined pursuing his journey without the *Teeka*, and has written accordingly to the Muha Raj upon the subject. *Ruths* of various kinds are in common use among the Rajpoots, but those drawn by camels are, as far as I have been able to learn, peculiar to them.

On the 11th the Baee completed her purification, by bathing for the third time in the river; the sixth, twentieth, and fortieth days after the birth of the child being those appropriated for this ceremony. A large suite of tents was pitched on the bank of the river for her accommodation, and a numerous retinue posted around, to prevent any intruder from violating the purity of the rites.

Old Anajee, who is now at Oojyn, and with whom a correspondence has for some time been kept up by the reigning favourites, has written to inform the Muha Raj of overtures having been made to him by Bala Ram, a leading personage in Holkar's Durbar, which he declined attending to, without permission from hence; but that they had been renewed with so much earnestness, as to induce him to accede to a personal and private interview with that Minister, who had made communications to him of such a nature and importance, that he deemed it advisable to despatch a confidential friend to camp, for the purpose of laying them before the Muha Raj himself. He adds, that it is his intention to follow his messenger in a few days.

The neighbourhood of Oojyn has lately been the scene of continued riot and disturbance. Muena Baee, the mother of the Muha Raj, who now resides there, and exercises a kind of sovereignty over the city, had insisted upon a man named Sambajee Ingria, with his riotous and turbulent followers, quitting the place; an order with which he thought it prudent to comply, but which he took so ill, that he intrigued with a large body of Pindaras in the neighbourhood, and induced them to ravage the whole country around, with the expectation of being himself recalled to suppress them.

All the personal troops of Surjee Rao, who since they quitted camp have remained in the vicinity of Oojyn, and even some of those under the command of Bapoo Seendhiya, have gone over to Holkar's army. Bapoo Seendhiya has also experienced a severe mortification, in the defeat of a detachment sent against the fort at Rutlam, a town and district in the western parts of the Muha Raj's hereditary states, and the Zumeendar of which was in open rebellion against his authority. The garrison sallied out during the night, and completely defeated the troops sent against them, with the loss of more than half their numbers, and all their guns.

Of the views and intentions entertained by Holkar's Durbar and Meer Khan, various conjectures are formed; the latter is become an object of peculiar interest and curiosity here, as well as at all the other courts of the Duk,hun. It is well known that he has assembled an immense army, and report adds, that he has crossed to the southward of the Nuhrbudda. Should his designs be against the Nagpoor territories, it is not improbable that the British government will be induced to interfere for their preservation.

Baptiste has been exerting all his influence to be reinstated in the command of those battalions of which he has been deprived, and has offered to divide twenty-five thousand rupees among the principal people of the Durbar, if he should succeed in his endeavours: he has also pledged himself, in that case, to put Subbulgurh into the hands of the Muha Raj, a strong fortress attached to the Soobuship of Nurwur, which Kundoojee does not seem inclined to give up the possession of.

There has been a grand *D,hurna* since I wrote last,

though it was not of long continuance. The dispute, as usual, was respecting the settlement of accounts, and all the Risaludars joined in supporting it; a monthly subsistence of thirty rupees per man to the Hindoostanees, and of fifteen to the Duk,hunees, was offered by Seendhiya, and refused; the claimants, with one accord, declaring their resolution to be blown away from guns, rather than compromise, what they termed, their just rights. These heroic resolves, however, were, as usual, overcome by a little patience, and a great many fair promises. The reason of a larger sum being offered to the Hindoostanees than to the Mahrattas, is, that the latter are supposed to reap some advantage from plunder, and the former not.

An old and faithful servant of Bala Rao, who went to Jypoor during the late negociations, and was suspected of having secured something handsome for himself while at that court, has been kept in confinement ever since the death of Surjee Rao; the counsellors of the Durbar hoping, by a little rigour, to extort some money from him. His courage, however, has remained hitherto unshaken, and he submitted a few days ago to four hours' torture, without yielding to the demands made upon him. The mode of compelling acquiescence, which is commonly had recourse to here, is to tie a quantity of cotton well oiled upon every finger of the person questioned, and having set fire to these living flambeaux, to let them burn, till the sufferer's obstinacy is overcome, or he is utterly unable to endure any more. Upon this occasion the Mamma interfered, and the unfortunate wretch was delivered over to his care and custody. The Mamma's own situation does not appear to have been rendered at all more comfortable by the fair promises made of a regular payment of his stipend; he has asked permission to go to Oojyn, for the purpose of marrying his daughter, declaring that he lives here in such a state of misery and distress that he *cannot eat*. Seendhiya, as usual, soothed him by promising magnificent presents upon the celebration of the wedding, and added, by way of comfort, that as to appetite, his own was precisely in the same state, and from the very same cause.

Bapoo Seendhiya's interest has triumphed over all his opponents, and the Soobudaree of Ajmeer is at length made out in the name of his brother Gomanjee *Tantia*, who received the *Khilut* of investiture two or three days ago.

We have been celebrating the *Diwalee*, a Hindoo festival in honour of *Luchmee*, the goddess of wealth, who on this night is supposed to descend from heaven to visit the earth, where she enters into those houses, whose doors are thrown open to receive her, where the floors are clean and well swept, and where abundance of lights are exhibited to invite her entrance. No Hindoo is so poor as not to make a little illumination on the night of the *Diwalee*. For this purpose small cups of coarse earthenware are used, in which a common cotton wick is placed, with a little oil, and which are arranged, according to fancy, on slight frames of bamboo or other sticks. The illuminations in the great camp produced a very pretty effect. Gambling is allowable at the *Diwalee*, and they whose principles would deter them at any other time from approaching the gaming-table, now try their luck, in full confidence that their various merits deserve, and will probably attract, the notice of *Luchmee*. With these rational expectations such large sums are often lost, that to guard against a repetition of such inconvenience, the unfortunate losers bind themselves by oaths never to play again, which oaths are rigidly kept, till the next *Diwalee* comes, to tempt them with fresh hopes and plunge them in fresh disappointment. There are two things which, if found at the *Diwalee*, are supposed by all classes of Hindoos to make the fortune of the lucky wight who finds them: *viz.*, the flower of the *Goolur*, a tree which produces a round red fruit, but never flowers, and the soul of a snake, that animal being supposed sometimes, during this festival, to deposit his spirit under the shade of a spreading tree, and wander about the world without it.

The former wonder is, in the conversation of the better sort, the black swan of Europeans; and though no one believes that either of these treasures have ever yet been seen, yet most are certain that they actually exist, and consequently may be destined for their more fortunate selves.

LETTER XXIX

Anajee's agent arrives in camp—The affair of the Teeka settled—Visit of condolence to Bala Baee—Character of the Mewar peasantry—Seendhiya's distress for money—Intrigues with Bala Rao—Jugoo Bapoo quits camp—Takoor of Juodpoor—Marriage of Narain and Toolsee.

CAMP AT ROOPAHELEE, *November* 27.

THE confidential servant of Anajee, whom I mentioned in my last letter, has arrived in camp; he was at the Durbar a day or two ago (whither we also went to deliver a letter from the Governor-General), and appeared to take a share in the business going on, being called to the Muha Raj's right hand while the letter was read, and receiving from him particular marks of attention.

The weighty affair of the *Teeka* has been settled, and in a manner truly characteristic. After the Wukeels had repeatedly refused to receive a present less in quantity than was customary, the Muha Raj was obliged to give up the point, and ordered the *Khilut* to be sent perfect as to the number of the different articles that composed it, but counterbalancing that required perfection by a woeful deficiency in their quality. Upon its reaching the tents of the Wukeels, the elephant was found to be lame and blind, and the *Sirpech* and collar of pearls so bad, that they refused to receive them, and sent the whole present back to be changed. In reply, they were desired to proceed to Jypoor, where an officer of Seendhiya's who was to accompany the mission, should purchase such articles as would be approved of, and they have marched accordingly.

We have paid another visit of condolence since I last

wrote; it was to Bala Baee, upon the death of her only surviving child Raja Desmook,h, an event which took place on the 22nd instant. The old Princess has been thrown into the deepest affliction by this heavy stroke, which seems, indeed, to have excited the sympathy and regret of the whole army. Seendhiya and the Mamma visited her immediately upon the event being made known, and remained with her for many hours: and Bapoo Seendhiya himself superintended the arrangements for conveying the corpse to the borders of a neighbouring lake, where it was committed to the flames. Desmook,h was, as I have before mentioned, presumptive heir to the *Musnud*, and there is now no nearer male relation of the family existing than Manajee Fankra (the man who murdered Surjee Rao), and one or two others in the same degree of affinity. Our visit was paid yesterday evening; Bapoo Seendhiya received us and did the honours, at the request of the Baee, to whom a message was sent, intimating the arrival of the Resident, and his anxious hope that she would endeavour to mitigate her grief, and resign herself to the dispensations of Providence. Bapoo Seendhiya held forth like a philosopher, upon fate, resignation, etc., and forgot not, in describing the excess of the Baee's affliction, to add that she had eaten nothing since the death of her son.

There is a little village within musquet shot of our tents the *Putel*, or Zumeendar, of which thinks himself under great obligations to us for the protection we have afforded to his villagers and his fields. He often pays us a visit, and came the other evening in great agitation to inform us that some of his people had fallen in with a large band of *Meoos* (a hardy race of robbers who inhabit the neighbouring hills and frequently make destructive inroads upon the villages of the plains), who inquired particularly which way our foraging party was gone. The old man entreated we would send a larger guard in future with the foragers and be more careful ourselves in taking our morning and evening rides; for that these people were very daring, and often made their appearance in parties of some hundreds, consisting both of cavalry and infantry. The more I see of the peasantry of this part of the country the more I am pleased with their sincerity and simplicity of manners. This old Zumeendar is one of the most interesting men of his rank in life that I ever met with. He has a large family of children and grandchildren, and has brought them all up to be respectable members of their society. We had an opportunity of showing him attention by giving medical aid to two of his youngest grandchildren, who were dangerously ill, an attention for which he has evinced the utmost gratitude; we have also greatly pleased him by a promise of making over to him, whenever we may march from hence, a little garden, well filled with salads and other European vegetables, which we have cultivated since our arrival here and which has excited his constant admiration.

Baptiste has been strongly urging an attack upon Subbulgurh, which place, he says, he has reconnoitred, and will engage to take if the Muha Raj will send him some money and the remainder of his brigade. He adds that the Qiludar, the son of Kundoojee, has fled from the fort, in which he has left only a garrison of one thousand men. That Seendhiya should wish to take the place is very probable, but that he should send him money is all but impossible; he has lately been making bitter complaints on this head to Gokul Paruk, declaring that he is not only unable to find cash for the payment of his troops and public establishments, but that he is in distress for funds to meet the common expenses of his family and household. He has also experienced some further vexations on account of Bala Rao, to whom he had caused it to be intimated that if he would send for his wife and family to camp, the Muha Raj would feel more secure of his fidelity, and would immediately employ him in some office of trust and emolument. These conditions he refused to comply with, and soon after a letter was intercepted from his brother Kundoojee intimating his intention to defend Nurwur against Baptiste, should he be sent against it, and strongly urging Balo Rao himself to make his escape from camp, to enable him to effect which he had despatched a confidential servant accompanied by two hundred horse, with orders to hover about in the neighbourhood, and watch for an opportunity of communicating with him. The party actually came, but after waiting some time, they discovered that the Muha Raj was aware of their design, and had taken measures for defeating it: they then returned to Nurwur, and Bala Rao was put under further restraint, in the charge of the Mamma, to whose tents three companies of infantry were sent for further security.

It is generally the Muha Raj's fate to be deserted in his greatest difficulties by some of the principal people of his army: Jugoo Bapoo, a Surdar of considerable rank and influence, left camp a few days ago, and a deputation was, as usual, sent to induce him to return, empowered to offer him bills for twenty-five thousand rupees. He rejected their offers, declaring, however, that he was willing to return to the Muha Raj's service if he would either assign him a separate jagheer or specify any fixed number of troops to be raised by him, whose pay should be settled by an account separate from his own, but that he would never go back so long as the present system of things existed, under which both he and his followers had been starved and ruined. He has hitherto kept firmly to this resolution, and is said to be actually on his march to the southward.

We have at present an illustrious guest in our camp, a Takoor of Juodpoor of high rank, who accompanied the Wukeels of that state, and has taken up his quarters with us, in the hope of being cured of a lingering and painful disease. His tents are directly opposite to mine, and ever since his arrival I have been kept awake for some hours of the night by a band of singers, whom he retains in his service to amuse him during the long periods when he is unable to sleep, the consequence equally of the pain he suffers and the quantity of opium which he takes to alleviate it.

A general salute was fired three days ago by all the artillery and regular infantry in the army in honour of a Hindoo festival, commemorative of the marriage of *Narain* and *Toolsee*, one of the most fanciful of the Hindoo legends, some account of which will perhaps amuse you. At the time when the *Deotas* and *Rachuses*, the good and evil spirits, were waging perpetual war against each other, there was among the latter one named *Jalindur*, whose prowess was so great that he had nearly succeeded in usurping the power of the *Deotas*. These in a body represented their situation at the throne of *Vishnoo*, who bid them be of good cheer and continue the conflict, and he would support them. Accordingly he entered the lists on their side, and for twenty-two successive days made tremendous efforts to secure a victory. All was, however, in vain: his arrows fell powerless when aimed at *Jalindur*, and the cause of the *Deotas* was at least not advanced. Astounded at his want of success, *Vishnoo* reflected, and at length discovered that *Jalindur* was rendered invulnerable by the virtues of his wife *Bindha*, one of the best and most zealous of his own votaries, and whose purity, while it remained unsullied, would for ever preserve her husband from all the efforts of his enemies. Upon this discovery, *Vishnoo* assumed the form of *Jalindur*, and appearing before the couch of *Bindha*, prevailed upon her, after suffering the keenest taunts and upbraidings for quitting the battle to indulge his own passions, to grant him the rights of a husband. He had scarcely risen from the bed, however, when news was brought to *Bindha* that her husband was mortally wounded. Shocked at the intelligence, she flew to the field of battle, and had just time to learn from the lips of *Jalindur* that she had been imposed upon, before he expired. The afflicted *Bindha*, snatching up some water in the palm of her hand, was about to cast it upon the earth and imprecate a bitter curse on whomsoever had thus cruelly deceived her, when *Vishnoo* in his own form appeared before her and stayed her hand, declaring himself the offender, and assuring her that what he had done was the only means of insuring victory to the *Deotas*, he added that he was so well satisfied with her piety and constancy that he would grant whatever request she chose to make. *Bindha* fell at his feet, and declared that her only wish was to burn as a *Suttee*[1] with her beloved *Jalindur*. The astonished deity raised her from the earth, and acceded to her request, but desired that she would add something to this pious demand, which should be more agreeable for him to grant. She then petitioned that when her present period of existence should terminate, she might assume some form, in which he himself would bear her upon his head, as *Seeva* did the Ganges. *Vishnoo* listened with astonishment, and told her that this request should also be complied with, but that its accomplishment must be deferred till the period of the *Kuljoog* (the present age), when he himself should appear on earth, in the stone *Salikram*, and she in the form of the plant *Toolsee*. Accordingly some leaves of the *Toolsee*, or sweet basil, are always placed on the *Salikram*[2] in all *poojas*, and in the month of *Katik*, in which the battle of the Deotas took place, it is usual to solemnize marriages between the sacred stone and the plant, which are conducted with all the splendour and formality of real weddings. They are seldom made but by those who can afford to expend large sums of money upon the occasion, he who proclaims the marriage considering the *Toolsee* as his daughter, and taking the same pains to regulate the various nuptial ceremonies as if she stood really to him in that relationship.

[1] Suttee is the term applied to those widows who burn themselves on the funeral pile of their husbands. B.

[2] Usually an ammonite.

LETTER XXX

March from Roopahelee—Opposition by the troops—Bala Qadir—Moohumedan Fuqeers—Designs upon the Raja of Shahpoora—Flocks of wild-fowl—Bapoo Seendhiya's domestic afflictions—Ceremonies of the Kiria Kurum—The Muha Raj's attentions to Anajee—Bala Chobdar—Battle between Meer Khan and the B,honslah—Pleasant weather.

CAMP ON THE TINEL, *December* 13.

WE have at length quitted *Roopahelee*, and are once more encamped on the banks of this river, near the spot we occupied in June last, and about eight miles from Shahpoora. We did not leave our old ground without regret; not merely on account of the vexations and trouble which always attend a march after a long halt, but because we had really enjoyed ourselves during our continuance upon it very much. Both the country and the climate were pleasant; there were many good rides in the vicinity of the camp, plenty of game, and the inhabitants of the neighbouring villages were peaceable and civil, advantages which we cannot hope to enjoy where we now are. We marched on the 10th, but not without much opposition being made on the part of the Surdars and the troops. Upon the report of this intended movement, the Silahdars[1] assembled, and sent intimation to Moroba Hurree, the agent of Anajee, who is now looked upon as a man established in power, that they were resolved not to stir, unless their accounts should be previously settled. He was directed by the

[1] *Silahdar* is the term used to denote [horsemen who furnish their own horses and arms. They who ride the horses of the Prince, or Commander of a corps, are called *Balgeers*. B.

Muha Raj to offer them thirty rupees per horse, according to the actual strength of the several corps; but this, as usual, was refused, and, as usual, other means were had recourse to, to keep them quiet.

The *Jinsee* was accordingly sent forward on the 7th, and the whole army followed on the 10th, except the battalions of Baptiste's brigade, who went in a body the preceding evening to the Deooree, protesting that they would not march from that ground till something was done for them in the way of settlement. Seendhiya told them that part of his baggage was to be left behind, from a want of carriage, and that they might stay to guard it, and escort it on the following morning to the new ground, when they might depend upon his listening to their complaints and settling their accounts. The Mamma and Bala Qadir both requested leave to quit the army and proceed directly towards Oojyn, instead of following the Muha Raj to his new encampment, but were both refused, with assurances, however, of their wishes being taken into consideration at the next ground. Bala Qadir, a Moohumedan Fuqeer, is the grandson of Munsoor Shah, who became the chief favourite and companion of Madoojee Seendhiya, in consequence of having predicted his future greatness, at a time when there were certainly no rational grounds for such a prophecy. He is the acknowledged *Peer*, or spiritual guide, of the Muha Raj, and is always treated by him with the utmost respect and attention. Seendhiya prostrates himself at his feet every morning before he performs the ablutions prescribed by his own religion, and, in the midst of all his distresses, can always find a supply of money for the use of his pious favourite. He has settled on him a considerable jageer in the *Duk,hun*, and lately presented him with twenty thousand rupees, to defray his expenses on a journey which he is about to make to that part of the country. At the *Oorus*, or funeral assembly, held in honour of Munsoor Shah, on the anniversary of his death, all the Surdars and principal people in the army make considerable presents to

Bala Qadir. The Muha Raj's favour, however, is by no means confined to him. All Moohumedan Fuqeers are well received and protected at his court, and many are supported in a state of comfort and even of affluence. One is retained for the sole purpose of proclaiming a march throughout the camp the evening before it takes place, to whom, if it should happen to be countermanded after such intimation has been given, the Muha Raj forfeits five rupees. It is common here to say, not that there will be a march to-morrow, but there will be the Fuqeer this evening.

The avowed object of this movement is to bring the Shahpoora Raja to better terms, who, it seems, has not yet fulfilled the engagements entered into with Surjee Rao. As he was besides the known bosom friend of that Minister, with whom he had gone through the ceremony of exchanging turbans (the strongest bond of eternal friendship), the Muha Raj's advisers have wisely concluded that his interest was too much attended to in the arrangement; and hope, by a little management, to bring him to a more favourable settlement. With a view to this, the *Jinsee* was at first directed to proceed immediately to the town, and open a brisk fire upon it; but Moroba Hurree, whose influence seems to be established at the Durbar, represented that it might, perhaps, be as well to try first what could be effected by fair means with the Wukeels, who had been sent by the Raja for the purpose of negotiating, and who were actually arrived in camp.

Our route lay again over the extensive plain which we passed over in June. At that time it had the appearance of a perfect desert, but was now covered with a thick crop of fine grass upwards of two feet in height. The baggage passed near some extensive lakes, covered with innumerable flocks of wild-fowl of various kinds, which, when alarmed and on the wing, resembled, at a distance, so many dark clouds floating on the horizon. Without having witnessed them, it would be scarcely possible to conceive the numbers and variety of these birds that are to be found in every province of this part of India.

Bapoo Seendhiya's philosophy was called upon, before we quitted Roopahelee, to enable him to put in practice all the fine sentences he so ably dealt forth at the tents of the Bala Baee. About a fortnight ago he received intimation of his wife's death, and, at the same time, that his father, who had selected another for him among the daughters of the Duk,hunee chiefs, was proceeding with his young charge to camp; but on the day before we marched, fresh news was brought that the intended bride had also been taken suddenly ill upon the road, and had, like her predecessor, paid the common debt of nature.

On the first instant, which was the tenth day from the death of Raja Desmookh, the funeral ceremonies, called *Kiria Kurum*, took place. It is customary, when a body is burned, for the nearest relation of the deceased to set fire to the funeral pile, after which he remains impure for ten days, if his relation were a male, but for nine only if a female. During this period he withdraws from society; bakes his own bread, and eats it at a distance from his own house or tent; sleeps upon the ground; suffers no one to touch him; and, in short, holds no communication with any one, except the Brahmun who accompanies him throughout the whole of the ceremony. These Brahmuns are called *Boora*, or bad Brahmuns, and form a distinct sect among themselves; it being reckoned unlawful for any other Brahmuns to eat or drink with them. On the morning subsequent to the funeral the *Boora* Brahmun suspends an earthen vessel, filled with water, from a tree—if possible, a Peepul-tree—in the neighbourhood of the pile, from which the water is allowed to drip slowly by a wick of cloth, fastened in a hole made in the bottom of the vessel. On every succeeding morning the stale water is thrown away and fresh put in by the Brahmun and him who performs the *Kiria Kurum*. On the tenth day a bed, with all its furniture, is presented to the *Boora* Brahmun, to which those who are able add a horse, an elephant, &c., according to their means, supposed to be for the use of the deceased in another life. On the same day little balls of boiled rice, called *Pind,h*, are exposed in leaves upon the open plain, which are also designed for the refreshment of the departed friend, and, after a certain time, are generally given to be eaten by cows. These officiating Brahmuns are also sometimes called *Muha*, or great, an epithet bestowed upon them by Hindoo delicacy, to avoid hurting their feelings by the offensiveness of the other appellation. The Mahrattas watch the *Pind,hs* with the utmost anxiety, in expectation of a crow descending to pick up the rice, a certain indication that the soul of the deceased has been received into heaven. The *Pind,hs* of poor Desmook,h remained throughout the whole day unhallowed by this wished-for omen. The Muha Raj and the rest of his family were thrown into the deepest affliction, and the fame of the unfortunate Raja remains, in consequence, stained with the suspicion of some great but unknown offence.

Baptiste's friends have been very urgent with Seendhiya to promote him to a higher rank, representing him as one of the greatest soldiers of the day. To which the Muha Raj replied that he had generally found these great soldiers were also very great rogues, and that the best policy was always to keep from them the possibility of rising above the power from whence they derived their greatness. To his old servant Anajee, however, who has quitted Oojyn, he writes in the most encouraging manner, inviting him to come on with as much expedition as he can conveniently use, and to rely upon a kind and favourable reception in camp. The old statesman will find a powerful rival, however, or else as powerful a friend (if he can contrive to make him such) in a man named Bala, who was but the other day a common *Chobdar*, the designation of a servant who carries a silver stick in the train of Princes and other great men. Seendhiya has lately promoted this man from such a situation to the command of one of his *Paegas*, or body-guards, and presented him with an elephant and a Palankeen, together with his permission to make use of both within the camp.

Information has been received of a battle having been fought between the armies of the *Bhonsla* and Meer Khan,[1] in which the latter was totally defeated, with the loss of his baggage, his bazars, and fourteen guns. Seendhiya has, in consequence, been advised to despatch immediately a small corps towards that quarter, lest the Nagpoor Raja should accuse him of not sending any assistance, and use that as a pretext for withholding all share of the advantages he may reap from the campaign.

We expect Mr. M——[2] soon in camp, to reassume the duties of Resident, and shall probably halt on this ground till his arrival. Our situation is agreeable enough, on the banks of a river, in which there is a clear and plentiful stream, and a great abundance of fine trout. The weather is cold and very pleasant, and we amuse ourselves in riding, shooting, and fishing throughout the day, without any fear of ill consequences from the sun.

[1] Or Amir Khan, a celebrated chief of the Pindarees, and the founder of the house of the present Nawab of Tonk. In 1817 he was confirmed in the possession of all the territories he held from the Holkar family, but was compelled to surrender his artillery to the British Government, and disband his followers who, for some years had been the scourge of Malwa and Rajputana.

[2] *See* footnote, p. 29.

LETTER XXXI

Negotiations with the Shahpoora Wukeels not concluded—Bala Rao escapes from camp—The Mamma's vexation, and message to Seendhiya—Disturbances in the first brigade—The Nuwab Moorteza Khan—Daring attack upon Puriag Das—Wretched state of the peasants—Their imprecations on the Mahrattas—Mr. M——'s arrival in camp—Ceremonies of conducting him into camp—Visit to the Durbar—Discussions respecting Khiluts—Seendhiya returns the Resident's visit—Superb barouche presented to him—His suspicions on the subject—The Ziyafut—Conclusion.

CAMP ON THE TINEL, *December* 31.

THE negotiations with the Shahpoora Wukeels are not yet brought to a conclusion, though the sum demanded, in excess to that agreed upon with Surjee Rao, is only fifteen thousand rupees, no sum being too small to be considered beneath the attention of a Mahratta court.

Bala Rao has contrived to make his escape from camp, greatly to the vexation of the Mamma, who looked to his influence and wealth as his main support in the Soobuship of the province of *Banswara*, to which he expected shortly to be nominated, but which appointment will now most probably be passed over, as the Mamma is, with respect to money, almost entirely dependent upon the bounty of his nephew. He has been loud in complaints of his salary not being paid, and even sent Wukeels to remonstrate with the Muha Raj on the subject, protesting in angry terms that his claims and interests were less attended to than those of the commonest Silahdars in the army. Seendhiya was exceedingly displeased with the bearers of this intemperate message, whose duty, he said, was to soothe, not to aggravate their master's wrath ; and added, justly enough, that when the members of his own family treated him in this manner, it was no longer to be wondered at that others took the same liberties. This rebuff, together with the flight of Bala Rao, has plunged the Mamma into great tribulation. He had left no scheme untried to get the latter completely into his power; to effect which, one of his plans is said to have been a projected marriage between his own daughter and the son of Bala Rao, an alliance not at all relished by that chief, as the Mamma is unfortunately sprung from a tribe held in utter contempt by all the Mahrattas. It was this sad deficiency of *caste* alone that prevented the lady's union with the Muha Raj himself; for when the Baee discovered that such a plan was in agitation, she fiercely upbraided her husband for his meanness, and proudly asked if it were only to plunge himself deeper in, that she had raised him from the *mud*, by an alliance with herself.

Baptiste has invested the fort of Subbulgurh, which the garrison have offered to deliver up to him, upon the payment of six months' arrears which are due to them. Seendhiya, in reply, has desired him to go on, and take the place in any manner he likes best, that he is highly pleased with his conduct, has distributed a lakh of rupees among the battalions in camp, which shall be soon restored to his brigade (though he has not in reality paid them a farthing), has presented his son with a *Khilut*, and is about to send another to himself. He is by no means so well pleased at present with the other brigade, in which, for the first time in my recollection, a very serious disturbance has been excited. It was conducted precisely according to the established forms, by seizing and confining the officers, immersing the paymaster in a pit of filthy mud, and then proceeding to the Deooree with all their guns. The suppression of this mutiny was also effected in the usual manner, by a great many fine speeches, to induce the men to return quietly to their lines, and as many positive assurances of speedy attention to their claims and rights. Upon what principle can we account for men entering into such a service, or, having once tried it, for their continuing in it?

Amidst all these vexations, which would be deemed serious evils anywhere else, Seendhiya continues to derive amusement from his usual impure resources. He has lately acquired an inexhaustible fund in the return of the Nuwab Moorteza Khan from Jypoor; a wretch who sprung from a noble family, and having been driven away from Lucknow, where he was married to a near relation of the Wuzeer's, is not ashamed to earn a precarious subsistence by filling the place of head buffoon at this profligate court, and submitting his person to the practical jokes and execrable tricks which are the glory and delight of the Prince who presides in it. This worthy associate of the Muha Raj went to Jypoor for the express purpose of marrying the daughter of a Moosulman of high rank and ancient family; and as Seendhiya was to have a strong personal interest in the wedding, he agreed to supply the funds for carrying it into execution. Moorteza Khan's character, however, had preceded him, and the hand of the lady was indignantly refused. Disappointed, but not mortified, at this repulse, he resolved to enjoy as much pleasure as Jypoor could afford him, though he had failed in his projects of securing a wife, and accordingly remained there surrounded by fiddlers, buffoons, and Nach girls, as long as the money lasted which was to have paid the expenses of his wedding.

Accounts have been received of the death of *Puriag Das*, the deputy Soobudar of Gwaliur, in consequence of wounds received two months ago from a man who rushed upon him while in the act of performing his morning ablutions, and surrounded, at a trifling distance, by his attendants, and who subsequently effected his escape undiscovered. It is conjectured, however, that the perpetrator of this daring act is the son of a Zumeendar in that province, and that revenge for some injury sustained by his father had instigated him to attempt so desperate an enterprise.

The villages around the camp are all in ruins, and in

some of them I have seen a few wretched villagers sheltered under the mud walls or broken roofs, and watching over a herd of miserable half-starved cattle. They assured me that the greatest part of the peasantry of the province had been driven to Kota or Boondee, to seek shelter from the repeated ravages of different Mahratta armies, and that of those who remained, most had perished by want and variety of misery. Their tale was truly piteous, and was accompanied with hearty curses invoked upon the whole Mahratta race, whom they justly regard as the authors of all their misery. You, my dear brother, will, I dare say, ere this, be inclined to join these poor people in detestation of a tribe whose acts I have endeavoured to make you acquainted with throughout one whole year. Unless we should go to Ajmeer, of which, by the bye, there is now some prospect, I shall, with that year, close my regular communications. To continue them would only be to go over again the same unvaried ground, to retrace the same acts of oppression and fraud, detail the same chicanery, folly, and intrigues, and to describe the same festivals and ceremonies. If I may judge of your feelings by my own, you are already heartily sick of them all, and will hail the letter that brings you the conclusion of their history, as I shall the day when I can turn my back on a people, proud and jealous as the Chinese, vain and unpolished as the Americans, and as tyrannical and perfidious as the French. Should we, however, proceed to Ajmeer, your curiosity will perhaps excuse one letter more, to convey a description of so celebrated a place.

Mr. M—— rejoined us on the 19th, to resume his charge of the Residency. We all went to meet him, and, at the distance of about a mile, were joined by Gopal Rao Buo, attended by several Surdars and a splendid retinue, who had also come for the purpose of conducting him into camp. On these occasions the parties only descend from their elephants and embrace; the Surdars on either side are introduced to the principals, who, after a few compliments have passed, and some common-place questions have been asked and answered, separate, and each returns to his own quarters.

That mixture of meanness with splendour, which is so striking a characteristic of Mahratta manners, was strongly exemplified on this occasion: many of the Surdars were mounted on elephants with silver howdahs, and covered with rich embroidered trappings; and into these magnificent carriages they mounted by the assistance of the tails of the animals and the ropes that fastened the howdahs, as if they were climbing up the side of a ship. Old Anajee arrived on the following day, but has not yet been nominated to any ostensible situation. We saw him on the afternoon of the 21st, when the Resident paid his first visit of ceremony to the Muha Raj. Seendhiya met us just beyond his own tents. He was attended by all the Surdars of the army, and followed by all the cavalry now in camp; but which I am convinced did not amount to more than three thousand men. They drew up in the form of a crescent, in the centre of which the Muha Raj quitted his Palankeen at the moment when the Resident did the same, this part of the ceremonial being regulated by the nicest punctilio. Seendhiya was superbly dressed in rich brocade, with a profusion of pearls aad emeralds about his neck and arms. After the usual ceremonies had taken place, he proceeded to his tents, and we followed at a little distance. At the Durbar nothing more than usual occurred, except, indeed, a profusion of civil speeches made to Mr. M—— on his return to camp. At taking leave *pan* and *uttur* were, as usual, distributed, and the customary *Khiluts* presented; as usual, too, the horse was lame, the elephant blind, and the shawls and other articles of the commonest description. In the evening a *Ziyafut*, or entertainment, consisting of several trays of sweetmeats, sugar, almonds, raisins, &c., and a purse containing one thousand rupees, was brought on the part of the Muha Raj, the whole of which becomes a welcome perquisite of the servants of the Residency, and the Surdar who brings it, is presented with a *Khilut* for his trouble.

After some days had been employed in discussing the important question as to what number of Khiluts should be presented to the Muha Raj's suite (in which discussion it is by no means deemed an indelicacy to dispute every inch of the way), the 27th was fixed upon for him to return the Resident's visit. Among the numerous demands which were brought forward and canvassed, was one for a *Khilut* for Raja Desmook,h, who has been dead for two months, upon the plea that the grief of the Bala Baee, which was now subsiding, would be again renewed by the recollection that, if her darling son were now alive, he, too, would have shared in the presents offered upon this occasion. This demand, strange as it was, was urged with such earnestness and obstinacy, that the Resident was at last obliged to give way, and the usual quantity of shawls and jewels, together with a horse and an elephant, were accordingly presented to the shade of the late heir to the *Musnud*.

When the Muha Raj pays a visit to any person of rank, he sends his own *Musnud*, or throne, on which he sits at the upper end of the tent, and everything is conducted precisely as at his own Durbar, except that he who gives the entertainment, rises to present him with *pan* and *uttur* upon his departure. On the present occasion, besides the usual *Khilut*, a superb barouche drawn by four beautiful Arabian horses was presented to the Muha Raj, on the part of the Governor-General: the lining of the carriage was of purple velvet, embroidered with stars of gold, and the liveries of the postilions in the same style of magnificence. Seendhiya appeared well pleased with this elegant present, but after his return to his own tents, some suspicions of witchcraft were instilled into his mind, and every cushion was examined with the nicest care, before he would venture to trust himself in the carriage. At length, about eleven o'clock at night, it was hauled within the walls of the enclosure, and he and the Baee having taken their seats, it was dragged about for an hour by the servants and attendants. Some little disappointment, too, was expressed in private by the Muha Raj, at the carriage not being a close one, in which he might have wiled away the time, upon a long march, in the company of some favourite fair, without being exposed to the prying glances of the envious and less happy vulgar.

But enough of Seendhiya and Mahrattas. Let me close my descriptions of them with a fervent wish that the coming year, and many successive ones, may rise upon my dear brother, not only rich in health and happiness, but in a mind more and more impressed with the blessings he enjoys as an Englishman, blessings which I hope may have been rendered more evident, and consequently more dear, by a perusal of my attempts to depict the manners and customs of a people as much separated from Englishmen by character as they are by actual distance upon the face of the globe. Farewell!

LETTER XXXII

March to Ajmeer—Description of the fort and city—Tomb of Moouen-oo-deen Chishtee—Ceremonies observed at the tomb—Visit to Pokur—Description of the different temples—The town, and manners of its inhabitants—Alarm of the Muha Raj; and preparations for quitting Ajmeer.

CAMP AT AJMEER, *February* 27, 1810.

THE hopes we entertained of seeing this once celebrated place have now been realized, and my dear brother will compound for the labour of perusing one more long letter, for the sake of learning something of a city so often mentioned in Indian history; I fear, however, that the expectations he may have formed will be greatly disappointed, as ours, I confess, have been.

About the middle of last month we quitted the banks of the *Tinel*, and returned once more to those of the *Mansee*, encamping a little to the eastward of the spot we were at last year. On this ground we continued till the 26th, when we marched to a village called Champaneree, about eleven miles on the road to this city. Seendhiya preceded us the day before, taking with him, however, only a small corps of horse, a couple of battalions, and a few small guns, the Bazars and the rest of the army continuing upon the old ground. The country we passed over this day was flat, well cultivated, and covered with villages apparently well inhabited and flourishing. The next day we made a march of twenty-one miles, in a direction almost due north, to a small village called Nandlee. By some accident or other the people who had been sent in advance with the breakfast things and tents mistook the road, and did not arrive at the ground till past four o'clock in the evening, till which time we were glad to take shelter under a small Babool tree, the leaves of which were so thin as scarcely to ward off the heat of the sun's beams, but which was nevertheless the largest tree which our eyes could distinguish on the neighbouring plain. The road was good, but the general appearance of the country flat and desert, with here and there a village, in the vicinity of which were to be seen some fields of corn, and a few trees. The luxuriancy of both, however, seemed to diminish at every village as we advanced. On this day's march I witnessed a painful instance of the distress to which women are exposed who spend their lives in a camp, which would in England have excited the liveliest emotions of pity and compassion, but which is here deemed a mere inconvenience, to which an itinerant life is necessarily subjected. A poor creature sat by the roadside just delivered: she belonged to the Muha Raj's own camp, and had been prevented, by approaching labour, from keeping up with her friends. She was quite alone, and had performed for herself all the painful offices of a midwife. She did not appear to be much distressed, and they who passed by merely observed that a child was born, without thinking it at all necessary to offer assistance to her who had given it birth. When a little recovered from the first effects of her illness, she probably took up her little burden, and walked on to camp; or, if her strength did not allow her to get so far, took refuge in some village on the road, till she was able to proceed and rejoin her family.

From Nandlee the fort of Ajmeer, called Taragurh, is clearly discernible, finely situated in the midst of several ranges of hills, all of which run in a direction nearly east and west.

On the 28th we reached Ajmeer, after a hot uncomfortable march of fourteen miles, though the straight distance cannot be more than nine, or at the utmost ten, the road, for the latter half of the way, winding considerably among the hills. Taragurh is built upon the north-east end of one of the ranges, and consists apparently of little else than a plain stone wall, running along the edge of the mountain, and strengthened by a few round bastions. The jealousy which pervades this court upon all, even the most trifling, occasions, has prevented my taking a near survey of the fort, much more attempting to visit it; but I should guess it to be inferior both in size and strength to Kund,har, Chuetor, and many other hill forts, which have not acquired half the celebrity of this one, whose principal strength doubtless lies in the ruggedness and acclivity of the hill upon which it is situated. The access to the fort is from the city, and is carried for more than half a mile over several smaller rocky hills, till it reaches the main wall of the fortress. Some of our people, who obtained admission with the crowd that were daily permitted to pay their vows at the tomb of *Meerha Sueyud*, a Moohumedan saint, complained of this road being so very steep and rough, that they were obliged to climb with difficulty for the greater part of the way. The city lies at the bottom of the hill, and is surrounded by a stone wall, with a *fause braye* and ditch, all in very bad repair. It could never have been extensive, and if it were magnificent, it certainly no longer retains any traces of its former splendour. The streets are narrow and dirty, and most of the houses small, and going fast to decay. It is adorned, however, by a palace, built by the Emperor Shah Jihan, which appears still to be in good repair. It is situated in the midst of a garden, but as the Muha Raj has taken up his quarters in it, I have had no opportunity of indulging my curiosity by a nearer inspection. Without the walls of the city there is an equal want of all traces of former magnificence: none of those fine ruins of baths, palaces, gardens and tombs are to be seen here, which render the environs of Delhi and Agra, and even of many inferior cities in Hindoostan, so highly interesting. I have been able to discover but two tombs that have the smallest claim to notice, and they are of a very modern date, and the garden in which they are built has been allowed to go quite to ruin. The whole country around Ajmeer, up to the very walls, forms a flat, sandy kind of amphitheatre, surrounded on all sides by ranges of high hills, and in consequence of this situation the place is, even at this season of the year, as hot as in the month of May in most other parts of India. The town is, however, well supplied with water from two fine lakes close to its walls. That to the northward, called *Unna Sagur*, is fully six miles in circumference, and very deep. The other, which is called *Tal Kutora*, is neither so large nor so deep as the first. Both are at this season covered with innumerable flocks of ducks and geese, among the latter of which is one species considerably larger than any I ever saw before. They are very shy, but I have succeeded in shooting one, which weighed sixteen pounds.

The principal attraction of Ajmeer is the tomb of Khwaja Moouen-oo-deen Chishtee, esteemed the greatest Moohumedan saint that ever flourished in Hindoostan, and who, in his later days, received the title of *Sooltan-ool-hind*, "Prince of India." He died upwards of six hundred years ago, and this mausoleum was erected over his remains by the Emperor Shah Goree.[1] It is of white marble, but remarkable neither for its style nor beauty. The main building is crowned with a dome, immediately under which is the tomb, covered with a pall of rich brocade, and surrounded by a square railing of solid silver, at each corner of which is a silver pillar supporting a canopy, also of brocade. Here it is usual for visitors to present some of the rupees with which they should come well supplied to answer the numerous demands made upon their purses. When the offering is made, the *Kadim*, or priest, who attends to show the place, just lifts the pall high enough to discover the lower step of the tomb, and lets it fall again immediately: the tomb itself, which is of white marble inlaid with cornelian, jasper, and various other coloured

[1] *See* page 180.

stones, being totally uncovered only on seven days in the year. A clamorous host of sturdy fellows are always thronging about it, each of whom asks some benefaction for himself in a tone and manner more resembling the demands of a footpad than the supplication of a beggar. They are all descendants, in a line more or less direct, from the saint, and I was assured that there are now more than eleven hundred of these *Peerzadus*, as they are called, who subsist entirely upon the produce of the tomb, and the revenues of a few small villages appropriated by the government to their support. Within the precincts of the building are shown the tombs of a daughter of the saint, and of the Princess *Jihan Ara*,[1] the favourite daughter of Shah Jihan, who often resided at Ajmeer, and added greatly to the beauty of the tomb, by a mosque of white marble erected in the style of simple elegance which distinguishes all the buildings of that accomplished monarch. There is also a spacious reservoir of water within the walls, supplied by a spring so abundant, that almost all the inhabitants of the city make use of it for drinking, though no one is allowed to bathe or wash himself in it. Before you quit the tomb, a quantity of sweetmeats is brought, which are purchased at an exorbitant rate: one of the eldest *Kadims* (generally he who attaches himself to you at your entrance, and accompanies you during your stay) says a prayer over it, and it is then called *tuburrook*, or consecrated: one half becomes his perquisite, and the other you are permitted to carry away with you. The entrance to the outer court passes under an arched gateway, remarkable only for its preposterous height, and one of the exhibitions with which you are indulged during a visit to the tomb is to be

[1] This is a mistake. Jahán Ara Begam, who died on the 5th September, 1680, lies buried in the enclosure of the mausoleum of Nizám-uddín-Aulia at Delhi. The tomb referred to in the text is that of Chimni Begam, who is *said* to have been a daughter of Sháh Jahán, This tomb lies to the south of the Saint's grave, next to that of his daughter Háfiz Jamál.

mounted to the top of this archway by a flight of steps so steep and narrow as to be really frightful to one not accustomed to them, and, when seated there, to scatter handfuls of *cowries* and copper coin among the crowd of *Peer-zadus* and beggars of all descriptions, who flock below, and scramble and fight for the money, to the great amusement of the exalted spectators. On either side of this archway, within the court, is an enormous copper boiler fitted into solid masonry, the larger of which is capable of holding seventy maunds, or five thousand four hundred pounds of rice, and the smaller, half of that quantity. When Princes or other great men visit Ajmeer, it is usual for them to order these vessels to be filled, which is accordingly done with rice, sugar, butter, sweetmeats, &c. It requires the whole night to boil this mess, which is distributed in the morning among the hungry *Peer,zadus*. The mode in which the distribution is conducted affords the chief amusement to the pious donor, who is generally seated half way up the gateway, to witness the extraordinary spectacle. Some of the oldest of the *Peer-zadus* are entitled to certain portions of the composition, and when this quantity is taken out and distributed, large shovelfuls are thrown among the rest of these holy persons, who scramble for them with such avidity that they soon begin fighting, while some, who have taken the precaution to wrap old clothes around their bodies and limbs, plunge boldly into the boilers, where a battle-royal takes place for every handful, but should an unfortunate stranger presume to intrude upon their prescriptive rights, and try his luck for a share of the *tuburrook* (for it is all consecrated), they join instantly to drive away the intruder, and make him pay dearly for his temerity. The *tuburrook* is afterwards sold by the *Peer-zadus* about the town, and anxiously purchased by the pious and devout. Seendhiya, whose devotion to Moohumedan saints and religious customs I have more than once had occasion to mention, has given this favourite entertainment three times since our arrival; he has also bestowed a superb pall and canopy of cloth of gold upon the tomb; and even the *Peer-zadus* seem to be pretty well satisfied with his pecuniary donations. There are generally one or two bands of Nach girls singing before the tomb, but on Thursday nights, all the sets belonging to the city attend, for the amusement of the devout Moslems, who upon those evenings flock there in numbers.

On these occasions the whole building is lighted up, and all the wealth of the establishment displayed, which consists of gold and silver sticks, canopies of rich cloths, and other similar ornaments. Opposite to the door of the tomb, I observed a small lustre, made, after the European fashion, of rock crystal, and within the dome are several ostrich's eggs suspended from the roof. To this shrine the Mahrattas resort, not merely to gratify idle curiosity, but apparently with the idea of performing a religious duty. The Hindoos of all ranks, belonging to our camp, have also gone to visit it, but with the same ideas only that would carry them to see any other object equally celebrated. It is among the Hindoos of the Duk,hun alone that a profound veneration for Moohumedan ceremonies and relics is observable; and I am not sure that they do not carry this veneration even to greater lengths than a large portion of the faithful themselves. I remember being taken to see a *Durgah*, or shrine of a Moohumedan saint, at *Kurera*, a town belonging to the Soobudar of Jansee, which was held in peculiar veneration, and to which a near relation of the Soobudar's, a Duk,hunee Brahmun, who governed the district, went every afternoon to make an obeisance before the marks of two feet impressed on a stone, and imagined to be those of the saint himself.

On the 1st instant we went to Pokur, or, as it is more classically called, Pooshkur; a place as highly venerated by the Hindoos as Ajmeer is by the Moosulmans. Its actual distance from the latter place is probably not more than three miles and a half, but travellers, even those on foot, are obliged to make a considerable circuit, to cross the range of hills which lies between the two places, the pass over which is by many degrees the worst I ever saw. Both horses and elephants can go over it, but at some places, where the narrow steep path winds round projecting masses of rock, and where the footing is only the naked stone, without any kind of parapet to prevent one's being precipitated down the precipice, the appearance at least of danger is so great that we thought ourselves safer upon our own feet, than when trusting to those of our cattle, and accordingly climbed up and down the hill on foot. After passing this *G,hat* the remainder of the road winds along a flat sandy bed, apparently a channel for the mountain torrents during the rainy season. The town, which is not large, is situated on the shore of a most romantic *Pokur*, or lake, from which it takes its name. Its sanctity is derived from a *Jug*, or sacred entertainment which *Brimha* there made, in the *Sut-joog* (or golden age), for all the *Deotas*. His wife *Savitree*, instigated by *Narud*, one of the sons of *Brimha*, refused to assist at this *Jug*, and retired to the top of a high hill, about a mile from the lake, where she has now a temple, which is visited by all the pilgrims who have strength and perseverance enough to climb so high, a labour which, from the description made of it to me, is fully equivalent to the reward of bowing at the shrine of the goddess. It is at Pokur alone that an image of *Brimha*, at least one of any celebrity, is to be seen: his temple is close to the margin of the lake, small, plain, and evidently very ancient. The image, which is about the size of a man, has four faces, and is in a sitting posture, cross-legged, but neither it nor the apartment in which it is placed is distinguished by any kind of ornament.

The largest temple at Pokur is one dedicated to *Barajee*, the third *Uotar*, or incarnation of *Vishnoo*. The building, as it now stands, presents only the small remains of the ancient temple, which was overthrown by the bigoted zeal of the Emperor Aurungzeb, and is said to have been one hundred and fifty feet in height and covered with the finest specimens of Hindoo sculpture. The old walls, to the height of about twenty feet, were left entire, and have been covered in, to form the present temple, by Raja Jue Sing,h, Siwue of Jypoor. The next, in point of sanctity and consequence, to this temple is one sacred to *Vishnoo*, under the name of *Budrinath*, but in which there is nothing remarkable to be seen. These four temples are of very ancient structure, and are held in particular veneration; but besides them, there are innumerable others, of more modern date, erected to every god of the Hindoo calendar. Among these is one dedicated to *Muhadeo*, which is by far the most remarkable, both for the size and elegance of its structure, and the nature of its ornaments, of all the temples that Pooshkur boasts of. It was built by Anajee Seendhiya, the grandfather of the present Muha Raj. The image, and the altar on which it is placed, are of fine white marble, highly polished, and executed in a style superior to anything of the kind I have seen in India. The idol is *Punj-mook,hee*, or five-faced, each face crowned with the *Jutta*, or matted hair of the *Uteets*, and exhibiting that harsh and obscene expression which is the characteristic of the Indian, as well as the Roman, Priapus. The image in question, together with its *Urg,ha*, or altar, is precisely what one would expect to see in a temple of ancient Rome dedicated to that deity. A large building erected by Madoojee Seendhiya next attracted our notice. It contains images of *Bawanee*, *Muha Deo*, and some others of the Hindoo deities, all of white marble, but executed in a manner very inferior to the one I have just described. The interior apartment is surrounded by a range of piazzas, also of marble, designed for the accommodation of the numerous *Bueragees*, or mendicants, who make pilgrimages to Pooshkur; and for whose support the revenues of ten small villages in the district were allotted by the illustrious founder. Into all these temples we were freely admitted, except that of *Barajee*, where the *Purohit*, or priest, who attended us intimated it would be proper to go barefooted:

S 2

as we were in boots we contented ourselves with observing everything from the door-way, though I make no doubt, had we pressed the matter, the objection would have been soon given up. *Purohits* are Brahmuns who attend at all celebrated *Teeruts*, or places of religious resort, to point out the most sacred spots, and to read the necessary prayers, &c., to the pilgrims, whose names, families and places of abode they enter carefully into a register, and receive some trifle as a compensation for their trouble. The pilgrims besides offer money, according to their means, at each of the temples they visit, and the *Ghats* where they bathe. With those who can afford such an expense, it is common to make the *Purohit* a present of a cow, with her horns tipped with silver, her hoofs plated with the same metal, and covered by a silken *J,hool*, or coverlet. The Muha Raj has not gone himself to Pooshkur, having been assured that it is unlucky for any reigning Prince to make this pilgrimage, though the true reason of his absenting himself is that his uncle Madoojee died soon after he had visited the place. He has, however, sent presents to the chief Pundits, though by no means so valuable as those given to the *Kadims* at Ajmeer. The Bala Baee was at the lake at the time we went, and our *Purohit*, for we also had one, told me that she had behaved with great liberality.

Besides the temples which I have described, the banks of the lake are covered with a number of smaller ones, pavilions, *chuoltrees*, &c., built by the neighbouring Rajas, at various periods. Many of those buildings are at present nearly, and some of them altogether, immersed in the water, the springs of the lake having risen within the last six weeks to a height beyond any that is on record. Some of the streets of the town are inundated, and the domes of the buildings upon the shores, with the trees about them, appear above the surface of the water at some distance in the lake. The inhabitants began to be seriously alarmed, but the water rose only a certain height, and is now slowly decreasing.

The town of Pokur is divided into two *Moohullas*, or quarters; one of which, called *Bara Moohulla*, from the temple of *Barajee*, contains about five hundred houses, the other not more than two hundred. The inhabitants, who are Brahmuns, are decent in their appearance, and simple in their manners; they are exceedingly poor, however, depending almost entirely for their support on charitable contributions. Some of our Sipahees, who visited the place after us, assured me that the sum we distributed at the different temples had excited the most lively sensation among all classes, who loudly expressed their wishes that they might be often favoured with visits from European pilgrims. The *Purohit* who attended us complained that the sanctity of the place was no plea with the Mahratta Soobudar for favour towards its inhabitants, who were assessed on a par with the rest of the province, and obliged to pay even to the last farthing. They have a curious custom here, similar to one which prevails in some town in Italy, I believe in Milan, on the second day after the burning of the *Hohlee.* The inhabitants of the *Bara Moohulla* make a regular attack upon those of the other quarter, who repel them as well as they can with stones and sticks, but the origin of this annual battle I could not learn.

The last thing we visited was a fine Moohumedan mosque, built at the *Gao Ghat*, the principal bathing-place, by Bueram Khan, the friend and tutor of the Emperor Acbar. Our *Purohit* urged us much to prolong our stay, and visit two other lakes, at some miles distance from Pokur, which are also esteemed sacred, but having ascertained that there was little worth seeing, except merely the lakes, and that they were much inferior to the principal one, we declined his offer of conducting us, and returned to camp in the afternoon, very highly pleased with our trip, and sensibly struck by the decency and civility of the Hindoo priests, as contrasted with the clamorous, and almost insolent, demands of the Moohumedan ones at the *Durgah.* I must not omit to mention that the marble used in most of the great buildings of this part of India is dug out of quarries about seven miles to the westward of Pokur, towards which quarter the view extends over a flat country, uninterrupted by hills, and apparently but thinly covered with villages or cultivation. It has all the appearance of the commencement of a desert, and we were told that it continued such to the city of Meerta, the boundary between the provinces of Ajmeer and Juodpoor.

We have now seen everything worthy of observation at this place, and begin to be anxious to leave it, a wish that will probably be soon gratified in consequence of an event that occurred last night which has excited great alarm throughout the whole of the Muha Raj's suite. The cattle of all kinds, bullocks, horses, and camels, were observed to be very restless, and to make much more noise than usual, bellowing and neighing in a very uncommon manner. This was told in the morning to the astrologers, who declared that it intimates some impending evil, which can only be averted by large presents to the Brahmuns, and a speedy departure from the place. Seendhiya has accordingly distributed twenty thousand rupees among the Brahmuns, and given orders for marching to-morrow morning. If the march takes place, you will hear no more from me, and will probably join with me in benedictions upon the unruly beasts that have been the cause of carrying me away from a hot, disagreeable place, and of sparing you the further trouble of reading my descriptions of it. Once more, farewell!

THE END.

INDEX

INDEX

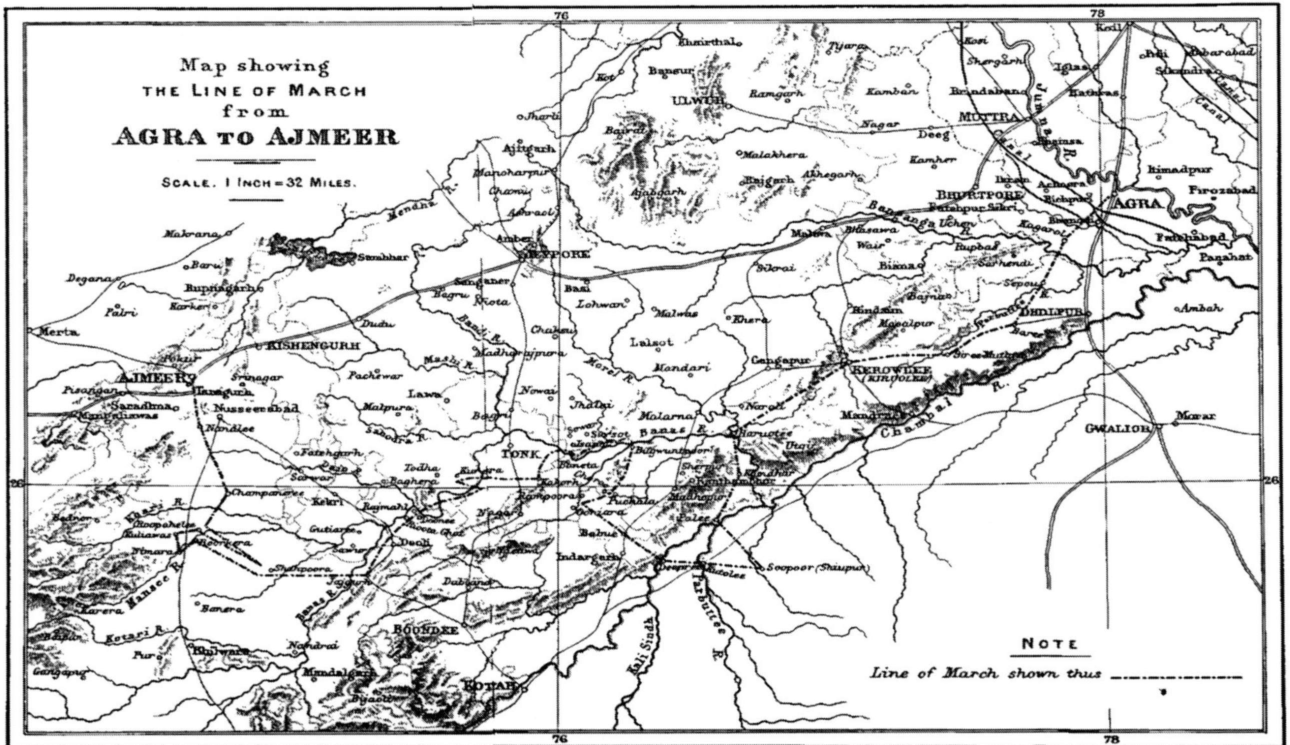

Compiled by A.C.

Westminster. ARCHIBALD CONSTABLE & Co

Stanford's Geog¹ Estab¹

ARCHIBALD CONSTABLE AND COMPANY'S PUBLICATIONS

CONSTABLE'S ORIENTAL MISCELLANY, a series that . . . . has the strongest claim on popularity.—*Notes and Queries*

Already published

Vol. I.

BERNIER'S TRAVELS IN THE MOGUL EMPIRE. An entirely new edition, with illustrations, and reproductions of maps from early editions. By ARCHIBALD CONSTABLE, Mem. As. Soc. Bengal, F.S.A.Scot. Cr. 8vo, pp. liv + 500. Price 6s. nett.

The old translation has now been revised and edited in very scholarly fashion.—*The Times.*

This is a scholarly volume, and bodes well for the success of the Miscellany.—*The Scotsman.*

The new Miscellany . has been right worthily inaugurated by a reprint of Bernier's Travels in India, which must delight the scholar and lover of books.—*The Bombay Gazette.*

An almost perfect instance of careful, painstaking, and judicious editing.—*The Pioneer.*

The excellent editing as well as outward get-up . . . . are a guarantee that this new venture . . . . will supply a long-felt want. —*The Times of India.*

The student will know how to prize the work, and the general reader will find it very interesting reading.—*The Manchester Guardian.*

Since their first appearance in Paris, in 1670, many have been the reprints and translations of Bernier's Travels. . . . . With all this, however, the book itself is not easily accessible. In offering the English Public a new edition of it, Messrs. Archibald Constable and Co. have therefore no need to apologize. It is a fact that until this publication no really satisfactory edition has existed. It is now edited not only with great care, but also with a laudable regard to the needs of the general reader.—*The Anti-Jacobin.*

The book abounds with curious scenes and anecdotes of native life in India, amusing in themselves and interesting for comparison with the ways, habits and ideas of modern India. . . . The running glossary of Indian terms and words is very useful; so are the brief notices of distinguished persons and remarkable places mentioned in the text; there is also a chronicle of Bernier's life, a bibliography of his works, and an excellent index.—*The Speaker.*

The book is of almost indispensable necessity to the reader of history, being accurate and painstaking to a high degree.—*The Academy.*

The volume has been admirably edited and illustrated. The numerous allusions in the text to individuals, places, productions of art and industry, &c., are well explained in brief but sufficient notes, which contain the results of careful research in contemporary historians, and of an intimate personal acquaintance with Indian life and industry at the present day.—*The Scottish Geographical Magazine.*

Vol. II.

POPULAR READINGS IN SCIENCE. By JOHN GALL, M.A., LL.B., late Professor of Mathematics and Physics, Canning College, Lucknow, and DAVID ROBERTSON, M.A., LL.B., B.Sc. With many Diagrams, a Glossary of Technical Terms, and an Index. Cr. 8vo, pp. 468. Price 5s. nett.

The authors lay no claim to originality, but have exercised a judicious choice in the selection of subject matter. . . . . The narrative style which has been adopted by the authors will make the book acceptable to general readers who are anxious to make acquaintance with modern science.—*Nature.*

It is hardly to be expected that this second volume of "Constable's Oriental Miscellany" will meet with such universal acclamation as the first volume, which consisted of *Bernier's Travels.* But when rightly considered, it equally shows the thoroughness with which the publishers have thrown themselves into the enterprise.—*The Academy.*

While the essays are such as would attract and instruct a general reader, they appear to have been written specially with a view to the needs of Indian students approaching the study of science for the first time. . . . They are well adapted to this end, and cannot fail to create in their readers a desire to push their knowledge further.—*The Scotsman.*

The new volume of "Constable's Oriental Miscellany" would have delighted Macaulay and the champions of "Occidentalism" in Indian education in Lord William Bentinck's day. . . . . Messrs. Gall and Robertson . . have prepared a collection of essays which will be at least as acceptable to the general reader as to the student, in which the results of the most modern researches in physical science are brought up to date. . . . . In each case the subject is treated in a clear and interesting way . . . . it is a most commendable undertaking.—*The Bombay Gazette.*

The title sufficiently indicates the lines on which the two collaborators have worked. Theirs is no dry-as-dust text-book; it is rather a collection of scientific facts forming chapters in what has aptly been called the romance of science. . . . . Messrs. Archibald Constable & Co. have a particular interest in this country, and their Oriental Miscellany is so well edited, printed, and published, that it is easy to predict for it a wide popularity.—*The Madras Mail.*

The second volume of "Constable's Oriental Miscellany," just published under the above heading, has been designed to meet an undoubted want, and will hardly yield in usefulness to any in the projected series. . . . . While elementary principles are explained with sufficient clearness to enable the work to be used independently of other text-books, the compilers have devoted much attention and space to many of the results of scientific researches which have mainly distinguished the present century. The Darwinian theory, for instance, is not only admirably summarized in itself, but we are furnished with a useful *précis* of the arguments *pro et con*, together with an account of the more recent discoveries of paleontologists which have strengthened the doctrine of the evolution of organic beings, and an outline of the views regarding it of the *savants* of all nations. The book is one which should secure a large number of general readers, who will find in it a vast store of useful information placed before them in a peculiarly readable and acceptable form.—*The Pioneer.*

This is a popular treatise covering a very wide range of subjects. . . . . A well-written book like a modernized Lardner, or a *fin de siècle* edition of the "Scientific Information for the People" of the "Useful Knowledge Series."—*The Educational Times.*

The authors write about what they know, and they write with clearness and precision, and on the topics which they discuss they have spoken with that accuracy which comes from full knowledge. . . . . The value of the book is enhanced by a glossary of technical terms, which will be of the utmost possible use to the beginner, and also of use to those who are somewhat advanced in their studies.—*The Aberdeen Daily Free Press.*

Vol. III.

AURENG-ZEBE, a Tragedy, by JOHN DRYDEN, and Book ii. of THE CHACE, a Poem, by WILLIAM SOMERVILE. Edited, with Biographical Memoirs and Notes, by KENNETH DEIGHTON, Editor of Select Plays of Shakespeare. With a Portrait of Dryden, and a coloured reproduction of an Indian painting representing the Emperor Akbar deer-stalking. Cr. 8vo, pp. xiii + 222. Price 5s. nett.

An interesting reprint of Dryden's tragedy. . . . . If anyone wishes to realize by an hour's easy reading the vast gulf which separates our knowledge of India and our conceptions about India, at the close of this 19th century, from the views of our ancestors about India in the last quarter of the 17th century, we recommend this book to his notice. Mr. Deighton's copious and suggestive foot-notes will render the perusal both profitable and pleasant.—*The Times.*

This volume, like its predecessors, is admirably got up, and is enriched by a fine portrait of Dryden, and a capital reproduction of a highly curious and interesting Indian picture exhibiting the youthful Akbar at the chase.—*The Scotsman.*

Mr. Kenneth Deighton supplies a short biography of Dryden, and a just estimate of his dramatic power, taking due notice of the improvement in the later tone of a poet who was largely made by his surroundings, and had to write to please. . . . . Ample notes, suited to the capacity of the Indian student, are incorporated in the volume.—*The Glasgow Herald.*

Forthcoming volumes, in active preparation

LIFE IN ANCIENT INDIA. By MRS. SPEIR. A new edition, revised and edited by DR. ROST, C.I.E., Librarian, India Office.

RAMBLES AND RECOLLECTIONS OF AN INDIAN OFFICIAL. By Major-General Sir W. H. SLEEMAN, K.C.B. A new edition, edited by VINCENT ARTHUR SMITH, Indian Civil Service.

Other publications

STUDIES IN MOHAMMEDANISM, Historical and Doctrinal, with a chapter on Islam in England. By JOHN J. POOL. With a Frontispiece and Index, pp. xvi + 420. Cr. 8vo, full cloth. Price 6s.

An interesting survey—all the more readable, perhaps, on account of its informal and even discursive arrangement—of Mussulman faith, practice, and history. . . . . A conspicuous feature of Mr. Pool's work is the account of the Moslem propaganda, which Mr. Quilliam, a Liverpool solicitor, is now prosecuting in that city. . . . . It is tinged by no rancour or contempt, and exhibits a conscientious endeavour to appreciate the Mohammedan standpoint. As a "popular text-book," dealing with some of the most picturesque aspects of Islam, it deserves more than ordinary attention.—*The Times.*

Mr. Pool . . . . has done good service in publishing this popular exposition of the doctrines and real character of Islam. So far as he errs at all, he errs on the side of too much leniency to Mohammedanism. . . . . Mr. Pool's too favourable account of the Moorish *régime* in Spain is the only part of his book that is open to serious question. The rest of the volume is both readable and instructive.

He has evidently studied Islam with great care, and he states his own views with exemplary moderation.—*The Spectator.*

The chapter which gives information on this matter [Islam in Liverpool] is naturally the most interesting in the volume. . . . . As to the other parts of Mr. Pool's book it is difficult to speak too highly. His account of Mohammed and his system is fair and full, abounding in all kinds of illustrative anecdote.—*The Glasgow Herald.*

In the forty-one chapters of this volume the promise of the title is well kept, and every aspect of Islam faith and practice is discussed in a clear, comprehensive, and interesting manner.—*The Liverpool Mercury.*

These "Studies in Mohammedanism" are conspicuously fair. The writer is devotedly attached to Christianity, but he frankly and gladly acknowledges that Mohammed was a man of extraordinary powers and gifts, and that the religion which bears his name has done incalculable service to humanity in keeping the sublime truth of the unity of God before the eyes of the non-Christian world steeped in polytheism. —*The Bradford Observer.*

This volume will be found both interesting and useful to the general reader, as supplying in a convenient form a very good outline of the rise and development, with an account of the more salient features, of the Mohammedan religion. There are short chapters also on the Turks, Afghans, Corsairs, crusades, literature, architecture, slavery, &c., which convey much popular information in a pleasant style.—*The Scottish Geographical Magazine.*

ILLUSTRATIONS OF INDIAN FIELD SPORTS : A Series of Ten Coloured Plates, after the drawings by Captain THOMAS WILLIAMSON of the Bengal Army, first published in 1807. With a Preface and Description to each Plate. Oblong 4to, printed on hand-made paper, gilt top. Price 10s. 6d.

THE HISTORY OF THE MOGHUL EMPERORS OF HINDUSTAN ILLUSTRATED BY THEIR COINS. By STANLEY LANE-POOLE. With a Map of Mediæval India, showing the mints of the Muhammadan Rulers, a Genealogical Tree of the Moghul Emperors, and Index. 8vo, full buckram, pp. 188. The impression for sale is strictly limited to 100 copies, numbered and signed. Price 8s. nett.—*Out of print.*

A valuable monograph on the history of the Mughal Emperors as illustrated by their coins.—*The Times.*

. . . . exemplifies in an interesting manner to what extent the researches of numismatists are of value to the historical student.—*The Saturday Review.*

A work of this character could hardly have been issued under better auspices. The collection of Moghul coins contained in the British Museum is the richest and most complete in the world: and few, if any, are better qualified, whether as orientalists or numismatists, than Mr. Stanley Lane-Poole to extract from it every ray of light whereby the history of the period may be elucidated and controlled. Not least should the history of this great dynasty [Moghul] interest us Englishmen, to whom has passed the wide empire over which it once held sovereign sway; and Messrs. Constable may well be congratulated on having within so short a time increased our knowledge of it by two books so excellent as this one before us and the *Bernier* of last year.—*The National Observer.*

Under preparation

ANCIENT INDIA, its Invasion by Alexander the Great, as described by Arrian, Q. Curtius, Diodôros, Plutarch, and Justin: Being Translations of such portions of the works of these and other classical authors as describe Alexander's Campaigns in Afghanistan, the Panjáb, Sindh, Gedrosia, and Karmania. With an Introduction, containing a Life of Alexander, copious Notes, Illustrations, Maps, and an Index. By J. W. MCCRINDLE, M.A., M.R.A.S., F.R.S.G.S.—*In the Press.*

THE PRESENT SITUATION IN CENTRAL ASIA; authorized translation of the work *Antagonismus der Englischen and Russischen Interessen in Asien*, Wien 1890. Brought up to date, with a Map embodying the latest information.—*In the Press.*

THE MOHAMMEDAN DYNASTIES: Tables and Pedigrees of the Princes and Khalifs of Islām from the Seventh to the Nineteenth Century; arranged with brief historical introductions and Indices. By STANLEY LANE-POOLE.

INDIAN CHRONOLOGY, being a Table of Authentic Dates, historical and literary, from the earliest period until 1500 A.D. By C. M. DUFF.

MEMORIALS OF THE DISRUPTION IN THE SCOTTISH CHURCH, Historical, Financial, and Pictorial.—*Early next year.*

THE MIGRATION OF SYMBOLS. By Count GOBLET D'ALVIELLA, Professor of the History of Religions in the University of Brussels. An authorized translation, edited by Sir GEORGE BIRDWOOD, M.D., K.C.I.E., C.S.I., LL.D., Officer of the Legion of Honour and of the French Academy. With five full-page Plates and 139 Illustrations in the text.—*Early next year.*

SOME MEMORIES OF BOOKS, AUTHORS, AND EVENTS, from the Life of a Publisher's Assistant. By the late JAMES G. BERTRAM. With a Portrait of Sir Walter Scott from an engraving by Lewis, after the drawing by Geddes. —*Early next year.*

PREM SÂGAR, or Ocean of Love. A new translation of Professor Eastwick's edition of the Hindî text of Shrî Lullû Lâl Kavi. By FREDERIC PINCOTT, M.R.A.S., Author of the Hindî Manual, Editor and Annotator of the Sakuntalâ in Hindî, and Translator of the Sanskrit Hitopadesa. With copious notes, philological, mythological, and historical, emendations of faulty readings in the text, and explanations of peculiar idioms.

ENGLISH SETTLEMENTS IN INDO-CHINA. By J. CHAILLY-BERT. Authorized English translation, with an Introduction, Maps, Notes, and an Index.

THE INDIAN MAGAZINE AND REVIEW. A publication which aims at interesting its readers in the people of India, in their literature, their history, their art, and their customs; their various phases of development, and particularly in their progress.

Published on the first of each month. Subscription, 5s. per annum, in advance, post free; single numbers, 6d., postage extra.

North Indian Notes and Queries. A Monthly Periodical devoted to the systematic collection of authentic notes and scraps of information regarding the country and the people. Edited by William Crooke, B.A., Member Asiatic Society of Bengal and Folklore Society, Bengal Civil Service.

Subscription, 10s. 6d. per annum, in advance, post free.

Westminster
ARCHIBALD CONSTABLE AND COMPANY
14 PARLIAMENT STREET S·W